The Black Dibiase:
Return of the Goon Squad

by
Swift Sloan

The Black Dibiase:
Return of the Goon Squad
by
Swift Sloan

All R H Publishing titles, imprints, and distributed lines are available at special quantity discounts for bulk purchases for sales promotion, premiums, fund raising, educational or instructional use.

Special book excerpts or customized printings can also be created to fit specific needs. For details, write to:

R H Publishing, P.O. Box 11642, Milwaukee, WI 53211
Or email us at: talk2us@rhpublishings.com
Visit our website: www.swiftnovels.com

ISBN-13: 978-0-692-88580-2

First Printing:
10 9 8 7 6 5 4 3 2 1

1. Urban   2. Fiction

Cover Design: Nuance Art

Editor: Gloria Palmer (movinonup57@yahoo.com)

The Black Dibiase:
Return of the Goon Squad

Acknowledgements

Much thanks to all those
who have supported my many works.
You are the real MVP's.
Thanks.
Swift Sloan

~ One ~

Dibiase Hammond stood in his bedroom looking out the window. He peered silently at all the luxury cars lined up in front of his home waiting patiently. The tall, thin man in the white suit emerged from the front car, placing flags on the driver's side of all the vehicles that were part of the homegoing ceremony. Dibiase had never seen so many people before, at least not at his home. He knew a lot of them were just pretenders, major wannabes—just there to say they were part of Rico's funeral. Ricky Costello Hammond, better known to the streets as Rico, had been gunned down coming from his best friend's wedding on the north side of Milwaukee a couple of days ago.

Dibiase turned to face the door when he heard a faint knock. Turning from his fixated position to face the intruder, the hurt plastered on his face was clearly seen. For seconds, he just looked at the door with a blank stare.

"Who is it?" Dibiase finally asked, really not wanting to see anyone right then.

"It's me, baby," Camille replied.

Camille was Dibiase's girl, his ride-or-die. She wasn't hood, but she was still down for her man, and he adored that about her.

"They're waiting on you, bae. Your mother wants you to ride in the limo with her."

"Tell 'em I don't want to ride in no-fucking-limo," he replied. He didn't want to be cooped-up next to anyone right now. "I'm taking my own-damn-truck," he continued, holding back the tears, stopping them from falling from the wells of his eyes.

"I ain't feeling no company-shit right now, baby. I just want to be alone," Dibiase said, turning to look at the Michael Jordan life-size poster tacked to the back of his room door. Jordan was taking off

from the dotted line and switching hands in the air from right to left, while the Lakers' defenders watched in amazement.

Camille didn't respond. She knew not to push the issue with Dibiase at times like this. Camille knew better than anybody the effect of his father's assassination on him.

Dibiase opened the door after he heard her footsteps departing and he knew she was gone before he headed downstairs. He watched her from the living room picture window as she got into the limo in which his mother, Cassie Hammond, and his younger brother, Ricky Jr., were waiting patiently.

Dibiase thought his mother looked stunning as always, fitted in her black Armani dress with the white flower perched in her hair. He punched the wall, upset, hoping he hadn't sounded too rough to Camille, knowing she was just trying to be there for him.

Golden Gates Funeral Home was where the service for kingpin Rico Hammond was being held. The parking lot was jam-packed full of people. It almost looked like an R. Kelly concert was going on instead of a man's funeral. Cars were backed up for at least two-and-a-half blocks in each direction. You would have thought it was someone of Barack Obama's stature's funeral as long as the lines were. Dibiase circled the block a couple of times in his black ESV Cadillac truck. The luxury vehicle was his graduation gift from his father when he finished school.

Dibiase looked up to check the scene again on his last time circling the block, and he noticed the two all-black, new-body-style Chevy Impalas parked across the street from the funeral home.

"Ain't this-a-bitch?!" Dibiase said to himself. He realized by the black bumpers who the rides belonged to. "The damn-feds won't even let the man be buried in peace," he thought out loud.

Dibiase mugged the two white federal agents who sat there observing and taking photos of the people as they went inside the funeral parlor. He pulled over and watched for a minute as he gathered himself. Dibiase watched as his mother went in, escorted by his girl and his brother. He saw his Uncle Mickey, who was a boss player, walking with Chi-Chi, one of the many girls he fucked with on the hustling tip. Ra-Ra, one of his father's old-school partners, was also there, standing out like he normally did. Ra was wearing stupid platinum pieces around his neck, and on his wrist was the bling of his favorite Presidential Rolex Sprayed Face with a million baguettes. Ra-Ra was shining so hard he was lighting the daylight up.

Slim was just pulling up in his ultra-gold 500 two-seater Benz with his new bride alongside him. Slim had just tied the knot and gotten married to some Hawaiian chick he'd met on a cruise. His wedding was where it had all ended for Dibiase's father Rico. Dibiase had known Slim since he was a baby. He and Rico were more like brothers than homies, and he knew Slim was taking it just as hard as he was. Dibiase knew Slim actually blamed himself for what had happened to Rico.

He saw a few chicks he'd always wondered about scattered around as well. Dibiase wondered if his father had messed around with them when he first came home from the service. He figured they would show their faces anyway out of respect for the street legend, overlooking any possible consequences that might jump off. He wasn't worried about them disrespecting his mother because whatever Rico had done in the streets he hadn't allowed it to affect their family life. Rico had always treated his mother like a queen.

Dibiase knew Cassie was the only woman who'd ever meant anything to his father. One thing for sure, Rico had always had strong viewpoints on family values and marriage, but Dibiase also knew Rico was still just a man with at least one flaw in one area. He remembered riding with his father one day and Rico telling him there were some things you didn't allow your queen to do or see because of the way

she would feel in the long run. No matter how tough her outside shell appeared to be, a scorned woman would be just that—scorned. Dibiase later understood this when he got serious with Camille. He never bought anything home—disease, lipstick stains, or extra jewelry—that he hadn't left with.

He finally decided to get out the truck as he stubbed out his blunt in the ashtray. Dibiase removed his I Am King cologne from the glove compartment and drowned himself in it so he wouldn't smell like the sticky green walking in his father's homegoing. He knew once he got inside to see his old man's body in a box he had to be high. It was going to be the only way he could stomach seeing his father laid up, arms folded, ten toes up. He had almost died when he went to the city morgue to identify the body. It was even worse when they wouldn't let him actually see the corpse, just Rico's driver's license and the rest of his personal belongings. The AK-47's the hitmen had used to kill Rico had done that much damage to his father.

Dibiase checked himself in the rearview mirror, making sure every facial hair was intact. He wanted to look his best in case the feds wanted his picture too. He smiled at the thought because he knew it was something his father would have said and done—not respecting the law. His black alligator Mauris hit the pavement and he strode inside. All funeral homes seem to have the same stale smell to them. It was a smell that made Dibiase feel like vomit was layered on the pallet of his tongue.

Tons of his father's people began approaching him, shaking his hand, while a lot of familiar and strange women hugged him, offering their condolences. People started telling him shit he already knew about how great a man his father was, saying Rico would be greatly missed in the city. 'Shit,' he thought, '*no one will miss Rico more than I will.*'

Dibiase felt a little dizzy as he entered the room that held his father's body. The same tall man he'd seen from his bedroom window approached him.

"Are you Dibiase?" the man asked.

"Yeah, that's me. What it do?" Dibiase asked, wondering why the man wanted to know.

"Well, our people did all they could to make this an open casket," he replied, pausing.

"Your father's face was too badly damaged to repair," he continued before touching Dibiase on the shoulder.

The closed casket wouldn't allow him to get one last look at his father's bullet-riddled body. The bone ivory, imported-marble case with gold bars sitting on the stand was what would go in the ground six feet deep, taking Rico with it. His Uncle Mickey walked up next to him as Dibiase stood in front of the casket. He was running his hand back and forth across Dibiase's shoulder, as the funeral home worker had just done.

"I can't believe dude's gone," Mickey said. He was Rico's only brother.

"I loved your father, nephew. This-shit's eating me alive to know I'll never see him again, you know? Like, man, he was the world to me," Mickey continued.

He couldn't ever remember seeing his uncle cry, but at the moment, Mickey was letting the tears slide down his face. Dibiase was choked up. It was like he was falling out an airplane and his lungs were full of air. He did his best to speak as he tried to muster out a few words. It was hard; his throat cracked and nothing would come out. It felt like he had swallowed a bag of cotton balls.

He wanted to say something because he knew Mickey was taking it hard, just like Rico's friend Slim was. Mickey was a fuck-up at times but Dibiase knew his father loved Mickey to death. He always made sure Uncle Mickey was eating good. Mickey put his hand on Dibiase's arm, offering as much comfort as that gave, seeing his oldest nephew couldn't respond.

Mickey, who they called Old Man Mickey in the streets, was the last person to have a one-on-one with Rico. Dibiase wondered if his father had said anything to him he should know about. Dibiase remembered Mickey had disappeared for a few days after their meeting and hadn't answered his cell for anyone. Today was the first time Mickey had come back around; at least he was there for the funeral. Mickey's disappearance wasn't odd; it was an MO of his. Mickey was a stone-cold hustler. He played the field with the whores and sold a little boy every now and then. He also got high every once in a while, but he was actually a good dude and a great uncle. Life was life and every man had his one flaw.

Dibiase stared at the casket again as he put his hand in his pants pocket feeling the eight-karat ring that was once his father's. He wanted to open the casket and kiss his father on the forehead but knew he couldn't. He felt another hand rest on his back and the smell of the Paris Hilton scent let him know it was Camille before he even turned to face her. Dibiase finally stopped fighting the tears back as she hugged him. He held on to her as tight as he could, wanting out of there. He couldn't take it any longer. Dibiase was in deep pain, and he no longer wanted to hear everybody reassuring him he would be okay and his father was in a better place now that he was a dead man.

'How-in-the-fuck could there be a better place than home with your family?'

Dibiase was just glad the other person he loved the most in the world was right there with him, standing by his side. He was having a

hard time accepting the fact that Rico had been shot down in the streets, murdered in cold blood. The police claimed they didn't have a lead; they didn't even know where to begin, as they told it. As far as Dibiase was concerned, he felt they didn't even give-a-fuck. Rico was just one more thug drug dealer taken off the streets to them. When, in reality, the streets had lost a true boss. He knew the police didn't see it as a husband was gone, a father taken from his kids, a provider of many was no longer around to provide.

'Fuck the police!' Dibiase thought.

Revenge was going to be inevitable. He knew he wouldn't sleep until the person or people responsible's family was packed in a funeral home somewhere just like his family was.

Whoever had done this to Rico had hell-to-pay. He wasn't sure exactly what he was going to do, or even who he was up against, but his ears were to the pavement, and it wouldn't be long before the streets talked. They always did. He knew it wouldn't be long before the ground opened up and spilled its guts about the lost player. When it did surface, whenever the information came out, whoever was responsible didn't have to worry about being judged by twelve, but by the one-hundred-twenty-round clip of his mini-14.

Dibiase knew the Golden Rule well: Do unto others as you would have them do unto you. He'd learned that in third grade from his English teacher. Whoever had merc'd his father had better know his wrath was coming. They'd waged war, so it was time to go to war. He was for sure bringing a gun to a gunfight. He didn't see it any other way.

Dibiase got in his truck, unlocking the door on the passenger side for Camille.

"Do you have your L with you, honey?" he asked. He had some plans he hadn't yet disclosed to her.

"Of course, baby," she replied. "I never leave home without it," she continued, wondering why he had asked if she had her license on her. She was hoping he wasn't going to ask her to drive. She was still a little shaken up and really wasn't in the mood to push the huge truck, but would if he needed her to.

A few minutes later, Dibiase pulled the ESV into the U-Haul lot on 60th and Good Hope Road. When he stopped at the front door, he reached in the glove compartment again, this time pulling out a wad of bills. Camille didn't have any idea what was going on as he looked at her and told her to get out and follow him. She didn't question him, just did as she was told. Dibiase had already phoned before they arrived and rented a midsize truck. They walked into the place and it smelled like fresh cardboard boxes. Dibiase thought about the smell at the funeral home and how everything in life had a smell to it, even a rat.

"Next in line," the attendant said.

Dibiase had Camille show her driver's license and the man asked if it was cash or credit.

"Greenbacks," Dibiase replied.

"In God we trust; all others must pay cash, right?" he continued, mustering out a smile.

Dibiase watched as the man punched multiple entries in the computer and instructed them about the usage of the truck. He gave them the mileage requirements and gas instructions.

"The truck must be returned with a full tank of gas; otherwise, it's seven dollars a gallon," the attendant said.

Dibiase knew the rules already and didn't give-a-fuck. He really wasn't in the mood for chit-chat. He just wanted to get the truck and go. Dibiase gave the man five hundred dollars, all hundred-dollar bills. The truck rental wasn't that much, but by paying cash, Dibiase had to leave a deposit.

Camille passed the man her driver's license and he turned to make a copy. She was still unaware of what was about to transpire and she still hadn't asked any questions. She knew ride-or-die chicks just rode to death.

Outside, Dibiase helped Camille in the truck and kissed her on the lips. "Follow me," he said and walked back to get in his own truck. He waved out the window to his girl Camille. He knew she was wondering what-the-hell was going on, but Dibiase had decided to make his next move his best move.

~ Two ~

Dibiase wasn't the least bit-concerned whether or not his baby could handle the box truck from U-Haul. He had let her push around the city in his truck at times, and it wasn't that much shorter than the U-Haul. Dibiase really loved her with all his heart.

The two of them had met in Zion, Illinois, at an all-night skate. Camille happened to be there with Donna, his godbrother J.C.'s main girl. It felt like just yesterday that he'd skated over to the concession stand to get a bottled water and check on his godbrother. J.C. and Donna were standing there sharing nachos when Dibiase noticed the thick, fine-ass redbone next to his godbrother's girl.

"Damn, will you two stop bitching about who's getting the last chip so Donna can introduce her homegirl," he said laughing.

He might have been laughing, but he was serious about knowing who the honey was with Donna. He had never seen her before around the city. She sure-as-hell didn't have that Milwaukee swag to her. She looked like she was from down south, maybe Cassopolis, Mississippi, or somewhere in Arkansas.

He could instantly tell that Donna's friend was the shy type the way she smiled and put the soft pretzel to her mouth. Her eyelids blinked rapidly as Dibiase checked her out from head to toe. When he saw she had sea-foam green eyes that matched her flawless skin, he was hooked. Donna introduced Camille as her cousin and Dibiase took it from there. The couple skated on a few slow jams and exchanged numbers. He knew she was going to be his woman.

Dibiase pulled the ESV in front of the house with Camille in the U-Haul right on his tail. He found reason to smile when he looked in the rearview mirror and saw her face. He looked around and was pleased to see that none of the people from the funeral were there yet. They had to be still at the church enjoying the repast for Rico. He

wasn't up to being surrounded by an army of fake-ass people just there to eat the chicken and dressing and tell fake stories about his father. Dibiase knew he didn't want to hear what anyone had to say about a man they thought they knew, especially when most of them were only around because of the generosity Rico had shown everyone. Rico had been like that. He was very kindhearted, whether he knew you or not. He'd had enough to make sure you were all right. Money was never an issue with him.

Dibiase use to smile all the time when his father Rico would talk and spit his game. Rico use to say it was because of him the rubber band companies stayed in business. He said he had more money than little girls had hair. It was still hard to digest the fact that his father's voice would never be heard again—on his cell, in the kitchen, period. He got out the truck, looking around. He'd seen one of his little partners standing at the end of the block and waved for him to come over. Little Ken, who they called 40 Ounce because whenever you saw him he was either chugging on a bottle of St. Ides or a bottle of Old English, came running to see what Dibiase wanted.

"Say, lil nigga, you want to make a few dollars?" Dibiase asked. Camille had gotten out the truck now and was standing next to Dibiase.

"Is the Pope Catholic? Hell yeah! I need some paper," Lil Ken replied.

"Well, put that damn-beer down and come help me move my stuff out my room."

"Shit, say no more, partner," he replied, ready to earn a twenty.

It was becoming clear to Camille exactly what was going on now and what the U-Haul truck was for. Dibiase was moving out of his mother's house. Seeing how he'd picked this moment, it was obvious to her he hadn't discussed it with his mother. Camille knew Cassie would most likely be hurt by him leaving. When they went inside, up

to his room, she understood now why he hadn't opened the door for her earlier. Most of his belongings were packed already and in boxes ready to be loaded.

Despite knowing how Cassie would feel about him moving, Camille knew Dibiase had something else on his mind. One thing that made her realize it was she didn't remember seeing J.C. at Rico's funeral and the two of them were inseparable. Also, the way he'd been acting prior to the funeral, and last, but not least, the fact he hadn't wanted to accompany the family in the limo. To her, it meant her man was up to something and he needed time to think things through. She knew Dibiase would act as if his father would have acted, and that was to protect the family by any means necessary. Now wasn't the time for her to try to hash it out, so she just continued helping by taking the smaller boxes out to the U--Haul. She was already exhausted from the day and she now had sweat beading on her forehead like she was Venus Williams. She said a silent prayer for Dibiase as she loaded the last small box.

Dibiase left the ESV in front of his mother's house for now. He told Camille to slide over so he could drive the moving truck to their new destination. She was more than happy to leave the driving to him. Besides that, she wanted to keep a watchful eye on him to see if she could get a read on whatever was on his mind. Dibiase drove to the new apartment almost in complete silence. There was no conversation, no radio playing, and no steering wheel tapping whatsoever. She kept cutting her eyes in his direction every few seconds to see if he was ready to talk, but nothing.

They were driving for about fifteen minutes when Dibiase finally turned into an apartment complex on Lovers Lane. He got out and went into a front office with a sign on the door reading Manager's Office. She watched as he walked into the building still wearing his dress pants and bow tie from earlier. Whatever it was he had to do took about twenty minutes. When he finally emerged again, he was carrying papers she assumed had to be a new lease.

Dibiase still didn't utter a word to her as he got back inside the truck. He just drove down a pathway and headed to the backside of the complex. Lil Ken came along, riding in the back of the truck. He seemed to be fine when they stopped and Dibiase opened the back of the truck. His forty-ounce St. Ides was now depleted of substance, so Dibiase knew a liquor store would be a required stop on the way back.

Dibiase went inside to check the place out; it was fine. The walls had been freshly painted, the carpet had been steam-cleaned, and the appliances were all updated just like he'd asked. Everyone started unloading the truck and he was grateful the unloading was going smoothly and quickly. When he noticed Camille started to look a little exhausted, he told her to stop lifting boxes and chill out. She had already dug inside one of his boxes and slipped on a pair of Old Navy shorts and a T-shirt. She had kept a whole wardrobe at his mother's house for when she stayed nights there with him. Now that Dibiase had moved out on his own, Camille was wondering if he was going to ask her to move in with him. She wanted to be by his side now more than ever. Camille hoped-like-hell, as much as she loved Dibiase, that he wouldn't shut her out. He was for sure the only man in the world she would ever love. In fact, Camille felt like there wasn't a world without him.

Just as Camille took a seat in the grass next to the walkway, watching Dibiase and Lil Ken finish with the last of the boxes, she noticed another truck pulling in, heading to where they were. A big red-and-white furniture truck pulled over and turned on the flashing hazard lights. Two men got out and she noticed the tall one who handed Dibiase his clipboard had a slight resemblance to the actor Brad Pitt. She watched as Dibiase intently scanned the man's manifest then nod with approval. Seconds after that, they went to work unloading the purchases Dibiase had set up the day before. The furniture was in clear plastic and Camille could see it was yellow Italian, most likely custom-made. She knew his father Rico loved the color yellow. He had driven a yellow Bentley, had yellow diamonds, and even wore custom yellow clothes at times. The two men finished unloading with two marble tables and a dining room set.

'Dibiase has it all figured out,' she thought.

As always, his timing was impeccable. He was so much like his father it was scary. Rico was a perfectionist when he did things. He was a very meticulous man. She knew calculation and perfection were in Dibiase's bloodline. When they say the apple doesn't fall far from the tree, it was an understatement when it came to Dibiase and his father.

Dibiase asked Camille if she wanted to stay at the apartment alone while he took Lil Ken and returned the truck. He was glad when she said she didn't want to stay alone nor did she want him to be alone at that moment. He knew how much she really cared for him and about his well-being. He curled the corner of his lips and managed to smile again as the three of them hopped in the front of the U-Haul truck.

After dropping the truck off and losing their deposit because Dibiase didn't gas it up, they hit his old block where the ESV was parked. There were at least two dozen vehicles parked out front of his mother's home. He could see the limo that had carried his mother and little brother was parked right up front by the main door. He could hear the loud music all the way outside and noticed a bunch of people crowded on the front porch. Some of them had plates of food in their hands, some had glasses full of Hennessey, some even already had to-go plates wrapped in foil. The screen door was shut but the front door was wide open, and he could hear Frankie Beverly and Maze's song *Back in Stride Again* blasting through the Bose system Rico had installed.

Dibiase was irritated, wondering why his mother wanted all the people from the church piled up in their home. His father's body hadn't been in the ground two hours and he felt she was making a party out of life. He saw a face he didn't mind seeing when he rounded the truck to give Lil Ken two one-hundred-dollar bills for his contribution. Ken smiled and dashed for the Love's liquor store a couple of blocks away.

His Uncle Mickey was outside mingling with the crowd of people. It looked more like he was trying to spit some game at Nicole Braxton, whose family owned a chain of watermelon stands throughout the inner city. It was rumored the green oval fruit had made them millions, and it was also rumored the Braxtons were related to them somehow. Dibiase knew Mickey didn't give two shits about rumors; if a-bitch's birth certificate didn't bear the last name of Hammond, to Mickey, she was workable.

There was a drunk who had fallen out on the lawn, crying and screaming out Rico's name. Dibiase remembered him from the gas station up the street. He was the man always begging for change when a person got out their ride. Dibiase remembered his father buying the man a bottle of window cleaner and a four pack of paper towels. He made the man wash his windows and the windows of every car that pulled in after him. When the man realized he had just made a hundred dollars in a couple of hours, he'd never had to beg again.

Mickey noticed his nephew and finally gave the Braxton girl a little breathing room. But before stepping away, he did let her know the conversation was far from over. Mickey was a player, he knew women inside out, and after talking five minutes to any one of them, he knew exactly what that particular one liked. He knew it wouldn't be long before he got a chance with Nicole. Distant relative or not, she was no different from any other-bitch he'd enticed into getting him some paper and giving him some pussy.

"Nephew," Mickey called out, waving Dibiase closer to him.

"What up, Unc? I see you're trying to work your cousin," he said playfully, but serious as a heart attack.

"That-bitch? Man, if I don't know her mother and father, she ain't my-muthafuckin-cousin. You know how much paper a face and an ass like that will bring in?" Mickey replied.

Dibiase just smiled at his Uncle Mickey's sure will to stay true to his nature.

"So what you need to holla at me about, Unc? I'm not staying long."

Dibiase had given Camille the keys to his ESV. She knew that meant she was back in the driver's0 seat, but she did want to go say something to his mother before they just bolted out of there. Mickey finished a piece of jerk chicken before he spoke. He licked his fingers, not wanting to let any of his sister-n-law's special sauce go to waste.

"So, neph, your old man left me with a few choice words for you," he said flatly.

"A few choice words, huh?" Dibiase questioned. He knew Mickey and his father had spent some time together before his father was killed.

"Your father knew how you are."

"I'm his-fuckin'-seed; of course he knew how I am," Dibiase replied, wanting his uncle to get to the point.

"D., look, for some odd reason, when I met with my brother, he said he felt death coming for him. He said he didn't know when or how, but something bad was going to happen," Mickey explained. "He also said, in the event of his demise, it wouldn't be from the hands of another man unless that man who took him away from his family was the Almighty."

Dibiase stood there in silence listening to the words coming from his uncle's mouth. It was strange because, as he flowed, it seemed like Mickey was Rico. The sound of his voice had changed to sound just like his father was talking directly to him now.

"Your father was a wise man, D. He knew if someone did something to him you would stop at nothing to find out who did it, and may God rest their souls when you found out."

"He did know me very well then, didn't he?" Dibiase said, watching the front door of the house.

"Yes, man, he knew you," Mickey said, removing a silver necklace from under his silk Brandolini shirt. Dibiase saw it was his father's old military dog tag but it also had a key on it.

"This is for you, Dibiase. Your father said, if anything were to suddenly happen to him, you should get this necklace and key." Mickey was sweating profusely from the spicy jerk chicken sauce.

"He said, if there was a change in you, you should have it. So, when I walked in from the church and saw your room was empty, I suspected that was the change he was talking about." Uncle Mickey paused for a second or two, knowing he was ready for another piece of chicken.

"So I guess you know what the key fits because he didn't tell me," Mickey confessed. "Nephew, all I've got to say is be careful out here, whatever you do. I don't want to lose another family member; you feel me?"

"I feel you, Unc," Dibiase replied, watching his Uncle Mickey turn and walk off. Mickey looked at Nicole as she was standing there talking with another woman. She had a nice shape underneath her dress, but Dibiase realized Mickey was more interested in heading to the kitchen to undress another piece of chicken first.

He thought about his uncle as he stood there. Mickey was a good man and Dibiase knew how much he loved his brother. There was no foul play even considered in his mind when it came to the relationship they'd had. Rico had given Mickey the game and Mickey had run with it, making himself a lot of paper in the streets. He had given up being big time almost a year ago when word got out he would be indicted. He still played around a little bit with his own personal clientele of white men who liked to endorse their fetishes with black women. He had a few doctors and lawyers who would come around and shoot dope, smoke crack, and write checks for black pussy. He was the man in their eyes, and it had worked out fine for him.

Dibiase saw his girl emerge from the front door. She was carrying two to-go plates and his mother was right behind her. Camille came all the way out while Cassie just stood there in the door jam. She knew her son well and knew he was hurting. She too knew he was like his father, so she just let him be, until he was ready.

"We leaving, boo?" Camille asked.

"It's about that time," Dibiase replied.

She started to ask him if he was going to go say something to his mother, but she thought better of questioning him. He jumped in the passenger side of his truck as she placed the plates on the back seat. He looked out the window, admiring the trees and everything they passed that had life. Life was precious, and no one had the right to cut down a tree and no one damn-sure had the right to gun down a man. People who did those type of things were supposed to be dealt with in a special way.

Dibiase continued to stare out the windows at the buildings and the skyline. It all seemed like a fictitious Polaroid picture to him. Camille went over a set of railroad tracks a little too fast and it jogged Dibiase out of his reverie.

"Are you hungry, honey?" Camille asked.

"Not really. I just want to get back to the new place and chill," he replied. "You know my head's still kind of fucked-up right now," he continued, still dealing with the death of his father.

"I know, honey; you're going through a lot right now. I lost my father when I was young, but even though we weren't as close as you and Rico were, I still felt the pain."

"Yeah, baby girl, this-shit hurts. My chest has been pounding like somebody is hitting me with a sledgehammer. Sometimes I feel like I can't breathe, and that it should have been me instead of him. I haven't even had time to talk to my brother and make sure he's okay."

"You sure you're okay, bae? Do you want to go to the emergency room and get looked at?" she asked, worried about her man.

"Trust me, there isn't a doctor in the world who can cure what I'm dealing with!"

Camille knew exactly what he meant and decided not to ask any more questions, to just let him vent and use her shoulder if needed.

She pulled his SUV into the parking lot of the new apartment and he pointed to the spot where they were assigned to park. They had an outside parking spot and an underground spot that cost fifty extra dollars a month. When they got inside, Dibiase looked around; he liked the place. He felt he could be himself and have some solitude if needed. He looked at the boxes on the floor and found the one marked bathroom. He knew there would be some clean towels and shower gel in the box so he could freshen up. He walked in the bathroom, turned on the water, and watched as steam filled the large bathroom like a sauna.

Camille undressed and joined him, stepping in behind him, touching his back. Dibiase rested his palms on the wall in front of him as she soaped up her sponge and cleaned him off. The feel of the hot water and her soft hands started to arouse him. He turned to face her, placing one of her legs on the rim of the porcelain tub. He gently rubbed her pussy with his index finger and felt how moist she was. His dick finally grew to capacity as he entered her eager insides. Camille rested her hands on his shoulders and thrust her torso back into his, meeting his every moment with precise timing. She kissed him, moving her tongue inside his mouth, causing him to pump harder.

Seconds later, Dibiase started to shiver and she began to do the same. He wanted to collapse right there in her arms; instead, he let out a loud sob, and said to her, "I can't believe some-muthafuckas killed my old man."

Dibiase was grateful for her. She had proven to be more than a queen, and he knew the right thing to do was one day put a ring on her finger. He took her face in the palms of his hands and kissed her softly on the lips before getting out.

"I see you didn't slip on getting some of that jerk chicken," he said, smiling.

"Your momma's jerk? Shit, I wouldn't miss it for the world," she replied, soaping her body, still in the shower.

Dibiase wrapped a towel around his body, telling her he would warm up the plates and be waiting on her. He walked back out to the living room, looking for a different box. He found the one marked 'jeans' and slipped on a pair of wrinkled Levi's. He saw he had left his dress pants in the middle of the floor and picked them up as well. He went through the pockets, removing his Rolex watch and money. He'd almost forgotten about the necklace with the key on it.

Camille was still in the shower and he could tell the sex had been good because she was singing a Beyoncé song. She always had a song to sing when he made her cum. He looked at the dog tag one more time before leaving the apartment, taking the back stairs that led to the basement storage area. He surveyed each storage space until he found the one he knew he was looking for. As soon as he slipped the key in the lock, it popped open.

~ Three ~

J.C. had finally gotten the chance to call Dibiase on his cell. D. answered on the fourth ring, stopping the voicemail from catching the call.

"Yo, bro; where-the-hell you at, homie?" J.C. asked impatiently.

"Calm down, bro," Dibiase replied.

"I told you I was copping Rico's hideout on the northwest side of town. I had to redo all the paperwork on the lease today." He continued relaying to his godbrother the day's events. Dibiase knew a few people would be curious as to why J.C. wasn't at the funeral, but it was none of their business as far as he was concerned.

"Where you at, my nigga?" D. asked J.C.

"Bro, check this-shit out. I was at some club up in Racine last night and I had to dump my-shit on some niggas," J.C. said.

"For real?" Dibiase replied, wanting to hear the details of what had gone down.

"Yeah, playa; some nigga called himself siccing his beat-up broad on me like I was green to the play, fam. Dude really thought I hadn't peeped his lame-ass move. First off, I knew the niggas was on some jack-ball-shit all the time. I had Don D. with me and already had sent him outside to be on-point, my nigga."

"That shit's crazy."

"Yeah, tell me about it. Weak-ass fools want to play cat-and-mouse games, but ended up getting themselves in a trap."

Dibiase smiled. He loved to hear his best friend and godbrother talk. One thing he knew was a lame-ass-nigga didn't have a-damn-thing coming. One had to get up pretty early to get anything over on J.C.

"So what-the-fuck went down?" Dibiase questioned.

"I played along and started mackin' on the little chick; shit, you know me. I was up in there shining, buying a few bottles, and had the bling on the neck and wrist like a Cash Money nigga, so I guess these bum-ass-niggas felt like I was a new dog pissing in the wrong territory," he explained, taking a puff on the blunt he was smoking.

Dibiase knew that was exactly what J.C. was most likely up to. He was as down as they come, and with J.C., it was never about where you were from; it was always about where you were now. Dibiase had played around with the game a little because of J.C. He'd grabbed a few extras here and there, but didn't really have to do much.

He had known the streets and the game well. He knew most of the players who had their shit together and the ones who weren't to be fucked-with. His father had put him and J.C. up on the do's and the don'ts, figuring they were going to creep and get a bag anyway. Dibiase knew his father didn't really want his firstborn son to have to be grinding, but he knew it was inevitable. His father use to say he had paved the way already for his family to eat for a very long time.

"Yeah, my nigga, I knew them cats wanted my pieces and that bankroll I was flashing at the bar. I was going to buy that-bitch out!"

Dibiase knew his brother was a hell-of-a-show-off. He had a certain swag about him that would make most men jealous if they were in the same club.

"You mean to tell me these niggas were actually going to try you? Huh!"

"Try me? Listen, Don D. hit my line and said these fools even had a wrecker pulling up to snatch up the Cutty!"

"They snapped! They were trying to get the '72 as well? They must really be some lame-ass-niggas who didn't know who they were fucking-with," Dibiase said, hitting his own blunt. He knew J.C. loved that car to death. The car was a gift from Rico. His father had found the car in Memphis, looking like it was on its last leg. He'd given J.C. over forty thousand to restore it back to its original look.

"I went out there and unleashed the twins. I mean, I aired out the whole parking lot. I sent the broad's nigga away in a black bag," J.C. said, not showing any remorse for just murdering someone.

"Damn, bro, you'd better be careful out there. Lay low for a minute just in case some other Milwaukee niggas hear about it. You know your car stands out like a sore thumb."

"Shit, I ain't too worried about it. You ask me, it was self-defense!"

"I feel you, bro, but you know how these laws are."

"I agree, but we still need to meet up."

"That's what's up. I'll be to get you shortly; we can hit Perkins," Dibiase said, forgetting about the jerk chicken he was supposed to share with Camille.

J.C. had just gotten out the shower himself. He was glad he'd gotten the chance to rap with his brother early. Chicago had been a dead trip for him and his cousin Don D. They'd gone over there looking for some cat named Dizzy, who was one of Rico's partners from the service. He knew Dibiase wanted to make the trip himself, but couldn't with the funeral and other things he was putting in place. J.C. understood his godbrother's position, and even though he'd wanted to be there for the funeral, he had elected to make the trip for Dibiase.

When the trip went bad, and he and Don D. were headed home, Don had suggested they stop in Racine. J.C. was reluctant to stop, wanting to get back, but had decided to check out the new club he'd heard about on the radio. Besides, he had known his cousin had a little skeezer in Racine he wanted to see, so he made the decision to go ahead and hang out for a few hours. It was a decision that had cost some hater his life. He hated now that he'd even exited the highway on Route 20.

J.C. wasn't the least bit upset he'd had to add to his body count. Killing had become second nature to him, and with Don D. on his side, it hadn't made matters any better. He had been trying to slow down, but he wasn't going to accept a jacking from anyone. He knew, since the death of his godfather, that the streets were about to do a drastic one-eighty—at least for everyone in his crew. Rico wasn't only his godfather, but he was his plug as well. He had put J.C. deep in the game and had given him game right along with it. He was like a father to him, and even though he was J.C.'s godfather, it had made him and Dibiase brothers. His death was heavy on J.C.'s heart.

"Yo, Don, I've got to make a run. Hand me a zip of that dro; my personal is on the low-low, homie," he said, waking his cousin up.

"I got it, big dog," Don replied, handing his favorite cousin the only medicine that kept his nerves intact.

"Thanks, cuzo. Hey, I'll be back shortly to scoop you so we can ride."

"One, cuz."

"Make sure you check on that broad you fucked-with in Racine. I want to know what their streets are saying. Don't do too much talking either; let the broad do all the talking, fam," J.C. said, making sure he gave Don D. the game.

"I'm on it, fam. You know I ain't going to say-shit. I'm going to call her in about ten minutes, right after I shower and blow one back," he replied, watching as his big cuz left out.

Don D. wasn't from the same set as Dibiase and J.C. He was J.C.'s mother's sister's son and had been raised in Baltimore. He'd come to Milwaukee and fit right in. Being from a city where they buried the enemy in vacant, boarded-up houses, and the police were all scared to come in the hood and do anything about the hustlers, it was only fitting that his mentality was a little outrageous when it came to getting paper. But nonetheless, J.C. loved his cousin and would die for him.

Don D. was happy he'd fit in with J.C. and Dibiase. He'd started making money right away and meeting plenty of chicks who were down for anything he wanted to do. There was plenty of money in Baltimore, but if you didn't work for one of the top players, you were subject to get killed. It was so crazy they had even made a television series about the way shit went down in his city. He was living proof of what went on in Baltimore. Some of the little homies use to love to hear him sit around and tell stories about how it went down.

J.C. pulled the strawberry-colored '72 Cutlass in front of the duplex where his girl stayed. He got out, looked up, and saw Donna was on the top porch doing her daughter's braids. Keava wasn't J.C.'s real daughter, but he had been in her life since she was able to talk, so he treated her like she was his own child.

"Hey, lil mama, you happy to see me?" he called up.

"YEAAAH!" Keava yelled down, causing everybody to laugh.

She knew J.C. was talking to her mother, but she'd answered because she was happy to see him too. She knew she needed a fresh pair of Air Maxes for school and J.C. wouldn't hesitate to give her whatever she wanted. Donna stood up and leaned over, showing the top half of her thirty-six double-C breasts through the tank top she had on.

"Bae, you coming up? I know you've got something good to smoke on," she said.

"I got a lil something, ma; you know how I get down," he replied.

"Come on, bae; come on up. I just fried some pork chops and made some rice."

"I'm on my way up, but I ain't hungry for food," J.C. replied, smiling.

"Ughhh, Momma! Y'all nasty," Keava said, eavesdropping.

"Don't get too grown now!" Donna snapped back at her daughter.

Keava knew exactly how far to go with her mother and didn't say anything else for fear of getting popped. J.C. made it upstairs, and sat at the kitchen table, removing his sack of dro. Usually when he and Donna smoked together, it led to the bedroom, and he'd add another hole to the drywall behind the headboard. He smiled thinking about it, knowing the smoke he had was grade A and would normally serve as the perfect aphrodisiac. Keava came running in the kitchen first to give him a hug.

"Hey, J., I need some new shoes. Can you help a sista out?" she said, giving him her 'I love you' face.

Keava had just turned thirteen and she wasn't his biological daughter, but she was his despite what other nigga's blood she had running through her veins. He had vowed to take care of her for the rest of her life when he'd first laid eyes on her as a baby. J.C. extracted the wad of bills from his pants pocket and handed her a fifty-dollar bill. She instantly changed her happy look to a sad one instead.

"Girl, what's that look for?"

"Pops, I want some Air Maxes and this won't be enough to even get some piss wipers."

He didn't hesitate for one second. He went to the middle of his bankroll and removed three one-hundred-dollar bills, giving them to her.

"Now, how's that for my little princess?"

Her reply was a big hug and kiss on the cheek. "You're the best daddy a girl could ever have," she replied.

He always wondered if he and Donna split up, would she still let him take care of Keava. He tried not to think about that because it wasn't often the two of them fought about anything. He kept the bills paid, the fridge full, and her booty satisfied. He knew she couldn't replace him with the slim picking of bum-ass-niggas on the streets. Donna was standing in the kitchen doorway, watching the entire transaction go down.

"Now, J., that little thang didn't need that much money for no shoes," Donna said, knowing her words were going to fall on deaf ears anyway.

"Hold up a minute," J.C. said. "Never once has she said, 'Daddy, why you giving Momma so much money on the bills; that sexy thang doesn't need all that money for the bills'," he continued playfully.

She just shook her head. Donna was actually glad he had the relationship he had with her daughter. Keava's real sperm donor was doing a life bit in Waupun prison for murdering a woman at a check cashing place in broad daylight over forty dollars.

"Now come on over here with your sexy-ass and give me some attention. You think you want to hit some of this head banger I got?"

Donna walked over to where J.C. was sitting and sat on his lap. She took the blunt from him and choked as the thick smoke coated her lungs. She was wearing a loose tank top and some tight-fitting white booty shorts. She knew what drove him crazy. He could feel Russell starting to swell in his pants as she wouldn't be still from the choking. He reached back and palmed her round, firm ass and it didn't take Donna long to feel the creation that kept rising between his legs. Donna whispered something in his ear and they disappeared ten seconds later into her bedroom.

J.C. heard his cell vibrating on the nightstand. It was obviously important because the caller dialed right back, causing the phone to make its way to the floor. He had fallen asleep after Donna had put in that real work. She was like a wildcat sometimes and today was one of those days. She only got like that on two occasions: either she was about to come on her period, or the good weed had her feeling herself.

He leaned off the bed, picked up his phone, and noticed he had several missed calls. He looked at his rose gold-colored Invicta, not realizing he had let that much time go by. Dibiase had tried to reach him three times. He knew Donna had probably heard the phone, but she never told him when his phone was ringing in fear that one day he was going to take a call and it would be the last time she'd see him. Street life made him accept her reasoning and they never argued about it. He dialed Dibiase's number, knowing he was wide awake and an hour late for their meeting. Dibiase answered right away.

"My fault, bro; I'm at Donna's spot and fell asleep," he said.

Dibiase knew exactly what had happened. "Don't trip, freak-ass-nigga, I know she put it on you," he said, laughing. "Just get up and watch out for me. I'm not far from there."

"That's what's up; give me ten."

"Cool; we can ride out by the new crib. We're only taking one whip. I don't want your hot-ass-ride out there. I told your-ass to grab a hoopty."

"Fuck I look like in a hoopty, nigga?" he asked, laughing but knowing his brother was right. "You're right and I'm going to head up to Harry's one day this week and grab something," J.C. replied.

"HARRY'S? Nigga, I said a hoopty. You'd better take your-ass to Bargain Bill's or CarMax. You know Harry don't sell hoopties."

"Just hurry up before this damn-woman of mine rolls over," J.C. said, ending the call.

J.C. rolled over and slapped Donna gently on her ass. Soon as she felt the contact of his hand, she rose up, still wet and ready from the first round. J.C. admired her body. She had a Halle Berry stomach with a Williams' sisters' ass. If you didn't know she'd had a baby, you wouldn't be able to tell just looking at her. She was one of the few women he knew who'd had a child and could still stand next to Nia Long in a two-piece and make your decision hard-as-hell. Her skin was that flawless.

"Baby, get up and throw me a couple chops in the microwave. I've got to get ready. Dibiase's on his way."

"Hmmm, I thought you weren't hungry? Besides, didn't you just get fortified with eight essential vitamins?"

He started to bend down and go right back between her legs, but he knew once he started putting that tongue on her, it would lead to round two.

"You talking shit, huh?"

"I'm just saying, baby." She smiled.

"If I didn't have this meeting with D., I swear I would finish tearing up this wall. Make your landlord come put your-ass out of here," J.C. said, wanting to stay.

She stood up in the bed with her hands on her hips. It was like she was daring him to pass up on what she had to offer.

"Come on now, girl, stop playing."

"Oh, you think it's a game? You think *all this* is a muthafuckin game?" she said, dropping to her knees, still on the mattress and crawling to his side. Donna reached for him, and in one swift movement, he was inside her mouth. She moaned loudly as she swallowed as much of his manhood as she could.

"Damn, baby!" he said, running his fingers through her hair.

J.C. took a handful of Donna's hair in his fist and guided her head back and forth. She had no problem challenging herself, taking in every inch slowly until her lips touched the base of his dick. His head snapped back as he came. His knees got weak and he almost buckled to the floor. He knew he had to keep his composure and get ready for business.

"Okay, baby, you win. I'll be in early tonight."

"I thought you would see it my way," she replied, smiling.

J.C. pulled up his pants and headed to the kitchen. He grabbed the loaf of Wonder Bread and forgot about using the microwave. She had fucked and sucked him up an appetite. Donna came out in a silk robe, telling him she needed some bill money for the lights. He didn't even argue with her. J.C. just took the rest of the money in his pocket and laid it on the table.

"Well, damn, I didn't expect all that."

"Shit, I started to go to the safe," he said, smiling.

J.C. rolled himself another blunt and wrapped his sandwich in a paper towel. He heard some loud music coming near and knew it had to be Dibiase. At the same time as Dibiase was pulling up, Keava was returning from the mall. She waved at D. and told him she was on her way upstairs and would let J.C. know he was out there.

~ Four ~

TWA flight 504 landed at McCarran International right at its scheduled time. Rico and his beautiful wife Cassie had a limo reserved waiting to take them to their suite at the Flamingo Hotel and Casino. Cassie had wanted to stay at the Excalibur but Rico had talked her into staying at the Flamingo. It was the first place the gangster Bugsy Siegel had built and had a lot of sentimental value to Rico.

The Vegas airport was crowded as usual this time of year, but Rico's experience taught him to just keep it moving and not get caught up in any of the tourist attractions the airport offered. A person could spend their whole trip gambling right there before even making it to their room. Now that was gangster for real. People who played the games at the airport had to be crazy. They obviously didn't believe the cliché: What happens in Vegas stays in Vegas. Well, it was the same thing when it came to gambling. What was won at the Vegas airport stayed at the Vegas airport. No one won there and turned around and took a flight back home; it was a pure-genius set up. Vegas had never been built on winners and Rico knew that firsthand. He gambled but it was only for leisurely fun. He already felt his life had been a gamble, and now that he was finally living, the risk had definitely been worth the reward.

The Chrysler 300 limo was waiting patiently outside concourse K for Rico and Cassie. When the Colombian driver spotted him, he rushed over to help with their bags. The driver didn't say much in the car and Rico knew his job was to just drive them straight to the hotel. The good thing about it was the ride from the airport to the hotel was short.

Once they got there, Cassie checked their confirmation number and they headed straight for the presidential suite on the top floor. Rico's people always made sure, since they were the majority stockholders in the hotel, he got the room he wanted. It was the actual room Bugsy had resided in when he was in Vegas. He had seen the movie and the room was exactly like it was on the big screen. The rest of the hotel had been updated a little and Rico had heard talk about the people he knew building a second Flamingo further down the strip. The new amenities were most likely going to be put in place to appease the younger gamblers, those who didn't know much about the history of Las Vegas. He didn't want anything to do with a new Flamingo; the insane feeling he got from staying in the old one was enough for him.

Cassie sprawled the luggage out on the huge double king-size bed and hurriedly unzipped her Louis Vuitton bag. She found an all-black sheath Gucci ensemble with a split way up the side she thought would be perfect for the Vegas heat. She knew they had front row seats at the Roy Jones fight in the MGM in a couple of hours. They had been to Vegas so many times, the normal person would have been sick of it, but not Cassie Hammond. She actually loved the heat, the shopping, and the shows with all the unsung music heroes who were given one more chance to perform before they were washed all the way up.

Cassie also had made a friend in Las Vegas, the beautiful Julia Hernandez, who was the wife of Rico's plug. Julia had begged Cassie to come to Vegas several times without her husband, and she had liked Julia so much it didn't take much convincing. The two of them had hit it off. She remembered her first trip to hang out with Julia well. She had spent over a hundred grand shopping. She'd purchased so many items she'd had to Fed-X most of the items she bought home. It was an amazing time. She'd had only nine thousand in cash and twenty thousand in cashier checks, but Julia had promised her the sky was the limit, and since money was no problem, the sky had become the limit. She was going to call her husband back home and have him wire her the money, but Julia Hernandez wouldn't have it.

Rico was in the shower, getting ready for the night's event. He heard his wife speaking but couldn't make out what she was saying because of the powerful shower head. He didn't answer right away because he wasn't sure if she was talking to him or on the phone with someone.

"HONEY, DID YOU HEAR ME?" *Cassie yelled as she walked into the huge bathroom that was done completely in marble.*

Rico was washing his hair so the water had his hearing halfway plugged.

"No, honey, I didn't hear you. I was washing my hair," *he replied.* "What were you saying?"

"Will Julia and Tito be there tonight?"

"Yes, of course, baby; it's a big fight. Everyone will be there tonight."

Cassie wasn't sure what he meant when he said everyone would be there tonight. She didn't care about what the men would be doing. Cassie just wanted to hang out with her friend. Something felt different about this trip anyway. It felt more like business than a vacation, so she was already mentally prepared to be spending most of her time without him.

Cassie and Rico had talked briefly about what his intentions were for them coming to Vegas this time. She was glad when she'd heard what he was saying to her. She was a little scared because she knew how those people got down, but she knew Rico and trusted he knew what he was doing. Nevertheless, she felt it was going to be okay, and she couldn't wait to see her friend and hit the stores.

The MGM was a beautiful casino and hotel on the main strip in Las Vegas. It was a premier spot where most of the stars hung out when they visited and the food at the establishment was to die for. Rico stepped out the Chrysler 300 limo first in his black-and-white Armani suit with matching bow tie and gator shoes. The lights that illuminated the outside of the lavish casino seem distracted by all the diamonds he wore on his neck and wrist. The patrons outside all turned to see if they recognized the distinguished-looking man getting out the car. *Vegas was a place if you wanted to compile autographs of the rich and famous you were most definitely in the right spot.* Rico heard a woman yell out, "IT'S DENZEL!" Then he heard her man tell her to shut-the-fuck-up; it wasn't Denzel.

He stuck his left hand out so his beautiful wife Cassie could emerge from the limo. Cassie Hammond was just as beautiful as any Hollywood star. Her long, sleek legs slid out first, exposing the black stiletto red bottoms she wore. The dress she had chosen was elegant and her jewelry accented well. She could have easily been the cover model for *Vogue* magazine or the centerfold for *Jet*, even at her age. Rico tightened his muscle so his wife could use his arm as a grip. They interlocked arms as she cleared the limousine. The tourists began looking at the couple even harder when Cassie joined him, wondering if she was the famous one. There was already a huge array of stars present on their way to see the fight.

Cassie began making out a few faces of her own: Eddie Murphy, Magic Johnson, and Baby Face. Michael Jordan was pulling up in a red-and-black Ferrari, and Cassie almost fainted when she saw Jay-Z and Beyoncé. She had never been star-struck though, and really, she was glad people weren't doing like they normally did, questioning her about what soap opera she played on. Last time she was there, the paparazzi wouldn't leave her and Julia alone. They'd thought she was Faith Evans and Julia was Christina Aguilera. They'd kept on asking her about the Biggie Smalls shooting. She could only imagine the real Faith had to disguise herself when she went out in public.

Rico and Cassie were ushered straight to the front, not having to wait in the lines like the other unknown people. Cassie's head kept turning from side to side in hopes of spotting her friend Julia before they got in the arena and got seated, but she had no such luck. They made it to the entrance of the arena and Rico handed the usher their tickets. Their seats were in the second row and the man escorting them had to radio to a lower-level usher to come meet them. One thing Rico always had was front-row seats at any event in Vegas. It was part of the perks that came with his kingpin status and Colombian connections.

When they finally made it down the aisle to their seats, Cassie's frown turned into a smile. She saw Julia and her husband, Tito Hernandez, had already been seated. The usher told them they were in seats thirteen and fourteen, which meant Rico would be seated right next to Tito. It was rumored the Feds came to boxing matches because a lot of illegal business took place during the fights. No one knew how true that was, but it didn't stop the Hernandez cartel from conducting their business.

On the way to their seats, Rico shook hands with some of the heads and bosses who ran other states for the Hernandez cartel. Tito was the main man though. He was in control of the entire organization and the only person higher than him was his father, which none of the other underbosses had ever met in person. Rico was the only black man in the family and the only one who had ever met Tito Hernandez in person.

He knew as he shook hands with Jimmy Mancini and his brother Carlos that they were jealous of him for having that one-up on them. Little did they know, Rico wished sometimes the meeting he'd had with Tito had never occurred. When Julia saw Cassie, her eyes lit up, glad Rico hadn't come alone. The women knew they weren't going to stay for the fight and risk the chance of someone getting punched and spit flying in their hair. They'd both rather spend their time catching up and doing some shopping. As far as they were concerned, boxing was for men; punching each other's lights out for a couple of bucks just didn't sit right with them. Rico had explained that boxing was a big-money sport, but to Cassie, it still didn't make any sense. First chance the ladies got they bolted out of there. Neither husband batted an eye, just kissed their wives and let them through the aisle.

The main event was getting ready to start as the last amateur bout had just ended. Tito was saying he'd made four million on the fight and had laid anther six on Enzo Maccarinelli. Rico thought he was crazy, but somehow Tito had a vested interest in Maccarinelli and some inside intel he would win the fight against the older fighter Roy Jones. The announcer introduced both fighters and the beautiful hot chick paraded around the ring with the round card.

Tito never talked during the rounds, so Rico sat and waited patiently to get to their discussion. He knew it wasn't going to be pleasant for either one of them. Rico thought about the Tyson-Douglas fight where Tito had lost two million dollars and hadn't blinked an eye. Rico had actually won two hundred grand betting on the right fighter that night. He'd decided not to bet on tonight's event because he truly believed in Roy Jones and wanted him to win, but he knew Tito was precise and really had great sources when it came to information.

Money wasn't an issue for Tito; being the head of the CCC had made him one of the richest men in the world, to the point he was almost becoming untouchable. If any product moved across the United States from the west, it was stamped CCC. If it came from the West Coast and wasn't stamped CCC, dead bodies followed. Rico knew the CCC survived because Tito was a tenacious leader. He also knew something he wasn't supposed to know about the family. He felt when they discussed what he wanted, that's when what he knew would come into play.

The underground city the cartel family had built ran from Arizona through Las Vegas right into California. It had taken ten years to perfect it, but it was the way the Hernandez family controlled the trafficking of their dope. Rico had seen it had working electricity, sleeping rooms, and railcars that traveled at a moderate speed to help with transporting. It had become enormously successful when they figured out how to bury a server down there so they could have some type of telecommunications available. Most of the remaining cartel families were now investing in submarines since the FBI had invested in speedboats faster and better than the ones the drug lords were using.

Tito always stayed a step ahead of what the FBI was doing and Rico knew this was due to the Washington, D.C., connections he had in the White House. Fifty million was a small price to pay for information when your empire was worth billions. Tito had a brother who was in jail doing a life sentence for trafficking. His whole empire in Florida had gone down because of speedboats. When Rico first got in the game with the Hernandez family, Tito had said something to him: "The government knows everything that goes on above ground, but what happens below ground, they know nothing." Rico remembered those words he spoke as if he'd just said them yesterday. "Dem mutterfuckas can control the top harvest, but da stinky bastards can't control what grows inward. I have control."

Sometimes Rico dreamed about that day and sometimes the dreams were more like nightmares.

~ Five ~

Dibiase pulled off in the Escalade, adjusting the driver seat with the lumbar control, relaxing in the plush interior as he leaned. He fired up another blunt he had pre-rolled and turned up the volume with the steering-wheel control. He loved to play a little old-school music, while J.C. was just the opposite. The Isley Brothers and Maze were Dibiase's shit; J.C. was more into Plies and Jeezy.

J.C. chilled and slumped his body back in the passenger side of his brother's black truck. He was thinking about his baby girl and that he needed to show her a little bit more about saving her chips for a rainy day. His stepdaughter Keava had spent all the money at the mall he had just given her and it bothered him she wasn't more currency-conscious. Dibiase admired how his boy had taken to Donna's little girl. He watched him on several occasions dealing with her, and even though J.C. had an itchy trigger finger when it came to the niggas on the street, he had a real soft spot for Donna and her daughter. They were his world away from the ghetto madness.

"My bad, bro, you know how it be when a-nigga's in them guts," J.C. said, giving his godbrother dap with the handshake they had made up years ago.

"What it do, my nig?" Dibiase replied, passing the loud smoke to his boy.

"Nothing, man. I hope this here is that head banger, bro. You know I don't be putting that huff in my system."

Dibiase looked at his brother and said, "Nigga, you ain't the only mofo with the-nigga Cheese's number."

Cheese was the-nigga in the hood who had the best weed product. Nobody knew where he got it from, but he always had some shit that had weird names and would get you as high as you wanted to be.

"That was some wicked-ass-shit that went down in Racine, bro," J.C. said, pulling on the cigar paper filled with the sticky.

"I knew I shouldn't have been hanging out in that dump-ass-city anyway. I mean everybody knows them-niggas in that town are starving like real mutts, but I hope they realize they fucked-with the wrong one today."

"Man, J, you're always smoking some-damn-body. You're a fool, bro. You know something?" Dibiase asked.

"What's that, my-nig?"

"Your crazy-ass is going to singlehandedly make the Mil the murder capital of the world. Shit, your body count is really piling up, my nigga," Dibiase continued as he accepted the blunt back.

"Your-ass was taking so long I stopped and grabbed some food too," he said, making sure his two Bungalow dinners didn't spill their juices all over his truck's carpet.

J.C. was listening as Dibiase was talking to him spitting his knowledge. "Hopefully not, my-nig, but you know how I roll. I let the chopper chop, especially if a fool's on that dumb-dumb." He chuckled. "And furthermore, bro, Racine technically isn't Milwaukee. Niggas need to realize they can get merc'd on the outskirts as well as underneath the skirt."

"Yeah, we both know that," Dibiase replied, turning right off Burleigh Street, heading northbound on Fond Du Lac Avenue.

"Say, bro-bro, I drove all over Chi-town last night looking for that cat you sent me to try to find," J.C. said irritably. He was thinking about how rough the city was, and his and Don D.'s trip over there.

"This-nigga must be like a ghost or something. Shit, I couldn't find a living soul to point me in the right direction. I'm telling you that-shit was a lost cause, looking for that-motherfucker."

"Honestly, I knew that-shit was going to be a tough assignment. I was really hoping he would show up at Pop's funeral, but he didn't," Dibiase replied, stopping at a red light on Capitol Drive.

He looked over in ZaZa's parking lot and saw one of his homeboys standing around trying to off his new mix tape. He really didn't have time to stop as the dude was waving him down to do so. Dibiase supported all his people who were trying to start a movement, didn't matter if it was mix tapes or some urban novel they had written. If you were on your grind, he respected you for that. Dibiase knew he would catch up with the homie later, so he just bumped the horn and put his thumb and pinky to his ear sending a signal for the homie to just call him. The light turned green and Dibiase rode off.

"Telling you, bro-bro, we found out where some-broad he was dealing with lived and rode through there to holla at ol' girl. I was surprised she even answered the door, but she told us she hadn't even seen him in weeks, and bro, check this shit . . ." J.C. paused while he hit the blunt.

"The chick was bad-as-hell too for an older broad. I ain't into older chicks but, baby, she looked just like the moms on the *Cosby Show*, dawg, when Phylicia Rashad was in her prime. Man, you can't tell a-nigga that every-nigga didn't wanna run up in Theo's momma." J.C. laughed and Dibiase had to laugh at the thought of him being correct.

"But, baby girl, had a look like she got high on that shit too. She did say dude just pops in and out when he wants to."

"She say when the last time she'd seen him?"

"Nope, not all. She thinks the Navy fucked-his-head-up," J.C. stated, wondering if the dude they were looking for was fucked-up upstairs from the Navy for real. He thought any-nigga who could leave a piece like that alone for weeks must be shell-shocked from the war or something.

"Don't trip; hopefully, this cat finds us. I got a pretty good idea he will come looking real soon; trust me on that one," Dibiase said.

"So, man, what else the-fuck is going down in our dead-ass-city? I see you stepped up the game, nigga, and moved out of Mom's crib. So, what, you ready to really get this paper out here in these streets, man?" J.C. asked.

J.C. knew how much his brother played with the game, which wasn't much at all. They both had paper, but J.C. was out there and Dibiase was on his way to getting out there.

"Looks like I don't have a-fucking-choice now, don't it? I don't play poker but I don't fold either. Somebody just stripped me of my full house and now I've got to flush them the-fuck-out, royal flush out, bro. Ya dig, my-nig?"

"That's what-the-fuck I've been talking about. There's a lot of money out here in the streets, so you know I'm down," J.C. replied, giving Dibiase more ghetto points.

J.C. was all about the paper and he knew, with his clientele, they could get it at the drop of a dime by the backpack. He had a quick vision of him, Dibiase, and Don D. doing it big like he'd always dreamed for the crew. With the bloodline Dibiase had and the way he spit knowledge, this was what he'd always wanted and finally it was coming to light.

"We're 'bout to get it in, fo' real fo' real, so, man, let me ask, how is the rest of the family holding up? I know Lil Rickey's fucked-up, and Moms, she's got to be all fucked-up too behind this bullshit. All this-shit's got me fucked-up too, bro," J.C. said, still not knowing why the Chicago mission was so important.

He really hadn't wanted to miss Rico's funeral. He'd wanted to pay his last respects to the man who'd raised him and treated him like his own son. He knew he couldn't wait to go see his headstone and show his respects to Rico.

"J.C., man, to tell you the truth, everybody's fucked-up. Even though I've been around as little as possible, I know how hurt they are. Financially, I know Moms is sitting pretty, but money isn't worth a life. That woman loved my pops, bro. Tell you the truth, I have never seen a couple like them before. Lil bro, he's just chilling. I think he still cutting hair at the shop and getting shit back to business as usual. Lil dude, he's really taking it better than I thought he would," Dibiase said, still tripping on how well his baby brother was taking the assassination of their pops. He'd looked at his little brother when they were at the funeral home and he had not even shed a tear. Dibiase figured he probably would break down soon, but he'd held up great in front of everyone.

"Man, I miss our pops like crazy all-fuckin'-ready. He always told us, 'Remember, the game is cold but fair'," J.C. said, closing his eyes. The blunt went out and he decided to relight it.

"You miss him. Can you imagine what's going on in my head?" Dibiase looked at him.

"I wasn't sure I was going to be able to make it. Fuck, that dude Rico was my life. I loved that man more than anything or anyone in this world. Half these-niggas out here don't even know their pops. My dude was there since birth, bro."

He continued looking in the rearview, making sure no police were in sight. When he looked at the speedometer, he realized he was going ten over on a city street.

"I'm so glad I never knew my real pop's punk-ass like that. I heard stories that the foul-ass-nigga died of Hepatitis B or some weak-ass-shit like that when I was three, but I also heard he wasn't a stand-up dude like Rico anyway. Man, Rico to me was my pops, you know that."

"Yeah, I guess when you don't really know your old man, it doesn't hurt as bad," Dibiase said.

"I don't think I was hurt like that at all over mine, but I think, at some point in every man's life, they want to know whose seed they are, you know, see if they have some kind of connection with the-nigga who made them. Shit, you know what I'm saying—like, check out his features and see if there's any resemblance there. Maybe even shoot a jumper together," J.C. replied, thinking not only about himself but about Keava's real father.

The-nigga had tried to call collect one day, and J.C. had accepted the call and checked him. He'd never called back. "Niggas got the fatherhood game fucked-up," he continued, glad that all she knew was him and that was how it was going to stay.

He had already promised himself to be all dude wasn't to that little girl. J.C. knew his promise had a lot to do with his own life, the disconnection with his biological father, and the connection with Rico, his godfather.

"That's some deep-shit, bro. I guess having Rico, you know, I never had to look at shit through the eyes of someone who didn't have theirs. But, right now, I can definitely feel where-the-fuck you're coming from."

"See, bro, you remember how it was when your pops first bought me in. I was lost and that's why I came in like I did as a shorty. D., man, your pops embraced me. Rico showed me mad love, you feel me, like I was his own seed. It was all foreign to me, man. I had my mother's love and shit, but Rico? That man was that-father-figure a-nigga needed," J.C. said, honestly knowing that, if it hadn't been for Rico, he probably would have ended up in Wales School for Boys or Green Bay Prison, which was gladiator school. His life as he knew it today wouldn't be what it was, that was for sure.

"He sure was that; you can say that again, my-nigga," Dibiase replied, thinking about the final day he'd spent with Rico before his demise. He reached inside his armrest and pulled out a bottle of D'Usse.

"One thing, and I might sound like I'm on repeat, but Pops always had that good game for a young-nigga's-ass too," J.C. continued his thought, finally getting a little smile to cross his brother's lips.

"Say, bro, now that's real talk," Dibiase said, busting the top on the bottle of cognac.

"Not that what we been talking about ain't some real shit, but I do have some real talk for yo'-ass, bro," Dibiase said, taking a swig and passing the bottle to J.C., who frowned as the liquor went down smoothly.

J.C. was about to comment on what Dibiase was on, but before he could say anything, his cell began ringing. He looked at the screen, thinking it was probably Donna, but it was his cousin Don D. calling. He hit the blunt again, took another swig, and motioned to Dibiase to hold his thought. He had to take Don's call to see if anything had come about with what had gone down.

"Yo, lil cuz, what's cracking?" J.C. asked, hitting the D'Usse one more time. He wasn't normally a brown liquor connoisseur, but he had to admit the taste of it was smooth.

"I just got off the line with ol' girl from over them ways," Don said.

"Oh yeah? What's that tramp talking about?"

"She said the cat who went out toe-tagged was the chief of police's nephew."

"For real? Well, I don't really give-a-fuck if dude was Barack's nephew, he was on some foul-shit and got exactly what he had coming."

"I'm just saying, cuz, that's the word on the street up there," Don replied.

Don D. was a little salty because he was thinking, now he wasn't going to be able to see the chick again and her head game was up-top.

"Yo, cuz, they're also saying they got a description of the getaway car, but they didn't get a plate or a description of the driver."

"The police chief's nephew, huh? That's like a little baby pig in a blanket," J.C. said, making light of the fact he'd smoked a police officer's kinfolk.

"Baby girl said the rollers are sweating everybody down there driving an old school. You know I might have to cut her water short and quit fucking-with her. That's a shame; she got that good too," Don D. said, contemplating whether he would really stop-fucking Tanisha.

"I feel you, cuz, M.O.B. We can't risk getting this paper, especially not for some-ass."

"Right, right, I feel you, cuz, but make sure you put the Cutty in a shop; at least get that-bitch painted."

"I got you, lil cuz. I'm riding with D.B. right now, but when I get back, I'm going to scoop you and we can step out for a second," J.C. replied, ready to end the call.

"Yeah, let's hit Connie's Night Life. They'll be jumping tonight," Don replied.

"Cool; one, fam."

J.C. ended the call and hit the blunt again. He cracked the window and tossed the roach out. Dibiase waited until J.C. had ended the call with his cousin Don before speaking.

"I hope everything is all good with that-shit, bro," Dibiase said.

"Shit, it is what it is, but I got the-shit under control though."

"I'm saying that because we about to get on some real-shit and I need you focused, fam. You know more about the-shit than I do, so your full, undivided attention is what's needed."

"I have never let our pops down before, so what makes you think things are going to change now? Whatever needs to be done, man, I'm with it," J.C. replied, as serious as he could be.

"What I'm on is a new takeover, bro. You're the one who asked me if I was ready for this street life, right? Like you were testing me now that Pops is gone. You wanna make sure I eat just as good," Dibiase said as he pulled the truck in the underground parking structure. The roof of the garage was barely high enough for the truck to clear it.

"D., I wasn't trying to come at you in a disrespectful way. I was just saying you know firsthand how I get down out here, so you're going to eat regardless. We are brothers in my mind and heart; can't no DNA test change either for me."

"That's what I'm talking about," Dibiase replied.

Dibiase loved J.C. like he loved Little Rickey, his blood brother. He knew J.C. wasn't disrespecting him or giving him an ultimatum. He just knew what he knew, and it was about to go down. J.C. was on a couple of bricks and it was good money enough to carry them to a certain extent, but life was about to change for the better. Dibiase had known when Uncle Mickey gave him the dog tag with the key on it what the key went to. He didn't let anyone know about the apartment because the place was Rico's spot. It was a spot he'd never taken anyone to. Rico had moved out one day prior to being gunned down and given all his furniture to charity. When Uncle Mickey had showed up with the key, it was easy for Dibiase to read between the lines. His father was a master at saying things without actually using words to convey his message.

Earlier, when Camille was in the shower and he'd gone down to the storage area, he really didn't know what to expect to find in the black footlocker Rico had left him. His heart was beating so fast he was almost reluctant to open the chest. When he finally got his nerve up and popped it open, there were fifty kilos of uncut, pure cocaine. Each of the bricks was wrapped in yellow plastic, secured with grey duct tape and an alligator symbol in the middle. Around the logo were the letters CCC, which Dibiase had an idea what it stood for. He broke out in a deep sweat. He had seen a lot of dope before, but never fifty kilograms at once. Dibiase did his thing on a different level, but J.C. was trained to go in a situation like this. Rico had fully given him the game and Dibiase was beginning to think that was all part of his father's plan.

"D., what's going on, bro? You've been acting a little strange ever since I got in the truck." J.C. asked, curious to know why something seemed to be bothering Dibiase.

He fiddled around for the key to the storage as he had J.C. follow him down the stairs.

"I'm not acting strange at all, fam. I feel strange; that's it."

"What's down here?" J.C. asked

"Just come on; I've got something to show you. I mean, I've got something that's about to change our lives forever," Dibiase replied.

He put the key in the lock then pulled the storage locker over to him. When he popped the top on it for the second time, J.C. couldn't believe his eyes. He knew the markings on the dope well. The alligator symbol and the way it was wrapped meant it was a part of a shipment Rico had gotten over a year ago. It was the best dope around and the godfather had niggas coming from all over to cop packages.

"Damn, D., I remember this-shit, man. Our pops was a motherfucker, wasn't he? This-shit right here was a beast, bro. I mean, a one could stand a two and it was like nothing had ever hit it."

"So you mean this fifty is damn-near like having one hundred fifty?" Dibiase asked.

"We can get deeper than that, but one-fifty would be the magic number," J.C. replied, licking his lips.

"What do you think the street value of this-shit is if we do it like you say?"

"Let's just say we're going to be living like El Chapo." J.C. chuckled, already devising a master plan in his mind.

"Say, D., you really ready for these streets on this level?"

"I don't think I have a choice in the matter."

"It's going to be hard-as-hell to move this much work at a discreet pace, but I know this for sure, my bro . . ."

"What's that?"

"Pops put us in and he's sending a message that it's retirement time after we finish," J.C. replied.

J.C. knew there was no-way-in-hell they would move that kind of work and their names not come across a federal agent's desk. But it was also a huge reward with the risk they were about to take, and if Dibiase was ready, he was ready too.

"Bro, we got to hash out a plan to move this-shit the right way," J.C. said, still looking at all the work in front of them.

"Say, I'm leaving the plan up to you."

Tito Hernandez didn't like what he was hearing from Rico. Rico had been his most important mover in the Midwest and had made him millions of dollars. Leaving the CCC family wasn't an option for anyone. That just wasn't the way business went. They had a private room and a VIP suite upstairs in the MGM, and Tito told Rico, after he made sure his winnings from the fight hit his offshore account, they would meet and discuss the bad decision Rico was making. He said they would talk about it like men.

Rico didn't understand what there was to talk about. Rico felt like he had made it. He wanted out of the game, at least as far as dealing with the Colombians was concerned. Rico would get shipments every month, either fifty or a hundred kilograms of cocaine; he would open them and reseal them, taking at least one kilogram for a rainy day. He knew he had a sizable stash for his retirement and he was ready to exercise the get-out clause, which he'd forgotten to ask in the beginning what that clause consisted of.

He figured he could take the stash and hit a few of the top players' hands, make a few extra million, then move his family to a sunny state. There were only a few in the game he trusted, and he wanted to make sure when he went out on top, they had the chance to do the same. He had been the steak for many people, made sure dozens of people ate in the streets, and his heart was telling him to retire. Even though his mind said it wouldn't be as easy as it sounded.

Rickey Hammond looked around for his wife, knowing when her and Julia got together, they got into their own little women's world. He knew the two of them were having a good time and not worrying about the men's business. He hadn't told Cassie what the trip was about. He just knew she would be glad when he sprung the news on her about him getting out. Rico had planned to take her to Paris for a two-week vacation to lay around a beach and shop directly with some of the fashion designers. He knew she was in good hands and didn't have to worry about her safety in case things didn't go as planned during the meeting.

He knew Julia also knew Vegas like the back of her hand. She and Tito owned several homes there and a few other clubs on and off the strip. He was glad the two of them had hit it off the way they had. His wife was smart and had her Ph.D., but she didn't work and she didn't have many female friends at home because of his lifestyle. It was too dangerous, and besides that, he had seen many players go out badly because of some leaked third-party information a bitch had given up. It was a burden on her, and he knew sometimes she was sad about having everything and feeling like she had nothing. That was another reason for him retiring.

There were also his sons he had to think about. Little Rickey was doing well in business and his oldest son Dibiase was maintaining. Rico knew Dibiase wanted to walk in his footsteps and be in the streets. He would be devastated if something happened to anyone in his family. He would kill the whole state if it did. That was one reason Rico was thankful for his brother Mickey. When the streets talked, Mickey was one to get firsthand information on anything going on out there.

Rico was standing in the main lobby of the hotel when he felt a tap on his shoulder. When he turned around, he was almost nose-to-nose with Tito, who wore a great big smile on his face. Tito had his gangster look going for him tonight in his all-black pin-striped Valentino three-piece suit and black hat. He had his security posted on each side of him, and Rico knew not many people got into the casino with guns, but Tito boys were always packing. No one in their right mind would try to do anything to Tito anyway. His reputation around Nevada was bigger than the whole Gaming Commission's. Rico knew Tito never worried about any trouble. He had never lived a day in fear on any man.

They all took the elevator heading to the VIP suite so the meeting could begin. Once they got there, Tito waved his security off, and Rico and Tito went in the room. He sent one of the men after two bottles of vintage alcohol and some caviar, which was his favorite. Rico knew Tito knew the nature of what was to be discussed. All along, his man had been winning the fight, but the look on Tito's face said he was nowhere near in a happy state of mind. Rico felt bad somewhat, but he had made his final decision—he was out of the game for good.

Despite quitting, it would still be many years, if ever, before Rico would be able to live a normal life. That was why he was thinking relocation of the family could speed-up the process. He'd had a long, extended run with no infractions, and enough was enough for him. There weren't many players who played the game on his level and had come as far as he had and still had a clean slate. He knew heavy-hitters from Harlem, Atlanta, and D.C. who had paper and were all either doing life in a dirty cell or life in the dirt.

"Please have a seat," Tito said to Rico, motioning for him to sit on one of the couches in the room.

Tito still had his accent and his English wasn't perfect, but Rico had been around him so much that he understood him perfectly.

"I don't want to sit in here and talk, Tito. Can we take a ride somewhere?" Rico asked.

It was a strange request but Tito didn't mind. He called downstairs and had the valet bring his Lamborghini to the front of the hotel so they could go out and talk in the hot Nevada air. When they got downstairs, the valet had the expensive car right in front, waiting on Tito. Tito handed him a hundred-dollar bill, and the valet smiled and closed his door for him.

When Tito pulled out the casino lot, he was doing almost seventy miles per hour onto the Vegas strip. He loved things to move fast—cars and women, especially. They drove for about fifteen minutes in silence, with Tito listlessly taking turns and dips at a high rate of speed. Rico wasn't scared of his driving or the speed. He just didn't like it because he was traveling on unfamiliar roads. Finally, Tito dipped through a causeway in the mountains that was almost as narrow as the car. He didn't slow down one bit, and Rico could tell by his calmness it was routine for him. Rico knew if another car was traveling from the opposite direction, there would be a head-on collision for sure. He just hoped no one else was coming.

They now had to be about forty miles from the casino, and Tito had left his two security men at least twenty miles behind them. There was no way they could keep up with the Lamborghini in the late model Impala they were driving. The wrought-iron fence they pulled up to was built like it was embedded in the side of the mountain. The double entrance had two initials in gold lettering on each side of the fence. The letter 'T' and the letter 'J', so Rico knew where they were had to be the new house Tito had been saying he was having built.

The driveway looked like a chunk of the mountain had been removed to build it. It wound in a circular motion and stopped in front a custom villa that had a completely-glass front. Rico's door opened automatically, raising in the air like a butterfly. He exited Tito's car and stretched his legs, looking at the amazing construction of the place.

When they went inside, Rico was amazed at how nice the place was. He'd expected everything to be top quality for a man like Tito, but Rico would bet his last dollar that Michael Jordan didn't even have a place as luxurious as Tito's new home. Now Rico could tell why it had taken so long to build. The glass appearance from the outside was one thing, but the house had been built inside the mountain. Parts of the mountain had been sandblasted and were visible inside the house. There was a natural waterfall that ran down the sides of the rocks with huge exotic fish swimming in the base of it. Rico walked over and looked at the fish swim for a second.

"I see you like fish," Tito said.

"I've done some catfishing before in my life, I guess you can say," Rico replied, looking at some of the prettiest fish he'd ever seen.

"You know why I chose saltwater fish, Rico? Because even though there are over fourteen thousand species of saltwater fish, the gold stripe maroon clownfish is one of the rarest saltwater fishes you can find," Tito said, emptying some food in the stream.

Rico looked around some while Tito fed the fish. The suede walls in the house were an interesting touch and something different. The whole place was either marble or stainless steel. Rico knew Tito had to have spent a small fortune building the place.

"Brother Rico, let me fix you a drink before we get down to business."

"Sure; anything you like."

"I had this bottle of 1738 bought here just for you when you finally visited; now look, I didn't even have to wait that long."

"Thanks," Rico said, holding up his glass of cognac.

"In fact, I think I'll drink the same thing you're drinking. Vodka doesn't agree with me unless it's with my breakfast," Tito exclaimed.

Rico knew Tito loved to drink cheap vodka with eggs in the morning. That was a little bit weird because he could buy a vodka company if he wanted, but his Skol and fried eggs were what got his day going every morning.

"I just stick to the basics, Tito; you know me."

"You're something, my brother. Sticking to the basics is a good way to be. Most times, when we go any other way, it complicates matters," Tito replied, now holding his glass in the air.

Rico knew Tito had other meanings behind his condescending comment, but he was ready to let the conversation begin so he could see just how things would play out. He'd had enough and it didn't take any more convincing for him that he'd had enough. In his opinion, there was only so much money one man could have if it was illegal, and Rico had his share.

Julie and Cassie had done a little shopping. They had hit the Forum first, then the Wynn Esplanade and the Via Bellagio, finishing up by spending about twenty thousand a piece at The Shoppes at Mandalay Place. Now It was time for a little R&R, so they went to a little club off the strip. Neither Cassie or Julia cared who'd won the boxing match back at the MGM that had kept their husbands engrossed—just as long as they didn't have to sit there and watch it.

Julia was a real shopaholic. She had talked Cassie into buying a pair of jeans that cost two grand, and matching Rolex watches that cost a whole lot more. Cassie never would have spent that much on a couple of pieces of metal that told time like her cellphone did, but she knew the money wasn't an issue and she didn't want to seem like a party pooper.

They stopped at a little club and the line was way down the block to get inside. Julia instructed Cassie to follow her as they proceeded past the line of patrons to the front.

"Hey, Jules, what about all these nice people waiting in line? We just going to skip ahead of all them?" she asked.

"Girl, I own this club," Julia replied.

Cassie wasn't sure if Julia meant she literally owned the club or she was a good-paying VIP customer. She knew being the wife of Tito Hernandez came with perks, but Cassie still liked being civil. The people seemed hot out there, like the heat had them all ready to faint. Good thing the club had outside sprayers that let out a mist of cool water—not enough to ruin anyone's outfit, but just enough to keep them cool in the hot night air. Soon as they made it to the front, the oversized bouncer, who looked like he was a retired linebacker, saw Julia. He said something into an earpiece and several more security men joined him. They formed a barrier so Julia and her guest could walk in before another person did.

"Mrs. Hernandez, glad to see you tonight," the big, baldheaded one said.

"Hey, boss; you're looking amazing as usual," another added.

Cassie had the answer to her question now. She knew Julia owned the place for real. Her club manager, Shone Adams, walked over to her and Cassie, sizing up their outfits.

"Wow, sugar plum, you look gorgeous as always," he said, flicking his hand.

"Thank you, Shone. Is my table available?"

Shone was looking Cassie up and down like she was a piece of meat. At first Cassie was uncomfortable, until Julia explained Shone didn't date women. The club was a fashion club that hosted shows for some of the top artists in the world. Tonight, Kimora Simmons was doing an event, and Shone had automatically thought Cassie, even at her age, was part of the show.

"Is this one of the models?" Shone asked seriously.

"No, not at all; this is my good friend. She's in town for vacation," Julia replied.

"Well, then, let me get your table ready and a couple of bottles for you ladies," Shone said, snapping his fingers and switching off so he could accommodate his boss.

Julia and Cassie were seated in front by the stage. Shone had the waiter place a couple of bottles of Dom Perignon on their table. The two of them enjoyed the show and shared conversation about the future. Julia was happy to have a friend like Cassie who she could relate to, but in the back of her mind, she knew something didn't seem right with Tito earlier that night, and she hoped-like-hell Cassie's husband Rico was okay.

"That Shone is pretty cute," Cassie said.

"Shone? He's a sweetheart. He runs this place for me and does a magnificent job," Julia replied.

Julia's club, the Grand Finale, didn't look that big from the outside, but it was huge inside. There was a large area in the club that dipped underground and made it even bigger. Cassie loved the décor of the place. The stage was mahogany wood that matched the table and chairs, and she saw the right side of the club was comprised of glass offices. There were some Colombian men in all three offices and each one looked busy on their phones.

The DJ was playing Y'all Know What It Is by the rapper T.I. and the show seemed to be going great as the models were now showing off the designer's latest swimsuit line.

"Would you like a more extended tour?" Julia asked.

"Of course I would."

"Well, come on; there's no need for us to be out here. I have a private domain in the back where we can see all this from the monitors," Julia insisted.

"I'm all yours, Colombiana; just lead the way."

~ Seven ~

Tango sat in his one-bedroom apartment on West Madison Avenue in Chicago. He was watching his black-and-white television set, laughing at the late-night reruns of Judge Greg Mathis' court shows. For some odd reason, he had a connection to the show and he couldn't figure out why. He was originally from Detroit before he'd gone away to join the Navy. He assumed, because he was once a problem child from Seven Mile, that he and the judge had a lot in common.

Tango's real name was Charles Oliver, which, when he was Charles the electrician, he was good. He knew people didn't want to really know Tango. Tango was the mercenary he'd been transformed into by the Navy. He'd tried to bury the SEAL training and live a normal life. Charles used his skills as a master electrician to survive in the real world, but at times, he still got the urge to use his old skills and rip somebody's guts out their body.

Charles paced the floor of his apartment, wondering what his girlfriend was talking about. She had explained that some strange young men from Milwaukee had visited her place looking for him. Charles only knew one person who was a cheese head, and he hadn't talked to his friend Rickey Hammond in almost two years. They had been part of the same group when they were both in the service. When their time was up, the whole squadron had gone their separate ways. Charles also knew Rickey had gotten involved heavily in the drug trade and had two sons who had to be around the age of the boys his girl had described.

It had been about three weeks now, and he'd decided to investigate because he couldn't sleep knowing someone was looking for him. When he found out his friend had been gunned-down coming from a wedding, he knew it had to be Rickey's sons. That meant some foul play had taken place. Charles dropped to the floor and committed himself to doing five hundred pushups. He counted as he did the first fifty on one hand and the second fifty switching hands. When he got to five hundred, he stood up and took off his shirt, using it to wipe the sweat from his face. There was a bottle of Grey Goose on the mantle and he pour himself a healthy shot. Once he took it to the head, he poured another one. It was hard to believe, with the skills Rickey Hammond had, he'd let someone get the ups on him.

He poured himself one more shot, almost finishing the bottle. He placed the bottle and the glass back on the mantel, and walked over to a closet in his living room. When he opened it, there was a black bag sitting on the floor with the letters B.A.G.S. in bold white letters. It had been a while since he'd opened the bag and had hoped he'd never have to see the contents again. He removed two AR-15 assault rifles that had been dissembled, and in four seconds, he had them both back in working order. He broke them back down and reassembled them again, this time reversing the springs to make them fully automatic.

He felt a mission coming on and knew it wasn't going to be a pleasant one. As hard as he'd fought his alter-ego Tango, Charles had known this day would come. He removed a picture from the bag of Rickey Hammond, his wife, and two sons. At the time, his boys were just teenagers but looked just like their old man. Charles took a couple of his blood pressure pills, knowing if he stressed too hard, the doctor said it would skyrocket out of control. Once he'd done that, he went back inside the bag and removed two nine millimeter pistols he kept inside with the rifles. He cleaned both pistol since they hadn't been fired for some time and placed them on top of his ironing board.

He took a break for a second, hearing the intro to another *Judge Mathis Show* about to start. The judge was hearing a case where the girlfriend was suing the boyfriend for wrecking her car. When the boyfriend didn't have his-shit together, Judge Mathis told him to shut up because he believed he was nothing but a crackhead. Charles fell out on the floor laughing. Now he realized why he liked the show so much. Every episode he got a chance to smile and laugh, and that wasn't something that happened outside his apartment. When he entered the real world, his look was always the same and it represented that he wasn't to be fucked with.

He went back to cleaning his heavy arsenal of weapons and thinking about what could have happened to Rickey. The drug trade was a tough business to be in and that was one of the reasons he'd never indulged. He knew Tango would have to be unleashed and there would be a lot of dead drug dealers in the streets. He made sure each weapon was perfect and wouldn't have a chance of jamming up when he had to use them. The worst thing that could happen was for a gun to jam in the middle of a battle. If you were up against another good shooter, the man with the jammed weapon was as good as dead. Charles grabbed the almost-empty bottle, sat in a chair, and turned off the television. He closed his eyes for a second and halfway drifted off.

"IT WAS ONLY SUPPOSED TO BE A TRAINING OP!" *a voice screamed through the two-way.*

The team had only been in Kuwait for ten minutes when whatever could go wrong went wrong. Operation Fifteen was a practice mission of extracting a friendly from a hostile hostage situation. The chief commander of the crew was wondering why no one was responding to his radio. Every one of his men could hear his crackle, but they couldn't answer because the enemy had the walkie-talkie in his hand and they were being held at gunpoint, face down in the Kuwait dirt.

The real mission was supposed to take place tomorrow at eighteen hundred hours. A Navy scientist had been taken hostage and the SEALS had been called on directly from the president to rescue him. It was the first time the country had had a black president, and when he was elected, he'd made a promise he was going to rely more on Special

Forces to handle some of the country's most important jobs. Bin Laden and Saddam were on the president's radar as well. Rickey (Rico) Hammond, Glenn Dixon, Foist Johnson, and Charles had been ambushed by a group of renegades ready to kill any American soldier they could.

Charles winced in his sleep now as he dreamed about the six-inch blade that had been plunged in his side. It was like he could still feel all the blood he'd lost. Charles was the squadron leader and the head renegade didn't want anyone around him with stripes on their uniform except him. He used the same knife he'd jabbed him with and cut the stripes right from Charles jacket. The olive-skinned man spoke in a foreign language, thinking they didn't understood his words, but they all knew he was saying he didn't respect American authority.

Rico could see his squadron leader and good friend was losing a lot blood from the wound. Charlie was drifting in and out of consciousness, and it wouldn't be long before he slipped and maybe never regained consciousness if something wasn't done. Rico began observing the renegades' operation, and by voice tones, he counted seven of them. There were three inside the mud hut they'd placed them in and four on the outside. Obviously, they were all well-armed with AK-47's and prepared to do battle. He heard one of the voices speak in their language, telling his comrades he was going in to the second hut. Rico didn't know how many huts there were or if there were more of them in the sleeping quarters.

Even though the renegades had searched them all, they'd failed to find the second .45 Colt Rico had in his back waistband. It was still there, but getting to it would be the problem. The renegades had them all bound in wire cuffs that tightened and penetrated the skin if too much movement occurred. Rico looked back over at his squadron leader and saw the grimace on his face. Charles was in severe pain, but he wouldn't make any noise and give the renegades the satisfaction of letting them know he was in pain.

There was a loud noise outside that caused the men inside the hut to rush out and see what was happening. Rico heard planes flying, but there was no way they were American planes, so he knew it wouldn't be that easy. The good thing was, when he heard the renegades talking, they didn't know if the planes were American. Rico knew, with all the confusion, if he was going to make some type of move, he only had seconds to do so.

"Dixon," Rico called out in a whisper, since Dixon was the closet to him.

Dixon had been hit in the head with the butt of one of the renegade's rifle, but Dixon was tough. It was going to take more than a measly blow to put him out of commission.

"What is it, Lt. Hammond?" Dixon responded.

"When I roll over to face you, stick your two middle fingers under my cuffs; when I make a move, make sure you don't release those fuckers."

"Roger that," Dixon said.

They both knew Dixon was going to lose one, or maybe both, of his fingers, but Dixon knew whatever Lt. Hammond was about to do, it was most likely being done to save their lives. Neither one of them spoke on the probable outcome, they just went into action. The scary part was Hammond was completely sure his plan would work.

"Well, here goes everything," Rico said.

He scooted his body as close to Dixon as possible, then rolled on his side. The cuffs were doing their job, starting to tighten more. The pain was starting to become excruciating, but neither one of them was ready to give up. The right wire finally popped, but not before the left wire tore through the flesh in Hammond's wrist. The fact that his hands were free overrode the pain for the time being.

He quickly removed his weapon from his waistline and bent over Tango, checking his breathing; it was faint but there. With lightning speed, he released his guys, watching as cover while Johnson gave medical attention to Tango. Dixon was wrapping the nub on his left hand where the wire cuffs Rico was wearing had torn off his finger. Two renegades were heading back to the hut they were in. The voices kept getting closer and closer until the front door swung open. Reflexes made the SEALS get into action. Dixon grabbed the barrel of the renegade's rifle, catching him off-guard. Rico put the second man in a chokehold, cutting off his circulation in exactly three seconds.

Tango had fully regained consciousness and joined in. He extracted the knife from the side of the renegade and stuck the first one in the heart, killing him instantly. The one Rico was holding was the one who had stabbed Tango and taken his stripes. When Rico released him, the man's body slumped to the dirt floor, but Tango was livid. He took the knife, slit his throat, then stabbed him several more times. He reached in the man's top pocket, took his stripes, and using his thumb and index finger, forced open the jaws of the dead renegade. Tango fed him his American stripes.

Finally, Tango lifted his head, looking at the bottle of vodka. He took one last shot and threw the empty bottle across the room. He knew something was wrong, and in the morning, he was Milwaukee-bound to figure it all out.

Eight

Dibiase dropped J.C. off back at his girl Donna's crib. J.C. said he had to go chill so he could think about the plan and how they were going to put it together. That was cool with Dibiase because J.C. was the only one he trusted, and he knew, whatever J.C. came up with, it would be bulletproof. Right now, Dibiase just wanted to get back home to Camille because he knew she would be worried about him. He decided to stop to grab something to drink and few blunt wrappers, thinking about what had gone down in the shower. He could use a second round to keep his mind off things.

He was in the checkout line at the liquor store, about to pay, when he felt his phone vibrating on his side. He didn't look, expecting it to be J.C. already ready with a plan. He knew how his godbrother was when it came to making money. His mind worked like a cartel family.

"What it do?" Dibiase said, balancing the phone between his ear and shoulder as he sat the two bottles of D'Usse on the counter to reach for his money.

"Yo, it's doing, but I need to holla at you, nephew," a familiar voice said. It was Uncle Mickey.

"Hey, Unc; I'm in the checkout line at Otto's grabbing some-shit. What's going on? Everything cool?" Dibiase asked. He was actually worried about the rest of the family even though he wasn't acting like it.

"Say, D., this really isn't one for the airwaves. I just need to get at you as soon as possible," Uncle Mickey said, sounding serious.

Dibiase knew it couldn't be about his mother or Little Rickey because his uncle would have just told him what was wrong.

"I feel ya, Unc. I was heading back to my new spot, but I guess it sounds like I need to detour and head back your way."

"Yeah, that sounds like a plan."

"Where you at, Unc?" Dibiase asked, knowing Uncle Mickey had a million-and-one women with a million-and-two spots in the city where he could be.

"I'm at this-bitch Shay's house, but I'm about to jet out of here in a minute. She ain't on-shit," Mickey said, sounding displeased.

Dibiase thought about it for a second and knew Shay was the chick on the porch at the funeral. Mickey had suggested they meet in the Burger King parking lot on Lisbon. Lisbon wasn't that long of a drive from where Dibiase was; he could be there in seven minutes.

"Let me grab some petrol and I should be there in about seven minutes, Unc."

He wondered what was so important that Uncle Mickey wanted to meet in a Burger King parking lot but, knowing his uncle, he knew it could be anything, so he had to go check it out. They disconnected the call and Dibiase finished paying for his goods. The girl behind the counter was eyeballing his wad and smiling at him. He had seen her around before and knew she wasn't-shit. He smiled back and kept it moving. He dialed Camille to purposely let the girl hear him talking to her before walking out. Camille answered her phone on the first ring.

"Hey, baby," he said when he heard her voice. When he looked back, the chick was giving him a funky look.

"Hey, bae; you all right?" she asked.

"Of course; I'm straight. I was just about to head to the crib, but Uncle Mickey called and said he needed to see me, so I'm going to ride down on him first."

"That's fine, baby; take your time. I've been arranging the place and it looks nice. Something feels strange though."

"What's that, baby girl?"

"This place just seems like we've been here before. I know we haven't, but it just seems like it to me," she replied, wondering why the place felt like that to her.

"It's all in your mind. Hey, I want you pick a day so we can go get the rest of your things."

"FOR REAL?"

"Hell yeah; what did you expect? I know you didn't think I was going to be doing dishes," he said, smiling.

"Well, let's see how glad you are. I'm going to be timing you, and you know, since I don't have anything here, I'll be waiting with just my T-shirt and my panties on."

Dibiase thought about what he had waiting on him at home. They had been together for a quite some time and he still treated her like the day they'd met. He wanted to have a son and knew Camille was one day going to be the mother of his seed. He pulled in the gas station thinking, now that Rico was gone, he wouldn't get a chance to be a grandfather.

"You timing me, huh?"

"Yep; this good-good's wet and ready for her daddy to come take care of it."

"Say no more, baby. I'll be there as soon as I can," he replied, ending the call with both of them smiling.

Dibiase got out and filled up his truck. He got back in and headed for the Burger King. He knew he wouldn't be long with Mickey now that his-shit was hard as a rock thinking about his girl.

J.C. knew Donna was tripping because he hadn't stayed and chilled with her, but he had to move around because he had a lot on his mind. He knew he had to formulate a plan to get rich, put his car up, then get Don D. so he could break everything down to him. He stopped at King's car lot on Capitol and talked to one of his homeboys who owned the place. The car he picked out was a new-body-style Avalon, navy blue with beige interior. The car was low-key and wouldn't draw much attention. It would be perfect when he added some tint to the windows.

About an hour later, he walked back into the spot where Don D. had been waiting on him. Don had blown about a half ounce of dro by himself and had fallen asleep with his cell phone flipped open on his lap. J.C. picked up the phone and could hear a female voice on the other end calling Don's name and asking if he'd fallen asleep on her. J.C. started to respond to the dumb-bitch, but when he looked at the caller display and saw the 262 area code, he knew it was the-bitch from Racine's phone number. Instead of saying anything, he just hit the power button, shutting the phone off. Hopefully, the-tramp would think the phone had died.

J.C. tried waking Don D. up. He had to shake him three or four times to get a response out of his cousin, but finally, Don jumped up, about to reach for his heater.

"Damn, man, you're sleeping like a bear," J.C. said. "I thought your-ass was in hibernation," he continued.

"Shit, I smoked some of that-shit, man, and couldn't keep my-muthafuckin-eyes open," he replied, adjusting his nine back in his waistline. Don picked up his phone, realizing he had been talking to his broad and saw it was off.

"I know one thing, I'm up in this-bitch hungry-as-fuck. That-shit makes a-nigga want to go to Golden Corral and clown."

"Well, get up and wash your crusty-ass-face. We need to hit the bricks; I've got some serious rap for your-ass."

"Cool; give me a minute, cuz," Don said.

"Hey, you see my phone charger?" Don D. asked, standing up, stretching.

J.C. didn't reply to the question but watched his cousin head to the bathroom to get ready. Don grabbed a towel and wondered again about his girl in Racine. He didn't even know why he liked her so much. He wasn't sure if it was the fat-ass under her back, or the fact that she didn't wear weave and her shit was past her shoulders. He just knew he couldn't wait to see her again. Don was figuring he wasn't going to wait too long. He was even thinking about getting a rental and jetting up there later on with a low-key whip. She was the type-of-chick who was always ready, and he knew he was the type-of-nigga who liked them always ready.

Dibiase pulled the Escalade into the parking lot of the Burger King on Lisbon looking around for his uncle's whip. Mickey was sitting in his lime green '76 Seville, finishing up a double whopper with cheese when Dibiase pulled alongside him. When his uncle saw him pull up, he let the driver's side window down on his car and tossed the whopper wrapper on the ground. He got out and walked around so he could get in the truck with Dibiase.

"Thanks for giving this your prompt attention, nephew. I knew you would," he said, checking his fingernails for dirt or food.

"Say, Unc, you don't have to thank me. We're family, man, and besides that, you know I have never been the one to act funny about anything," Dibiase replied.

He remembered the time his uncle had messed up some money and called on him, not wanting Rico to know, and Dibiase and J.C. had given him the paper he needed to get back right.

"True that, neph; that's why I called you in the first place," Mickey replied.

"So what's up, Unc? What is this emergency about?"

"I fucked-up, D.! I fucked-up bad, man. I accepted a sack from this West Lawn-nigga right after your pops' death. I only did it because my money was fucked-up and I needed to stay above water. You know I got two-bitches in the A on the blade, and I had to bail one of them-hoes out."

Dibiase listened as his uncle talked. One thing about his uncle was Mickey wasn't a liar. No matter how bad things were, he'd always tell the truth. Somehow, bad luck stayed with him, and he always got himself in some funky-ass-predicaments. But Mickey was the shit! He would give a-nigga the shirt off his back, just like Rico would. Dibiase knew it was the pimp-game that had screwed his uncle. He was trying to mix too many hustles and couldn't quite nail any of them.

"Man, the-shit the-nigga gave me was some garbage too."

"Look, Unc, you don't have to explain," Dibiase said, knowing his Uncle was responsible for him getting his first piece-of-pussy, and for that, he was grateful.

"I wasn't going to pay that-nigga, that was my first mind, but my second mind said I'm too old to be going to war with one of these young hot heads," Mickey explained. "You know your pops kept me straight when he was here. I just bought that new Eldorado and sent these-bitches on the road. I have to keep the money floating."

Mickey was still explaining, but Dibiase had already made up his mind to help his uncle rectify the situation. He knew if his uncle had chosen not to pay the-nigga and wanted to go to war, they could have gone that way too. Dibiase knew Mickey wasn't any different than anyone else. He, too, had depended on Rico's tutelage to make it in the game. Rico had paid lots of rents and car notes, and bailed a lot of players out the county jail. He even had a lawyer on retainer for anyone who needed him. That was his father's nature as the godfather of the city. You fucked-in Rico's business and handled your business, he made sure you were good. He always said, "If you treat people right, the money will triple itself." Dibiase had thought it was going to be fucked-up for so many, and just hearing his uncle's new confession, he knew his theory was right. It was bizarre sitting alongside the godfather's brother, hearing he was the first one to make a mistake and so soon.

Dibiase knew the-nigga they called Peanut. He knew the-nigga was a hot head and want to be chemist. He used to get work from Rico, but Rico rolled like Frank Lucas and Peanut was more like the new millennium Nicky Barnes. Rico didn't play that mix-master-shit with the work that came from him. If it was going to be stepped on any, it would be done by him, and that was the way it was to be sold. Peanut was from a different breed, and he told Rico one day to his face that he wasn't Frank and he wasn't trademarking Blue Magic. Rico just cut him off instead of killing him.

Peanut had gotten away with what he was doing for a long time because he was re-rocking the dope and making the product look untouched. Somehow, he'd figured out how to step on it and bring it back to looking like it looked when he'd originally copped from Rico. The alligator stamp on the bricks was a sure sign drama could come to the godfather because whatever Peanut was doing, the product wasn't straight. Rico had cut him completely off and things could have easily escalated if Rico hadn't been cool with Peanut's old man, who'd begged and pleaded to Rico not to kill his son.

"Damn, Unc," Dibiase said, feeling like any infractions right now were terrible timing. "Just tell me how bad the debt is. I'm going to handle it."

"I owe this-nigga four racks for that-bullshit. I feel like such a fool, knowing about his reputation," Mickey replied. He knew how bad it looked to be fucking-with the same person who had crossed his brother.

"Nephew, I meant no disrespect, but I was just making a way out of no way."

"Don't sweat this-shit, Unc."

"I'm telling you, D., it's bad out here. I called a few other-niggas first before I even rang this-bitch-made boy's line and they all said the same thing: Since the death of your father, they ain't been plugged," Mickey confessed.

Dibiase rubbed his chin, listening to his uncle give him some important information he didn't realize he was giving him. That meant he could tell J.C.—if he didn't already know the streets were facing a drought—and they would probably have that shit off in no time.

"I understand, Unc; it ain't like I'm mad. You just made a mistake."

He told his uncle he wanted him to flush the rest of the garbage down the toilet right away. He didn't want any more repercussions behind some weak-ass-bullshit. He knew, not only would the hustlers try to take you out, but the hypes would even try to kill you if you gave them some fucked-up dope.

"So, what you think I should do about dude's ends?" Mickey asked.

"I need you to stall him for a day or two. Let me think about how I'm going to handle this. Unc, I'm going to need you to chill too for a second, okay? I mean, don't go calling anybody for-shit," Dibiase instructed. He reached in his pocket and gave his Uncle Mickey the money he had on him.

"What's this for, nephew?" his uncle asked. Looking at the money, he could see it was about two racks, all in twenty-dollar bills.

"This is just a stop-gap, Unc, so you can get your bills paid and take care of the problems you got with your people who're stuck on the road. I don't care what you really do with it, just lay low on the hustle tip until further notice. Trust me, it won't be but a second."

"Damn, you sounded just like your father when you said that-shit."

To Mickey, not only did his nephew sound like his brother, but they also looked just alike. The age difference was what made the difference in a person telling them apart. Other than that, you were looking at twins when they were side by side when Rico was alive. Little Rickey favored his mother, but did have his father's nose.

"I really miss my brother, nephew. Already it seems like four walls are closing in around me."

"I know, Unc; you can imagine how I feel."

"I know exactly how you feel."

"Hey, Uncle Mickey, I'm going to need to roll out. I stopped and got something for me and Camille, and I need to make it to the crib," Dibiase said, looking at the clock on the dash.

"Man, neph, you know you got you a ride-or-die by your side, kid. If I ever leave these-hoes alone, I'm going to find one just like her. In fact, she got any sisters?" Mickey asked playfully.

"Gon, get up out my truck, Unc. I'm on deuces, baby. Hey, I'll call you soon though. Be smooth," Dibiase said, watching his only uncle get back in his ride.

Dibiase pulled out the parking lot with a lot more on his mind than he'd anticipated. Mickey's conversation kept playing over and over in his head. *'I just didn't know what to do since Rico's gone.'* That specific line was going to be a lot of people's song. Dibiase knew what Rico had left him was the key to the city. Fifty bricks was a lot of weight, and with J.C. and Don D., they were going to move it. He thought about the way to handle Peanut, and the simple way was to pay him, but the way he was going to handle it was different. West Lawn was a spot where you could break down a brick and move it in two days in small packages. Peanut was about to earn himself a second chance at getting some real paper.

He was almost home and the thought of his brother, Little Rickey, crossed his mind. He knew he needed to call him and check on him since he hadn't seen his brother since the funeral. Little Rickey wasn't in the streets at all, nor did he care to be in the life. He was a straight shooter who owned the city's largest barbershop. His thirty-chair barbers' side and twenty-chair salon side did very well for him. Besides that, he had his own hustle. His pool game was up-top and he trimmed a lot of people every weekend for big money. Dibiase thought about how independent Little Rickey was, which was something he got from their mother. He'd wanted people to realize at an early age he was his own decision maker. That was why he'd saved his allowance, and at the age of seventeen, found a condemned building, and with his father's help, created the most lavish shop in the Midwest.

Dibiase finally made it home to the new apartment. He tried his brother's cell before he went in and got voicemail. He smiled, knowing what was upstairs waiting on him. Dibiase grabbed the drink off the passenger seat and hit the alarm on his truck. When he got upstairs and entered, he saw Camille stretched out on the bed. She was almost asleep now that he had taken longer with his uncle than he had expected. He removed his heater from his waistband and set it on the dresser.

Camille was lying on top of the sheets in one of his silk dress shirts and nothing else. Her legs were long and void of any blemishes, just like the rest of her body. She spread them a little so he could see what he had been missing. Dibiase quickly removed his shirt and displayed a pushup body that was rippled with midsize muscles. He didn't work out at the gym as much as he use to, so he did five hundred pushups a day to compensate. It didn't take much for Dibiase to get aroused when Camille was in her freak mode. She knew exactly what to do to make his dick stand up. Camille slid the shirt up above her head until it was completely off. Her nipples were erect and she now felt a throbbing sensation pulse between her legs.

Dibiase was licking his lips as she lay back, spread her legs wider, and began playing with the piercing that stimulated her clitoris. He watched as he rolled a blunt and enjoyed the moaning she was doing. He took several hits of the potent drug and passed it to her. She licked the fingers she was using to play with her pussy first, before accepting the weed-filled cigar. Dibiase slipped off his pants and climb down between her legs. While she took several hits, he was using his tongue to taste the juices she had conjured up. Her love pocket grew more anxious for him to put something inside it.

"Baby, I want to suck that-dick," Camille said, climbing up on top of him backward.

They gave each other the best oral sex. Camille was going all the way down on Dibiase, until her lips touched his balls. Dibiase rolled over and guided her to the edge of the bed, entering her from behind. He was slow and easy at first, until her muscles relaxed and allow him to penetrate her deeply. Camille crunched the sheets as she arched her back to allow more of his massive head to roam her insides. It didn't take long for her to reach a climax. When her warm juices covered him, Dibiase couldn't control the explosion that was ready to gush out. Camille always knew when he was ready to bust because he would grab each of her cheeks and apply a painful pressure that was intensely pleasurable to her. When she joined his rhythm, he exploded inside her. Dibiase slid out slowly and another gush came from her wet pussy.

"Damn, I love when that-pussy squirts like that," he said, smiling.

"This is the only set of sheets we have," Camille replied, collapsing on her stomach.

"You know I love you."

"Not as much as I love you," she replied, rolling over.

"You want to watch a movie?" he asked her.

"I think I just want to lie here next to you."

Dibiase climbed on the bed and they held each other. Three minutes hadn't passed and she was already snoring. All he could think about was everything that had been going on. His father was gone and had left him out here in the world to be the man of the family. He was the oldest, so he knew it was his job to become the heir to Rico's throne. Dibiase thought about J.C. and the fact that he was a stone-cold killer as well as a good hustler. He knew he didn't want to add to the body count, but knew, most likely, it was going to be inevitable dealing with as much weight as they had.

One thing Dibiase knew he had to do when he woke up in the morning was go by his mother's house and check on her. Cassie was also his life, just like his father had been. His family was all he had left: Cassie, Little Rickey, and Uncle Mickey, even J.C. and Don D. A lot of responsibility had been bestowed on him; he knew his father could have left the drugs with anybody. Rico chose him because he knew Dibiase would do what was right and make it happen. He looked in

Camille's face and kissed her softly on her lips while she slept. Tomorrow was a new day and things were about to get poppin'.

~ Nine ~
Las Vegas, Tito Hernandez

Tito was showing Rico how to use the reins on the horse to maneuver the stallion do what the rider wanted it to do. Tito was on Gem, the meanest horse he owned, while Rico rode Seth. Seth was more of a show horse and would allow a new rider like Rico some comfort. Tito knew Rico wouldn't stand a chance on Gem. Gem was a mare that didn't allow anyone on his back except Tito. Tito had decided to get into the racing of horses, then decided against it when his million-dollar prize horse had been poisoned. Since then, he'd had the designers build a trail at the new house that was just for pleasure riding. There would be nights when he would get Julia, and they would just go out back and ride the horses for hours.

Rico was just like Denomination, Tito's prize horse that had been expected to bring home the Triple Crown. Tito had been impressed with the way Rico worked since day one. He had other shakers and movers, but none of his people had been more productive than Rico Hammond. Now the fact that Rico was talking about bailing out the game was like disrespect to Tito.

Tito was raised with the belief that family was family and they were the people who were supposed to come first in your life. A person didn't have to have the same mother and same father to be considered family in Tito's opinion. It was the embracement of two souls, combining to form a bond of trust. That was what had happened between him and Rico; he trusted Rico like a blood brother.

The Colombian city Rionegro was where Tito's father, Draco, was born and raised. It was the same city where Pablo Escobar was born. Draco's father had worked the fields for Escobar until the day he'd overdosed sucking the product straight from the plant. Draco still lived back in the old country, but he was now filthy-rich thanks to the way he'd raised his son. The cocaine business was a one-hundred-million-dollar-a-year business, and certain people in the United states who acted like they wanted it stopped were the same people who were taking payoffs.

Tito Hernandez had gotten his start by using his engineering skills to help the cartel families find different ways to get their drugs into the states. He had held back the biggest secret of them all for himself and his father. Now that it was all said and done and the plans were implemented, anyone who knew the Hernandez secret was bound for life by their rules. You were in and there was only one way out.

Tito looked at Rico as they went up the trails on his property. He admired everything Rico had done in the game, even the way he'd learned to ride horses so quickly. Draco and Tito had had no intention of letting Rico in too deep into the family business at first. There were several branches run by other family members who wouldn't understand a black man having his own chapter, but Rico had what it took and that is why he had the Midwest. What they knew about Rico was he wouldn't be an order taker anyway. He surely was a great listener and a strong survivor. Tito was very upset this meeting was about him leaving the game. It felt like he was being betrayed and that was a no-can-do. No one left the CCC and lived to tell about it.

"I know what's on your mind, Tito," Rico said as they finally pulled the horses back into Tito's stable.

Tito laughed at his comment. "You don't know what's on my mind."

"Listen, Tito, I feel there comes a time when a man has to make a final decision about things going on his life. I know it's because of the CCC that my family and I want for nothing. For that, I'm grateful, but I can't see myself forever in your debt," Rico said.

He didn't mean to sound disrespectful, but Rico knew he had to tell it like it was. Tito understood exactly where Rico was coming from, but as a boss, he couldn't afford to start a trend of letting people leave. So he had to tell it like it was as well.

"Rico, I must be totally honest with you. You have been with the family for years and you know things no else knows. Frankly, it behooves me to say this, but business is business, never personal." He paused.

"I'm sorry my friend, but I just can't allow you to part with the family," Tito explained.

His words were a sharp knife that sliced through Rico's heart. Honestly, Rico hadn't flown all the way to Las Vegas thinking it was going to be that simple. He knew rules were rules and that some engagement might take place. Some things were totally inevitable, even though Rico had hoped Tito would find some love for him deep inside his heart and spare him. Now he knew that would not be the conclusion at all and he needed to figure out what was next.

"Take me back to my room at the casino please."

"I can see, Rico, that your mind and heart are settled. I expect you will send your last take in when you make it back home."

"I have never crossed you, Tito, never stolen a dime, never shorted or had some lame-ass-excuse for anything. So there is no reason for you to expect anything less from me now," Rico said with sadness in his voice.

It was partly due to the comment and partly due to him knowing where Tito's head was. Rico could have easily killed Tito right there with his bare hands. None of his henchmen were around to save him. The only reason he didn't was because his family would never be safe. He had to figure out something else; that would negate his very reasoning for leaving the game. He wanted his family safe.

ॐ ✿ ॐ

Julia and Cassie were still hanging at her club, having the time of their life. They were in her private office watching the cameras that looked out into the dance area of the club. They knew people came from all walks of life to party in Las Vegas. It was the town that seriously upheld to its popular cliché: What happens in Vegas stays in Vegas. Las Vegas had been deemed one of the best places to vacation for over sixty years. You could win big in Vegas or lose big in Vegas, but you would most definitely get the chance to enjoy adult nightlife whatever your fetish was.

Julia had a black leather set in her office and they sat there while she popped the second bottle of champagne. Both ladies were already tipsy and not worrying a bit about what time it was. Julia slid in closer to her best friend as she poured their flute glasses full to the rim.

"Here's to a lifelong friendship," she said, holding up her glass.

"Amen," Cassie replied as they bumped glasses.

Julia couldn't help looking deeply into Cassie's brown eyes. Her beauty was electrifying and she was indubitably very stunning. The color of Cassie's complexion made it hard to tell she wasn't mixed with something else. Her hair was long, way past her shoulders, and was naturally-silky, almost reminding Julia of her own hair. If a person didn't know better, they could mistake Cassie for being Cuban or Dominican. Cassie was really tipsy now and she could feel her friend moving closer to her as the expensive drink coated her insides.

"Hey, you wanna have some fun?" Julia asked.

Cassie answered right away because fun was what she was there for. "Hell yeah; let's have some fun. What . . . umm . . . kind—" she tried to ask, but before she could complete her sentence, Julia already had her tongue probing the inside of Cassie's mouth.

Cassie started to push her off, but her lips were soft and Cassie started feeling herself get aroused by what was happening. Julia was exotic and Cassie had always thought she was amazingly gorgeous herself. Never before had she thought they would end up kissing. The way Julia's lips felt was unbelievable though. It was a totally different feeling than when she kissed Rico. The emotion was there but in a different way. She tried to attribute it to the tipsy feeling she was getting from the sweet champagne—until she felt her pussy soak the back of her dress.

Cassie started returning the passionate kiss, sliding her body even closer. The heat between them had become hotter than the weather outside the club. Julia slid her neatly-manicured fingers under Cassie's dress, using her index finger to guide her Victoria Secret wear to the side. When her finger entered Cassie, she knew Cassie was just as excited as she was. The feeling of her thick pearl tongue aroused Julia even more as she gently caressed Cassie. Cassie reacted in a way she'd never thought she would. She began sliding the dress Julia had on down over her shoulders, exposing her perfect C-cup breasts. What would normally seem nasty or uncivilized to Cassie felt really good now.

"You like it, su madre?" Cassie asked.

"I don't know what I like. All I know, Jules, is I don't want to stop!" she exclaimed, taking one of Julia's breasts in her mouth.

While she inserted Julia's breast in her warm mouth, she managed to ease her hips to the edge of the couch, allowing Julia's fingers to penetrate her even deeper. The pleasure Cassie was feeling was undeniable. She loved making love to her husband, but there was something totally different about making out with Julia Hernandez. Cassie was wondering what was next and it didn't take Julia long to make her move. She slid the black dress above Cassie's hips, exposing her neatly-shaved pussy. Julia didn't waste any time lapping at her juices, causing Cassie to scream with pleasure. When she exploded in the most powerful orgasms she'd ever felt, she took one look at Julia before she fainted.

Julia placed a cool towel on her friend's forehead and finally Cassie came back to life. They kissed one more time and Cassie spoke.

"I think I'd better be getting back to the hotel. I'm sure Rico will be waiting for me."

~ Ten ~

The little green Honda Prelude shifted into its final gear as it hit the Dan Ryan Expressway. Tango looked at the signs on the highway. One said left if you were heading to Wisconsin, and Milwaukee was his final destination. Charlie Tango was going to find out exactly why the two young men had come looking for him.

J.C. woke up a little earlier than usual. The shit his godbrother had shown him in that footlocker had been embedded on his mind since they'd parted ways. Fifty bricks of pure china white was a monster shipload, and still unbelievable, it was all theirs to push. J.C. had been feeling for quite some time it was his time to shine. He had been out there hustling hard and pulling his way up the ranks to becoming the man. He had once been fronted a brick by the godfather, but when he came back to see Rico, he'd had his money and the funds to no longer need fronting.

He knew Dibiase wanted him to put together a foolproof plan to move the work Rico had left. J.C. knew Dibiase was okay in the streets, but he wasn't what J.C. was to the streets. That was because Dibiase had everything he wanted and had never had to get out there like that. His getting paper on the hustle tip was a choice. All he had to do was ask Rico for what he wanted and needed, and it was done. J.C. helped Dibiase play in the streets when he didn't want to go to his father for certain things, and from that, Dibiase had built a small clientele who managed to keep a bankroll in his pocket.

J.C. rose up and was still a little tired. He had spent the day with Don D., rounding up a few new soldiers to put in that work. His plan was going to be set in motion. He thought about the way he wanted to move the work and personally felt moving weight would bring the heat on them relatively quickly. Although they would have to service a few players to keep the street heat at bay, he knew most of the work was going to be broken down and moved in small quantities out of spots. They already had a spot that was booming, but now it was time to get on the incline and do some real numbers. He also figured, if they were going to be out there like that, he had to up his heat game. He'd already made contact with a-nigga he knew who had that real heat.

He decided to roll out of bed so he could think a little more. J.C. looked over at Donna and she was still sleeping as peacefully as a baby. He finally went and showered and found an outfit for the day. While he slipped on his Red Money jeans and hoodie, he thought about his car and didn't trip. He assumed he would be comfortable in the new one. Once he found his matching Havana Joes, he was set for the streets. Only thing he needed now was a fresh ounce of dro.

J.C. dialed Cheese on his cell and set up a quick meet. The potency of the drug made him relax and think things through. He climbed into the Avalon looking through the bag of discs he'd taken from his car. He was missing the Cutlass he'd had to put in storage. He knew they would have plenty of time to stunt in whips later. That-Racine-shit had to die down first though.

At a time like this, J.C. would normally play his Plies *Definition of a Real Goon*, but he was feeling like listening to something a little smoother. He popped in his Jay Z's *Empire State of Mind* and pulled off slowly. He knew music was a real state of mind for some niggas. He loved the rap game and could even spit a few bars himself. He thought about the lyrics Jay was spitting as he cruised. *I used to cop in Harlem, all of my Dominicanos, took it to my stash spot, 5-60 State Street, catch me in the kitchen like a Simmons whipping pastry.* Yeah, Jay was spitting the same-shit that was on his mind at the moment. Whipping up fifty, bringing back the triple-up.

He knew he and Dibiase were going to be the epitome of the popular cliché niggas were running around biting. They were surely about to get rich or die trying. He thought since the two legends of the game were gone, maybe he would take some of the proceeds and produce his own mix tape. He knew Big Meech had done the-shit for Young Jeezy, and that-nigga was holding the mic down. He felt the rap game was similar to the dope game. Once you put out your best product and grinded to the top of the charts, the label was just like the Feds: They came for your ass and you were done. Not him, he thought as he pulled up to Cheese's spot. He was going to one day clown the industry like Master P had. Instead of making a deal, he was going to be the deal.

He hit Cheese's cell, and the nigga came out the crib in his Pokémon pajamas. J.C. laughed at his little homie when he got in on the passenger side.

"Man, what's up with the nightwear, homie?" J.C. asked, counting out his bread for what he wanted.

"It's just a good cover to hide my heat," Cheese replied, pulling out a nine that was damn-near bigger than him.

"That's a bad-muthafucka right there, homie."

"You know a-nigga's got to stay strapped out here, big homie. These-niggas are starving and looking for their next meal any way they can get it."

"I feel you on that, my-nigga."

He was thinking about making Cheese a proposition to really step his game up. He knew Cheese knew a lot of people because he sold the best weed in town. He wondered if Cheese wanted to flip the game and see what it felt like to hold some real bands.

"I might have a little something for you, lil homie. Just keep your cool out here and give me a minute."

"That's word, my nigga. You know you and Dibiase are like big brothers to me. I know he's fucked-up in the head about losing his pops, man. Had to be some bad-muthafuckas to fuck-with a-nigga in the house of God."

"You're right about that. Let me get-the-fuck out of here, but keep your ears open on that-shit. I'm going to get back at you with the rap I was just giving you."

"One, fam."

"One," J.C. said and pulled off, taking a Dutch wrapper from his inside hoodie pocket.

He changed the disc to Cube since he felt today was going to be a good day. He pulled the Avalon up to the spot and hoped Don D. was up and ready to roll. Before going in the spot, he had hit up Kisha, his plug at the rental car joint they fucked-with. She always plugged them by letting them rent cars in fictitious names, which came in handy in case they had to bail. They needed a couple of rentals on deck, so he hoped she was working. He was in luck as it was her who answered the phone. Kisha had a good head shot on her too.

"What's up, baby girl? Y'all got some incognito joints on the lot?" J.C. asked.

"Wait a minute, I didn't sleep with you last night," she said, expressing a little attitude because she had called his phone, wanting to see him.

"My bad, baby girl; let me start over. Good morning, Kisha baby."

"Now that's more like it. I ain't going to trip on the fact you didn't answer my call last night since you ain't bringing it up. I know you love that-redbone-bitch you're shacking with," she said, feeling a little jealous.

"Come on now, Kish, you know the deal with that," he continued, knowing she was tripping, but that extra five hundred he always gave her when she plugged him would override whatever she was on last night.

"I ain't going to keep being a side-bitch, J.C., but yeah, we got a new-body-style Durango and a Ford Fusion," she replied, now thinking she would at least get her hair and nails done.

J.C. let her know the cars she told him about were cool and they would be there before closing time. He ended the call, thinking about the last time they were together. She put in that work, but he knew that was what chicks did when they knew the main-bitch wasn't going anywhere. He had watched the movie *Belly* too many times.

"I see somebody's up ready to handle some business today," J.C. said, looking at Don D.

"Fuckin'-right, cuz," Don replied, handing J.C. the twenty-five hundred from last night's take.

J.C. looked at the money and knew the change they had been making daily was about to be jack-ball cash compared to what was on the horizon for them.

"I almost let that-broad from Racine come get a-nigga last night. I was horny-as-a-bitch and you-niggas were probably digging in some-bitches' guts."

"Actually, playa, I went straight to the crib last night. I had to think about this paper we're about to get. A-nigga better get his mind right," J.C. replied, not just talking about his cousin, but the whole crew needing to be on point.

"A-nigga gets his mind and paper right, he can have any-bitch in the world, dawg," he said, spitting some game to Don D.

"I feel ya, cuz. Shit, we don't really do that bad now with the pickings, so I know for sure when we get it up, I'm going to get me a Beyoncé-looking-ass chick," he replied smiling, having premonitions about the future.

Don D. knew the pretty chicks only fucked-with the cream-of-the-crop niggas. He loved him a-broad with a big ass, big titties, and a big weave, but he knew those-chicks all wanted 'the man'. He was part of a plan that would soon make him just like 'the man'. He smiled at the thoughts he was having.

They walked outside the spot, eyeing the block and everything looked to be in order. J.C. pulled out the Dutch package and took the second cigar out, emptying the contents out right on the sidewalk. When they got in the car, he passed the new sack to Don D. so he could roll up as he headed to pick up Dibiase. Cube was still playing in the deck, and today was really going to be a good day.

Eleven

Since birth, James Contrill had been around the hustle. His mother, Teresa, had been a junkie who sold her body when the money was low to get what she desired, and his aunts, her younger sisters, had followed directly in her footsteps. He grew up moving from rooming house to rooming house, until the last move his mother made was to a rooming house on the corner of 19th and North Ave. James would never forget the black-and-white corner house that catered to many different people, mostly on a month-to-month basis. It still stood, and when he visited his favorite corn beef joint, he would ride by and have visions of torching the place. He was reminded of his past every time he saw the tenement building they'd called home.

The nine-room duplex was nothing but a flop house for junkies and hookers who couldn't keep a normal roof over their and their children's heads. He remembered the times he'd stood in the bedroom where he was confined to a window that faced the busy street and watched as his mother flagged down vehicle after vehicle, hoping to give some stranger head in the back alley for small change.

Sometimes the vice squad patrolled the area, but Teresa had been to jail so many times they didn't even sweat her any more. The most the cops would do was tell her to take her narrow-ass back into the house. Teresa was a charmer without a pimp. Her only pimp was the monkey attached to her back. The times she went to jail were the times she dreaded not having a pimp to pay her bail. She always had to sit three or four days at a time, leaving James to fend for himself. He remembered the time she'd called the young hustler she'd spent all her money with and he'd hung up on her, choking almost all the life out of her the next time he'd seen her.

Teresa had the street name of Sugar. She'd earned the name because that was one of the tricks she used on the men. She would get the tip and shaft of a man's dick totally wet, then open sugar packets she had stolen from the McDonald's down the street, pouring it all over the men she serviced. The sugar must have given her an adrenaline rush because her performance enhanced and she never left any customer unsatisfied. Sometimes she would bring the men up in the rooming house and James was made to face the window while she did her thing. He use to always ask his mother why she did what she did, and she would simply tell him that was how he got the clothes on his back and the food that went in his belly. James had never respected the answer because every pair of pants he owned—there were only three pair— were from the thrift store, his shoes had holes in the bottom, and most nights, his stomach and his back danced together from hunger.

It was a shame when James thought about his mother's life. She was once very beautiful and had held a great job at the Urban League, which was a foundation built to help black people in the community. Things had turned terrible a few years back when his older sister was killed by a drunk driver. It seemed Teresa lost her will to live and that was when her normal weed consumption turned into a daily coke habit. She was still with his father at the time, and his father blamed her for the death of their child. The two of them began fighting all the time, making matters worse. It was when Teresa decided she was tired of going to work with black eyes that she started playing hooky from work, taking up with strange men she would meet at a bar she frequented.

When the two of them separated, it didn't really bother James that much. Monty was his real father, but he was a drummer for a local band that only played a gig at a place called Bobbies twice a month. He never had any real money and he never did anything with his kids. He had another family, and most of his time and money were spent taking care of his new girl and his step-kids. But James loved Teresa no matter what her flaws were. It didn't matter if she sucked one hundred dicks a day, she was still his mother, the woman who'd given him life.

Everything that happened was normal life—until she met some super black-ass-nigga who looked like he was related to Kunta Kinte named Tim. Tim was a booster and a crackhead who was also abusive. Not only was he abusive to Sugar, but he also had a thing about kids not listening to him, and he would smack James whenever he felt like it. Tim was a big liar who always claimed he had lots of money and was one day going to take care of the two of them. James knew firsthand he was a liar because the meals didn't change nor did what his mother did to make it change. What Tim manage to do was make Teresa lose everything she had, then not allow her to see her sisters any more. When her closest sister passed away, Tim wouldn't allow Teresa to attend the funeral, telling her why would she go to someone's funeral who wouldn't be able to come to hers.

James would never forget the April Fool's night his life changed forever. Tim was now hanging at the rooming house, but he wouldn't allow James to sit in the window while they did their thing. James knew it wasn't the sex, but Tim was embarrassed about being a crackhead. Tim would make sure none of the other tenants minded James being in the kitchen alone, and would make him sit in there and do his homework while the two of them handled business.

He'd just had an eerie feeling that that day wasn't going to be like most days. Usually, he would pop in on them, knowing they were going to be sleep after the drugs and sex and more drugs they'd done. His intention was just to put his finger under his mother's nose to make sure she was still breathing; he really didn't give a-flying-fuck if Tim didn't have a breath left.

When he entered the room, James saw Sugar on all fours and Tim had stuffed a sock in her mouth. He couldn't make out what she was saying, but he stood there and watched this big black-ass-man pumping his dick into his mother's anal hole. He still had a needle hanging from his arm along with a belt. James could tell his mother was in pain and it seemed like she was begging him to stop. Tim had transformed into a total different man. It wasn't until sometime later that James found out they had elevated once again from smoking cocaine to shooting heroin, *but from that moment forward, James began to want to kill Tim, and his love had started depleting for his mother as well.*

"Bitch, I know you got some ends round here," Tim said as he exploded, pulling out and dumping his load on her back.

"Baby, ain't no money. I don't have shit left. I spent the last little change on something from the dollar menu for the boy," she replied, talking about James.

James was still there, just outside the room door, where he couldn't see them but he could hear everything.

"SOME FOOD?! Bitch, you tripping! How old is that little-nigga, twelve? Thirteen? That little-bitch-made boy should be out there getting his own food!" Tim replied, disgusted they couldn't cop another hit.

His words were cutting James like a knife. He couldn't believe the man was in their room, talking to his mother like that. Besides, he wasn't twelve or thirteen; he was fourteen and he'd tried putting in applications to work after school, but all the jobs had said he couldn't get a work permit until he was fifteen. He felt that black-ass-nigga didn't know anything about him and had no right defacing his adolescent character the way he was doing. He figured that should be the last straw, that Tim had said enough, that there was going to be no more sugar for him. She was going to toss any man out her room who talked-shit about her son. That was all wishful thinking as James listened closely to the next words Teresa said out her own mouth.

"Baby, I think James has some money saved."

"Some money saved?! And he ain't gave nothing on no bills?"

That was all Tim needed to hear before slipping on his high-water jeans to get the search on. James heard the room door open as he slipped back into the kitchen, acting like he was doing his homework. There were two sets of footsteps, so he knew the woman he'd once known as Mother Teresa, now Sugar, was accompanying her man to come rob him. He knew it would only be a matter of seconds before they both would be all up in his grill.

He had a couple of bucks he had been saving from ripping open people's garbage and collecting cans to take to the junkyard. He thought about all the times he'd had to dig through dirty diapers and flies and them snail-looking creatures just to get a can. He needed a plan because he wasn't ready to part with his money to no junkie-ass-booster. He quickly turned to see someone had left a steak knife in the strainer. It was rare because usually everybody who roomed there kept all their personal belongings in their own room. He jumped up as the footsteps got closer and concealed the knife in his math book.

When Tim walked in the kitchen, he didn't say anything at first. He took a paper cup and filled it with water several times, drinking it as fast as he could each time. He opened the fridge and found someone else's half-eaten chicken breast, an open can of peaches, and a box of baking soda he knew would come in handy.

"Ain't never nothing to eat in this roach-infested-ass-house," he said, slamming the fridge after biting into someone else's sandwich.

James remained silent, knowing Tim was waiting for him to say something so he'd have a reason to address him back. When he saw James wasn't biting, he started the conversation.

"Yo, little-nigga, did you drink all the Kool-Aid out the green pitcher?" he asked.

"We didn't have any," James replied, not realizing the opening he had just given Tim.

"Y'all didn't have any? Well, what kind of man are you to sit around this nasty-ass-house dying of thirst all-fucking-day? Boy, you can't wait on your momma forever to feed your trifling-little-ass. What kind of sense does that make, young blood? You a man or you a little-bitch?"

James just sat there now. What Tim was doing was apparent and he just hoped-like-hell his mother would put a stop to it before it got out of hand. But the more Tim rattled on, James had to realize she wasn't coming. He figured now the monkey was scratching at her and she needed a fix, so she was going right along with whatever Tim wanted to do.

It instantly made him think about his sister's death and what his father would say. "If you had kept a watchful eye on her, none of this ever would have happened." He would insist she get help and get admitted to a clinic for help, but she had never listened. Even though James had never forgiven his father for walking out, his father words played in his head like a tape recording. The same thing was happening to him now that had happened to his sister, who would have been eighteen in a few more days. Teresa was once again neglecting her responsibilities as a parent.

James thought about the news the investigator had given him about his mother being in the front seat of some white man's Buick giving him a blowjob while her child was left outside the car to wander. James figured maybe his father had left to keep from killing his mother, but the sad part was, he should have taken his only son along with him.

"Say, young-punk," Tim said, finally invading James' personal space.

James kept his head down for a second, hoping he would take his hot breath and forget about any foul idea he might have.

"I heard you're holding on to some secret paper round here," he continued, now leaning over James.

Tim was sweating from whatever had been going on in the room and some of it was dripping down on James' homework, leaving water marks on the paper he had to turn in. James tried to act like he didn't understand the slang terminology for money, but he knew exactly what Tim was talking about.

James had been saving his money every day. He would collect a bag of cans and walk to American Junkyard, which was a nice walk, to cash them in. The grown men who worked there liked him and always gave him a few extra cents per pound. He knew he had over a hundred dollars, and he wasn't about to let the boogey man come and take one red cent of it.

"I'm only going to ask this one time: Do you have some money you're hiding from me and your mother?"

"That's what you mean by paper?" he asked. "Oh yeah, I got some of that kind of paper hiding for sure, but it isn't for you or my momma's drug habits. That money is being saved to buy my sister a headstone for her grave since we didn't have any life insurance. My sister ain't got nothing there and all them dead people around her got nice rocks with their names on it. Their families can find them, and people walking by can read their names and see when they were born and when they left. So I'm saving that paper you talking about so my sister can have one too!" James exclaimed.

Instead of his words touching his mother, who was now standing in the kitchen doorway, she took Tim's side.

"Baby, I think he's got some good money saved."

That was all Tim needed to hear. They both trotted back to the room so they could see if they could find where James had stashed his money. Teresa was going right along with Tim and helping him search. Her first mind had told her to stop Tim when she heard her son's story, but the monkey was in control of her subconscious and her rational thought process wasn't the same. She wanted her daughter to have a headstone, but she wanted a stone for herself right now, and that was more important.

James walked behind them, knowing they wouldn't find the money. He had managed to pry up one of the floorboards and hide the money in there. When Tim got frustrated with his search, he turned and grabbed James around his neck, choking him severely, almost cutting all his wind off.

"Boy, why don't you realize you need to be a man and pay some bills around here and give us some money for something to drink," he said, applying enough pressure that you could see the color change under his fingernails.

James now had the knife in his back pocket and he was feeling himself slip to the point where he might not return. He used his dangling arms and reached behind to his pocket, catching Tim completely off-guard. The knife slid into the dope fiend's belly, releasing an ocean of blood. The first poke caused his grip to loosen a little, but not completely. James started poking him over and over, until eventually, Tim's hand came from around his neck and he released him. Tim fell to the floor, holding his chest, with blood coming from his mouth.

James felt an instant rush of relief when he saw the life seeping out the man—not only for him, but for his mother and his sister as well. After he'd stabbed Tim and stood there watching him die, he silently made a deal with himself that he would never again in life let anyone take advantage of him or do him any bodily harm. That, if it was a matter of him or them, it would be them. He looked at his mother as she began crying. She had slid to the floor in her dirty nightgown and he didn't know if she was crying for his safety or the fact that the monkey had to go back in the cage for now. But he wasn't going to wait and find out. James packed his three pair of pants and two shirts into his school backpack, and lifted the floorboard and removed his paper. When he saw his mother crawl over to Tim's body, he turned and threw the money at her.

"Is this all my-fuckin'-life was worth to you?!" he asked, watching the bills fall into the pool of blood surrounding her lover's body.

He stood for a brief moment, waiting for her next move. A part of him wanted her to grab and hug and reassure him that his life was worth much more than a high, but the other part knew, as she gathered the money up trying to wipe the blood on her nightgown, the monkey was all she was thinking about. It was at that point James decided he didn't care if he ever saw her again. She was in the same boat to him that his father was in. When she left to go purchase the drugs, he disposed of Tim's body and left—fourteen years old, homeless and broke.

James only had one real friend. It was a kid he went to school with named Dibiase, who apparently came from a nice home. Dibiase's parents liked James and always made sure he ate good when he came by to play with Dibiase and his little brother Rickey. Now he hoped-like-hell he could turn to Dibiase and his family so he wouldn't be in the streets.

When James made it to the Hammonds' home, Dibiase's mother Cassie opened the door and saw him covered in blood. She rushed him inside, screaming for her son Little Rickey to bring her some hot towels. So many young kids were getting shot and the police killings were at an all-time high. She was too frantic to even question James about what had happened. Finally, when she'd calmed down and gotten him cleaned up, giving him an outfit of Dibiase's, he explained to her and Dibiase's father Rico what had happened. They embraced him and told him he didn't ever have to go back. Their house was huge and they had a spare room in the basement. James was ever so grateful to the Hammond family that day for taking him in and making him their third son.

~ Twelve ~

James Contrill, now known on the streets as J.C., pulled into the parking structure of Dibiase's apartment complex.

"What it do, bro?" Dibiase said. He was on the phone with J.C. as he and Don D. were pulling in.

"I'm pulling up, bro; let's roll so we can hit up Enterprise. Baby girl's on deck and we need to get that way to scoop a couple joints she's got for us," J.C. replied.

Don D. was on the passenger side, high-as-hell from the last blunt. Cheese had really outdone himself this time with the quality. All Don had heard was a couple of whips were being placed on order, which meant he wasn't going to have to wait for a ride any more and he could go see his little broad at will.

"No sweat, fam; give me a sec and I'll be right out," Dibiase said, happy J.C. was already thinking and putting things in motion.

Dibiase went into the bathroom, where Camille was putting on her eyeliner, getting ready for work. She worked at a travel agency in Brown Deer called Fun Jet. She didn't make a lot of money, but the perks she could get on flights were well worth it. He walked up behind her, putting his arms around her waist.

"Hey, baby; I'm about to bounce. J.C.'s outside and we've got some business to tend to. I left the keys to the truck on the table," he said, rubbing her flat stomach through her blouse.

She turned and kissed him on the lips, then wiped the MAC gloss off so her man wouldn't be shining.

"Okay, bae."

Dibiase went in his pocket, gave her some lunch money, and told her to have a good day.

She sensed he and J.C. were up to something she couldn't quite put her finger on. She had been worried since the day he'd gone to identify his father's body that he would be looking for revenge on the person or persons who'd caused Rico's demise. It scared her immensely but she knew Dibiase was smart. She felt whoever had done the murder wasn't local. She knew Rico and Cassie had taken many flights out to Las Vegas because she was the one who'd always booked them first class. She never knew why they'd traveled there so often, but she had known Rico for some time and he wasn't loose with his money, so she didn't figure him to be a gambler.

One thing she remembered the homicide detectives saying to Cassie was, when the street camera caught a shot of the getaway car, the plates were from Arizona. Camille knew Arizona was only four hours away from Vegas. If she was a betting woman, she would bet it had something to do with Las Vegas.

'Maybe,' she thought, 'Rico owed a huge gambling debt and someone had come to collect.'

It wasn't impossible. People rumored it had happened to Michael Jordan, even though it had never been proven. She decided, before she left for work, to take the police report Dibiase had so she could thoroughly look it over. She'd seen him reading it over and over, and knew he wouldn't go on with his life unless there were some answers.

She finished putting on her eyeliner and opened the cabinet to place it back in its spot. She looked at the unopened box of tampons and realized she was two weeks late for her cycle. With so much going on, she had forgotten all about being late for her period. She made a mental note to stop by Walgreens on her way home to grab an EPT. She didn't want to say anything until she was sure. It could just be the stress from everything that was transpiring. It wouldn't be the first time stress had caused her to be late. But one thing she knew for sure was the little stick would turn pink or blue, and the truth would be revealed. At the moment, with Dibiase acting so strange, she wasn't sure what she wanted the truth to be. Then she remembered how badly Rico had wanted a grandson, and she knew she hoped the truth was in favor of a growing belly.

They rode in the Avalon and Dibiase was impressed at what J.C. had selected. It was about twenty minutes later when they pulled into the Enterprise lot on East Silver Spring where Kisha worked. The dark red Durango and the Ford were parked right up front like Kisha had promised they would be. Before they got out, J.C. peeled five one-hundred-dollar bills off the take from last night to slip to her.

When they walked in, Kisha was standing behind the service counter, waiting on a white man who looked like he was a golfer. When she finished, she used her index finger to call J.C. up to the counter. Kisha was a bad-little-bitch. She looked so much like the rapper Eve with her light-brown eyes that she'd even gone and imitated Eve's tats on her breast. She leaned over the counter and demanded J.C. kiss her since her manager had gone on break. He wasn't a-nigga who kissed anyone but Donna in public, but as fine as Kisha was and as much as he normally wouldn't, it was business.

He didn't know why the girl had the notion she could step up in the main spot and move Donna around. That wasn't going to happen! As crazy as J.C. was about Jada Pinkett, if he ever ran across her, she would just have to accept her spot as number two. He truly loved and cared about Donna. He knew, if anything ever went down and he had to go away, she would be there. If he had to go on the run, she would have all their stuff packed before he could tell her. Point blank, Donna was irreplaceable.

"Hope you like the vehicles. They're both brand-spanking-new and haven't been issued to any customers," Kisha said after tasting J.C.'s soft lips.

"Yeah, baby girl, they're straight," he replied.

"Straight my-ass, James." She used his government name, knowing he hated that. "Straight, as you and your people cannot, I repeat, *cannot* smoke that loud-ass-weed in them. Last time, I had to give the porter fifty dollars to do a special detail on the car!" she exclaimed.

"Okay, okay, baby, we won't blow our brains out in these pieces-of-shits," he said smiling, knowing good and well, they were going to smoke in the cars.

That was the one perk of Kisha: She didn't drink, smoke, have kids, or eat fried foods. All she did was fuck-and-suck a mean-dick and that was why J.C. kept her on the side. J.C. slipped her the extra money and used the pre-paid debit card to pay for the cars. He signaled Don D. to take the Ford because he knew his brother was a truck man. Don D. didn't give-a-fuck which car he used. All he could think about was getting Highway 20 in his sights. Ten minutes away from the exit and he could be knee-deep in some fine-ass-pussy.

~ Thirteen ~
Don D., The Baltimore Kid

Baltimore was a tough place to grind and hustle. You had to know *somebody who knew somebody who really knew somebody. The Barksdale crew had taken over like the Chambers brothers had done back in Detroit, Michigan, some years ago. The city was a cash cow full of crackheads, and if you had money and rank, you could buy your neighborhood from the police. There were plenty of spots in Baltimore, that if you dialed 911 and told the operator your emergency situation and your address, the reaction was a hang up.*

Don D. had been climbing the ranks in his city quickly. He went from lookout boy to package handler, straight to chief, for one of the big men in his town. But he had a weakness for pussy that would soon be his downfall and cause him to have to flee Baltimore or be killed. His tendency to let his small head outthink his big head had been something he was dealing with ever since he'd lost his virginity in middle school to the queen of the hood, Monique Grace. She was the hottest thing in Mount Vernon since Heavy D's first album had dropped. Monique had the face of a princess and the body of throwback Coke-bottle goddess. The issue was she belonged to the street-nigga named Pork Chop, who was the second biggest baller.

Don D. had caught finally caught Monique alone at the Lexington Market and figured, if he was ever going to shoot his shot, now was the time. He spit a few lines at her and was amazed she was listening. Don D. figured Pork Chop had a lot of people on his payroll, so if he took Monique out of the way, they could parlay and not be seen by any potential snitch. He knew Pork Chop was also a banger in addition to getting money. He was the-nigga who had a thousand send-offs who would try Fort Knox if he told them to.

Don ended up taking Monique to the Red Roof Inn out by the airport. The ride there was all he'd anticipated and more. He didn't have to do much talking because she couldn't respond to anything. The moment they had hit the highway, Monique was unzipping his zipper and removing him, administering to him oral pleasure. Don licked his lips as he drove listlessly at a high speed. All he could think about was smashing her and having a good time.

Don knew the airport wasn't anyone's territory because too many Feds patrolled the area, looking for dealers who were bold enough to try to get their packages in by air. He felt his phone ring and realized it must have slipped out his pocket and landed in the crevice between the Acura's seats. His first mind was not to answer, but he didn't want to miss a dollar. Besides, he wanted to take Monique shopping. If things went right, he would ask her to sneak away and accompany him on a trip. Don didn't stop her from doing what she was doing as he kept one hand on the wheel and the other reaching back, feeling for the phone. When he looked at the caller display, the name said Mega, one of his good-paying customers.

Reluctantly, Don D. answered and he was glad he did. Mega explained he needed a four-and-a-split. Don had the work in his trunk, and sticking true to his hustle, he told Mega to meet him at the motel where he was taking Monique. Don D. pulled his light-blue Integra into the parking lot of the Ramada Inn and jumped out, zipping up his pants. Monique was looking at him, smiling and telling him to hurry with the key because she was soaked thinking about his dick inside her. When Don emerged from checking in, he drove to the back of the place and they went in the room.

He'd always had his share of women, but none as sexy as Monique; none even close. She was like eating a box of Taraji Henson cookies. When they got inside, Monique didn't waste any time. She pushed Don to the bed and turned her phone to Pandora so the music could set the mood. As Jahiem's song Me and Bitch played, she started seductively undressing for him. Her matching lace panties-and-bra set fit her like they were part of her skin. Don D. felt his manhood rise and was ready to get it on. He was so engrossed by her performance he almost didn't hear his phone ringing. He had forgotten he'd told Mega to meet him.

"One sec, baby girl, let me take this. I've got to get this money," he said, watching her frown.

Monique was use to it because Pork Chop, her man, barely gave her any time because of his currency chasing. Don jumped up and left the room to meet Mega at his car. He popped his trunk, taking out the work Mega had said he wanted, and jumped in the passenger side of Mega's black Beamer. The two of them shook hands as Mega opened the package, tasting what he was getting.

"Yeah, boy, this is that flame right here," Mega said, liking the numbness that covered his tongue.

"Come on now, playa; you know how your boy gets down," Don D. replied, bragging on the quality of his work.

Mega began counting out his money as Don D. took his blunt out of his ashtray.

"I bet this-shit ain't that fiyah and desire," Don said, taking a puff and choking.

"Hell naw!" Mega replied.

"I know it."

"Not the weed, my nigga; look at that-bitch up there on the balcony."

Mega pointed in the direction of Don D.'s room. When he looked up, he couldn't believe Monique was standing on the balcony in a robe that had been in the bathroom.

"Man, that's a-bad-bitch up there; that-hoe looks familiar too," Mega said.

"I don't know that trick-ass-bitch. She was with a few niggas at the front desk when I was checking in," he claimed, taking the money and counting it.

Monique was out of order coming out the room like that, he thought. He knew he was going to head back up there and take it out on that fat camel toe between her thighs. When he got back upstairs, he didn't even say anything to her about the compromising position she had put him in. He just did what he'd thought he was going to do and she loved the way he fucked.

Every night for two weeks straight, the two of them hooked up. Don was giving Monique a few ends here and there, and they were careful to keep it secret. It wasn't until the third week of them seeing each other that things went terribly bad. Don was waiting on a package and he couldn't service Mega. Everyone knew selling dope was just as bad as using the work. When the dope man was out, he went on a mission like a crackhead to find his next package.

Mega had plugged-up with one of his cousins who worked for Pork Chop, and since his cousin was trusted, Mega was invited to the spot to cop. When he walked in and saw the chick sitting on the couch, there was no mistaking it was the same chick he'd seen at the Ramada when he was with his big homie.

Monique was none-the-wiser when Pork Chop walked up on her and slapped the blunt out her mouth. She felt the warm trickle of blood slide from her bottom lip to her chin and did all she could do to keep her wind. Pork Chop was furious and he was out for someone's head. He picked up her phone and went through her messages, finding a long text between her and Don D. That was enough for him to know whose head he wanted, and now, if she didn't do her part, it would be two heads he would serve himself on a platter.

Monique was baffled, not knowing how to handle what her man was proposing. She really enjoyed Don's sensual touch and the way he listened to her when they finished making love. Don wasn't tight with his money and he could eat pussy like nobody's business. Monique was trapped between a rock and a hard spot, but she knew it would cost her her own life if she didn't come through.

The following week, they missed each other and she had done that on purpose, hoping Pork Chop would calm down and come to his senses, but it was wishful thinking. The following Friday after that, which was the day they normally hooked up on, he made her call Don and set things in motion. Pork Chop had even gotten Mega involved, knowing Don D. would serve his boy a brick if he had it. Pork Chop's mind was made up though; he was killing Don D., Monique, and Mega. He didn't give-a-fuck; he was as ruthless as they come.

Pork Chop didn't want Don D. to get suspicious, so he allowed things to transpire the way they usually did. He made Monique turn on her locator that connected with her social media page. He was going to give them time to get into the act, then come and splatter some brains on the room walls of the Ramada.

Don D. picked Monique up at the mall like he always did, having had her park her car in the back by one of the stores where no black folks shopped. She climbed in his car, wearing a short skirt, way up past her knees, and a DKNY tank top. Don D. noticed her mood was a little different when she didn't seem as cheerful and as happy to see him as she normally did. He was about to say something when his phone started vibrating.

"What up, Mega?" he said, turning down his new Future CD.

"What it do, my-nigga? Say, I want to know if you can handle a huge order. I got that paper up like you been screaming and I want to go all the way through the woods to Grandma's house," he stated, talking in code.

Don D. knew all the way to Grandma's house meant Mega wanted a brick.

"I can handle an order from El Chapo, nigga. Your-ass just always calls me when I'm on something, or should I say about to get on something," he replied, looking over at Monique.

"Where you 'bout to be, my nigga? I got this paper on me and ready to ride down on you."

Don D. had changed plans. He was tired of the same old beat-up room at the Ramada, so he'd gotten them a lavish suite for the night, something special. He'd booked a top-flight room at the Country Suites out on Inner Harbor. He told Mega where he was going to be and Mega told him he would meet him there in ten. Don hung up the phone, watching the road, and at the same time, noticing Monique was more into her phone, sending texts and tweeting. He wasn't upset at all. He knew he would do like he always did and take it out on that pretty-pussy of hers.

They checked into the lavish suite that had its own whirlpool tub and sauna right in the room. The bed was twice as big as the bed at the Ramada and so were the flat-screen televisions. Don didn't want to get too deeply involved in his routine with Monique until after Mega had come and left.

When Monique saw the inside of the suite, her eyes lit up. Pork Chop had major loot, but always fucked her in one of his spots. Monique started undressing slowly, still not talking much. Don D. just chalked it up to her being overwhelmed about how nice the room was.

His phone rang again, and he looked at the caller display and saw it was Mega. Mega had gotten to him rather quickly this time. Don didn't have a whole brick with him, so they were going to have to ride and leave Monique to enjoy the amenities until he returned. He kissed her softly on the lips and told her he would be right back. She smiled and lay on the bed naked.

Once outside, Don D. jumped in Mega's ride, giving him the shake. They were from different sets, but they had gone to high school together and had always been tight.

"Yo, man, shit's 'bout to go down with you, playa," Mega said, catching Don off-guard.

First thing came to his mind was Mega was wearing a wire and working for the people. That would explain why he hadn't heard from him in a couple weeks.

"You with them people?" Don asked.

"Get-the-fuck out of here, my-nigga. Shit's deeper than them people. In fact, you're probably going to wish it was just them people."

"What-the-fuck you talking 'bout then, my-nigga?"

"That-bitch you're fuckin' with. Don't play dumb, my-nigga. I know how you are with them-hoes with your little tender-dick-ass, but I know I don't have to tell you Monique is that-nigga Pork Chop's main ride-or-die," he said, getting Don D.'s full attention.

Mega figured, since he already had Pork Chop's money to get the brick, he might as well watch the-shit play out, and hopefully, walk away with the paper. He didn't want anything to happen to Don D., but he knew Don was liking on another man's property and the game had rules.

"Man, this-shit you telling me valid?" Don asked, not knowing which direction he was about to take it.

"On the one, my-nigga."

Don felt the butterflies in his stomach moving around at an all-time fast rate. He had really taken a liking to Monique and tonight was the night he was going to ask her to leave the-nigga for good. He knew that meant he had to find her a place on the outskirts and take care of her, but he was willing if she was ready to be his permanent piece.

When he got back in the room, he wasn't sure how much time he had before the posse showed up. He knew Monique wasn't going to live to tell about it either way, and if he wasn't careful, neither was he. He fixed a Hennessey and Coke, and took it in the bathroom with him. As he looked at himself in the mirror, he knew exactly what he had to do. Monique should have told him what was up and they could have gotten through it. He figured she was scared, but two wrongs wouldn't make a right. He had to kill her.

When he came out the bathroom, he heard a bleeping noise from her phone and figured that was her man. He'd probably gotten messed up when the locations had changed and they were a little further than their normal spot. She was sitting, still naked, rolling a blunt and playing everything out like they normally did.

"Baby girl, let me take off these-damn-jeans while you get my drink out the bathroom for me."

"Anything for my love bug," she replied, trying to act like nothing was bothering her.

When she came from the bathroom with his drink in her hand and her nice tits bouncing free of their restraint, she found herself looking down the barrel of his .357 Magnum. She instantly dropped the drink, causing the brown poison in the glass to splatter everywhere. He was holding her cell in his hand, scrolling through the text message between her and her-nigga.

"You punk-bitch! You didn't even have enough sense to erase the damn texts," he said, steaming mad.

He was ready to plant two to her dome, knowing her banger-ass-boyfriend couldn't be far away. He was still trying to calculate just how much time he had.

"I'M SORRY, BUT I HAD NO CHOICE. THE-NIGGA SAID, IF I DIDN'T GET YOU, HE WAS GOING TO KILL MY-FUCKIN'-GRANDMOTHER!" *she yelled.*

"Call the-nigga back and tell him I went to the vending machine. Find out how much time I've got before he gets here," Don said, still holding the pistol on her. He was really upset he wasn't going to get one last nut off in her.

"I swear, bitch, if you want to get out of this alive, you'd better act like Halle Berry going for a Grammy nomination."

"Okay, daddy, but you know I didn't want any of this to happen. What was I supposed to do when he called his people on the phone right in front of me and gave them the name of the nursing home my grandmother is in? I hate him, Don! I hate him!" she replied, trying to save her life once again.

Don D. had scrolled to Pork Chop's number and hit 'send', passing her the phone so the show could start. Pork Chop answered on the first ring.

"Bitch, why you calling me? I got the text and I'm almost there." he said, wondering why she was going off-plan.

Don was right there listening to every word.

"Where's that fuck-boy and does he have that money I sent by Mega on him?" Pork Chop questioned, wanting his thirty grand back.

Don was waving his hand in a motion she understood.

"Yeah, Porkie; the-nigga was bragging about the money and he was even saying he's got some more dope in the trunk of his car," she replied, feeling like Don was going to help her out of the mess she'd gotten into.

He did like the way she'd sweetened the conversation and was thinking about giving her a pass. One thing he knew was, if he killed her, he was surely going to miss fucking her.

"Yeah, baby, that's what big daddy's talking about. Now, where is that punk-ass-nigga? Sounds like I hear running water."

"Yes, daddy, we're about to get in the shower. That way, it should be a total surprise when he steps out all wet and sees your handsome face."

Monique was acting her-ass off. She was better than Halle Berry and deserved the award for the year's best-slut. Pork Chop was digging the way Monique was handling things. Don wasn't their first victim, and they'd played it to the max. Anyone who'd had any inclination of what was going on had thought Monique was being raped. That was how they'd played it. This time, Mega had gotten in the way when he'd discovered Monique was the girl at the hotel with Don D. Monique had just known Don D. was going to be easy prey. He didn't know just how good of actress she really was.

"Turn the shower off, baby," he told her.

Monique walked into the bathroom, knowing her-nigga would be there in a few minutes and it would be all over. They would have Don D.'s money and dope, and be on their merry way. She could finally take that cruise she'd been planning. When she turned to walk back out, she was surprise that Don was right there. Things got dark in her world. The first bullet struck her in the face, sending her tumbling into the once-white porcelain tub. The second one, he stood over her and took precise aim at her no-good heart.

Don dimmed the lights in the bathroom and left the door cracked. He turned the shower back on so things looked like she'd said they would. He even turned on Pandora on her phone and let the Jagged Edge station play. Don unlocked the room door when he heard the small roar from Pork Chop's pearl-white CTS pull up. He peeped out the window and saw the big burly, Rick Ross-looking-nigga dressed in all black. Don knew Pork Chop thought it was sweet. He heard the footsteps heading to his room as he parked himself behind the door. It was seconds later when he heard the cocking of the unit Pork Chop was carrying.

He hesitated, making sure he'd pulled his mask all the way down before entering. When he silently pushed the door open, he could hear Let's Get Married playing through the cracked door to the room with the dim light shining. He knew that was the bathroom and headed right for it, knowing Don D. would be none-the-wiser. When he took a few more steps toward the direction of the bathroom, Don D. emptied his gun, making his back and the back of his head look like a dartboard.

Don heard tires screeching and looked out the window to see the pearl-white car bolting from the hotel's parking lot. When he rushed to Pork Chop's body, he unmasked the villain, seeing it was just a fat kid. Pork Chop had never left his vehicle. Don raised up the plaid sleeve on the kid's shirt and saw his tat was fresh. He knew Pork Chop had just given this young dude his first initiation into his world. Don D. rushed to his house, packed all he could, and headed for Milwaukee.

~ Fourteen ~

Dibiase was pleased with the way things were starting off with them. He knew he could count on his godbrother to handle shit the way it was supposed to be done. He main concern was that, once things got running and money was coming in, he could focus on who'd killed his daddy and handle that business personally. He was tired of spending countless hours reading over and over the police report that didn't make much sense to him.

Rico never talked much about his street business with Dibiase, so it was going to be hard for him to have a leg to stand on. But he knew, if a person wanted to go to war, they had to have their paper straight. That went for anyone—the United States, the terrorists who fucked with the United States, and anybody else who wanted to wage war.

Dibiase thought about the conversations his mother was having on the phone with a woman named Julia. It was weird that his mother had a friend who never came around. It raised a little suspicion with Dibiase, but not much at the moment. One thing he'd figured was that his father's connect was in Las Vegas, but that was also confusing if the connect had anything to do with it because the police report said the car was stolen from Arizona.

Dibiase thought about Chino Mares and knew he was one person he had to pay a visit. He just had a gut feeling that, between Chino, his father's plug, and a few other weak-muthafuckas, somebody knew something. Who and what didn't matter because, in just a few weeks, he would have enough paper to finance a private party. If that was what it was going to take, he was with it.

~ Fifteen ~
Rico's Return

Rico and Cassie were flown back to Milwaukee in Tito's private jet. At first it worried him to accept the accommodation Tito had offered, but he knew he would still be flying the friendly skies. Tito wouldn't do anything to harm Cassie because of Julia, and Rico felt that wholeheartedly. Tito also worshiped the female species and he held that close to his heart, so Rico accepted the flight knowing it would give him time to think.

One thing for sure Tito had confirmed with him was he'd chosen his path and he would issue a hit, leading to the demise of the Midwest Godfather Rickey 'Rico' Hammond. Rico knew he didn't have much time to get his life in order, but whenever the hit came, he knew it would be a solo hit and his family wouldn't be part of it. Word had come from Tito's old man that it had to go that way.

When the plane landed, Cassie noticed Rico had been silent the whole ride home. He had drank two glasses of brandy and that was something else odd. Rico wasn't a drinker or smoker, but he'd had two glasses. When she mentioned the money she'd spent on the watch, he didn't say anything about it. Normally, he would have had some type of joke about her spending when she was with Julia, but he was like a dead man all the way home. She knew when it was time to stop talking and let her man think. Cassie relaxed her head and decided to think about her friend Julia.

Mickey had driven the Vanden Plas to the airport and was waiting to pick up his brother and sister-in-law when they landed. Since Timmerman was a private airport, Mickey was allowed to drive the car almost to the landing strip, so when they got off, they could get right in the car and head for the security gates. He saw the Hawker Beechcraft land and watched his brother get off.

"Hey, bro; how was your trip? You see that-fuckin'-fight?" Mickey asked.

"It was cool," Rico responded in a dry tone.

Mickey had been around his brother all his life and he knew right away something was bothering him. If Rico wasn't going to talk about it, Mickey wasn't going to push it. He hoped Rico hadn't wagered too much money on the fight, but he also knew gambling wasn't much of Rico's style.

"Same-old-shit, my brother; you go out to Vegas, eat good, party good, and gamble a little. I tell you what though, next fight I'm going to have my-ass sitting right in my living room," Rico said as he tossed his last bag in the trunk of the beige Jaguar he loved.

Mickey still felt something was bothering him and directed his casual conversation to Cassie.

"Well, did you at least have a good time?"

"Yes, I did; thanks for asking."

"I see your wrist is lit up like a dancing globe," Mickey said, admiring the nice watch.

"You know I don't know a thing about this kind of stuff. A friend of mine took me shopping and we ended up buying these time tickers," she replied, smiling.

"Well, if you decide you don't want it, I've got a few chicks wrists it would look nice on," he replied jokingly.

He was hoping to get a rise out his brother, but still nothing as he looked through the rearview mirror at him.

⮞ ✸ ⮜

Cassie Weatherspoon was born in Gary, Indiana. She worked as a waitress after school at a Waffle House on the outskirts of town. She had to work because it wouldn't be long before her sick father could no longer do the job in the mills and her mother didn't make a whole lot cleaning houses for small business owners. She figured, taking on a job, she could help with the bills and the groceries, and take some of the weight off her aging parents. At least she could buy her own clothes. It didn't matter that most of her outfits came from the Goodwill, she prided herself on knowing how to pick out good things that didn't show too much usage.

She had come from a good, honest, hard-working family who had been putting any extra money away for her education. The one time she'd wanted something was her sixteenth birthday when her school was having a dance. She only had five dollars saved and she knew she didn't want to go to the school dance in one of the five outfits she mixed and matched daily. She decided to ask her parents, and when they told her they couldn't afford a new dress, her feelings were crushed. She knew before asking they might say exactly what they'd said. She'd just had hopes things would be different. The words her mother had said played over and over in her head.

"Cassie, now baby, you know we can't afford to buy you a new dress. That just isn't in the budget right now. Soon you'll be heading to a big school, and we want you to be comfortable and study."

She knew it had probably hurt them more than it had hurt her not to be able to get the dress. Her mother was starting to suffer from arthritis in both her hands from ironing so much that she couldn't even sew her one. Cassie respected them a lot and knew they were busting their tails to make sure she had a future. She made sure they didn't see her cry.

Two days later, on her walk home with her best friend Tangela, they were discussing the dance and Tangela told her about the rumor. It was said the principal was inviting some special guest to the dance. Mr.

Sharpe was an ex-Navy SEAL who kept in contact with most of the new recruits. He loved to have the men come in and talk to the young men to try to keep their heads on straight. This year he'd invited them to the dance. When Tangela told her that, Cassie continued walking with her head down, feeling now like she had to have the appropriate attire to even attend.

She knew her parents had a point. She just felt like she never got the chance to do any extracurricular activities. She really felt she never got a chance to dress up and it made her sometimes feel like the black Cinderella.

"Hey, Cass, why you looking so sad?" Tangela asked.

"What makes you think I'm sad?" she responded, not really wanting her friend to know she was sad or the reason for her sadness. "I'm happy you're going to the dance. I know you'll just have a grand old time," Cassie replied.

"What? Now, Cass, don't tell me you aren't going! Don't be playing with me," Tangela said with a note of sincere concern in her tone. They had been best friends since last year and they hung out together almost every day.

"Honestly, Tang, I don't have a-damn-thing to wear to a dance and you can bet I won't be parading around the gym in these ugly-ass-clothes. You can take that to the bank!" Cassie blurted out.

Tangela was shocked at the language coming from her best friend, straight-A, perfect-attendant comrade. It was actually funny hearing curse words spoken in proper English.

"Well, that ain't no reason, shit!" Tangela said, now using profanity herself. "I've got something in my closet that could fit those model hips of yours. I'm sure of it."

"You sure?"

"Listen, my aunt has been sending me clothes once a month from Rhode Island, some nice shit too. Some of the dresses still have tags on them."

"Damn!" Cassie replied, wishing she had an aunt who would send her some nice clothes.

"Cassie, you're my girl and that's what friends do. They stick together. Only one thing: I get the hottest soldier," she replied, laughing.

They shared a laugh as they walked past Cassie's house to the other side of the projects where Tangela lived. Tangela took Cassie up to her room, and when they opened the small closet door, Cassie's mouth fell open at how packed her friend's closet was with clothing she had never seen her wear before. It felt like she was in a section at Macy's with the freedom to roam and shop. After a few minutes of looking, Cassie selected an off-the-shoulder, above-the-knee turquoise dress that still had the tags attached to it. It was the most gorgeous dress she had ever seen in person.

"Good choice," Tangela said as she finished rolling a joint.

Normally, Cassie wouldn't smoke with her friend because she didn't like the feeling the drug gave her, but since it was a special occasion, she decided to take a few pulls. Cassie choked on the first pull and Tangela laughed as she coached Cassie through the next hit. A couple of pulls later, Cassie was a semi-pro.

"Hey, let me give you a shotgun," Tangela suggested.

"Tangy, you're tripping. It's bad enough I'm smoking weed, now you want me involved with firearms."

"Girl, you're so silly," Tangela replied, knowing just how green her best friend was.

Cassie was one of the prettiest girls in school, but most people didn't know it because she always wore her hair in an ugly style and wore baggy clothes that looked old and worn. But she and Tangela had been close. They had done sleepovers and played dress-up many weekends, and she'd seen Cassie in a whole different light.

Tangela took a fresh joint and lit it to show Cassie what a shotgun was. Cassie was already high and didn't know how much more of the substance she could inhale before she passed completely out. She watched closely as Tangela turn the lit in and placed it in her mouth. As she walked up close to Cassie, she instructed her to open her mouth so the other end could slide in. When Tangela removed the joint, she was still close to Cassie. Leaning in, she kissed Cassie on her lips, feeling how soft and wet her lips were. It took Cassie by surprise and she didn't know how to react. It felt kind of sensual, but Cassie wasn't use to kissing a boy yet, let alone kissing another girl.

"You know you have the biggest brown eyes I've ever seen," Tangela said.

Just as Cassie was ready to thank her friend, she felt the pressure of Tangela's lips a second time. She was ready to protest until she felt the texture of Tangy's tongue dance around inside her mouth with her own tongue. There was nothing to protest any more because Cassie couldn't deny that the feeling was intriguing.

It was obvious Tangela had been keeping a few things from Cassie. She was experienced in the sex area, or she'd watched a lot of television and learned very quickly. Tangela had skilled hands that roamed from Cassie's face to her breasts to below her belly button, causing Cassie to shudder and her knees to buckle. What Cassie did know was about masturbation, but it was what she did when she was alone in her room three or four times a month. Cassie had just finished trying on the dress for the dance, so she was still in her panties and bra.

Tangela was breathing heavy as she inserted her hand in Cassie's panties, feeling the thick bush of hair followed by a wetness that Cassie had never caused herself. They made it to her friend's bed and Tangela took over like she was Roxy Reynolds in one of those X-rated movies. She sucked Cassie's nipples, biting down on them and causing Cassie excruciating pain that also felt good. The two of them made love to each other every day afterschool for a week straight.

Cassie parents were very happy she'd somehow worked it out and was able to make it to the dance. Her father had originally felt bad that he couldn't bend the rules and get his baby a new dress because he knew she deserved it. He had tried to make a bet at the OTB on a horse that was a long shot and was supposed to be a sure win. He was now working overtime just to make up for the bet he'd lost.

It was the day of the dance and Cassie had dolled herself up. She wouldn't allow her mother to see her before she was ready. Cassie was finally finished and headed downstairs where her parents were watching reruns of The Jeffersons. When they saw her, they stood up and smiled at how beautiful she looked. Her mother hugged her as tears rolled down her face, thanking God that her daughter had gotten a blessing.

Her father offered to drive her to the dance, but Cassie declined, telling him Tangela was picking her up. He'd figured, if he dropped her off, he would have time to sneak and grab a racing form to see who was running in the Belmont Stakes tomorrow. He knew he had to win a bet soon because he had been dipping into his daughter's college fund money.

Tangela pulled up in the rental car her aunt had wired her the money to get. They rode together, talking about the past week at school and making a bet that the men who were going to be guests were all going to be either crazy or ugly. When they walked in the gym, the dance was just as crowded as they'd suspected it would be. When the girls had heard about the guests they were having from the Navy,

Cassie knew all the freaks would come out. The music was blaring and the young women were crowding around the Navy men as they all asked for dances.

Cassie and Tangela stood in a corner, holding up a wall, just observing the scene. Cassie decided to get up to get herself a glass of punch. She was moving so fast she didn't notice the Navy guy who had been staring at her trying to get her attention. Soon as she made it to the punch bowl, she heard a voice behind her say something. She knew it was a male voice that didn't sound familiar, like any of the staff members. At first, she was just going to walk away and ignore the person, but she decided to at least turn and get a look at who was probably standing behind her looking at her ass.

"I hope that isn't the spiked stuff," the deep voice said.

Cassie turned to stare into the face of a gorgeous young man. He didn't even look old enough to be a Navy man, but his features displayed a ruggedness that showed he was most likely physically tough. He had her attention now as she started to blush watching him smile.

"Well, I hope it is the spiked stuff. Might do me some good," she replied. "By the way, if that was a pick-up line, at least follow it up with a name," she continued, sipping her punch, hoping one of the ghetto-ass-girls had spiked it.

"I apologize. My name is Rickey, Rickey Hammond."

~ Sixteen ~

Mickey pulled the car up in front of his brother's crib. He really didn't want to stick around much longer, seeing Rico wasn't in a good mood. Rico was very observant of people, especially those he was close to. He saw his mood had been taken to heart by his brother and that wasn't his aim. Mickey was the only brother he had, and all through their childhood, Mickey had been a great big brother and a hustler by nature.

Rico remembered one time they were hungry and Mickey was just turning fourteen. He didn't know anything about the drug business yet, but he was good at fixing plumbing. Rico knew they were too young for someone to trust them, so he'd had Mickey hire a crackhead to pose as the company manager and had gotten a job right away that paid two hundred dollars.

After they unloaded the luggage, Rico noticed Mickey was anxious to hit it. He didn't want his brother to feel any kind of way, plus, he needed to prep him with some important information.

"Wait before you leave, bro. I need to holla at you about something," Rico said, stopping Mickey in his tracks.

Mickey turned around and followed his younger brother into the house, down to the basement where he had set up his office. The basement had two different-size pool tables and a bar. The tables were for Rico's son Rickey Jr., who lived to play and had become pretty good at it. Rico walked behind the bar and poured them each a shot of Remy 1738.

"What's going on, Rico? You seemed to be agitated about something. I've never seen you like this before," Mickey asked, worried because Rico wasn't a heavy drinker. He had buried his first shot while Mickey was babysitting his. Rico poured himself another one.

"Listen, brother, I didn't mean to seem like I was taking my frustrations out on you. Mick, you know it isn't like that at all. You've been there for me since day one. I'm just going through some real-deep-shit right now," Rico said, almost having second thoughts about what he wanted to say.

"Well, what? Do we need to ride on some-niggas over some paper?"

"I don't have ghetto problems, bro; you know that. I just know the problems I do have nobody would understand them, not even me."

Mickey was all ears now because he had never seen such a serious look on his brother's face, and he damn-sure had never heard him speak with such sincere fear in his voice until now. He knew whatever the problem was, it was big. In fact, whatever it was, it was starting to make Mickey nervous.

"Rico, you know you're like Gotti around this-muthafucka, so whatever it is, the-shit can't be that-damn-bad," Mickey said, trying to ease the tension in the cool basement air.

"Mickey, listen to me and listen carefully. If a man can conquer himself, there is no way that man can be conquered. All this power and all this money I got don't mean shit, bro. Who am I? I'm not that untouchable-nigga all these thug-niggas make me out to be. I know I can afford a bigger house or a mansion, but I know I don't want to have to pay for armed guards walking around my lawn with fully-automatic weapons. I would never live in no-damn-house like Scarface with monitors and machine guns. That shit looks good on television, but not this real thing we call life."

"But you've made it, little brother. Not many-niggas can say they had a career as a kingpin and made it," Mickey said.

Rico listened to his brother's comment and felt worse. He had made it as far as the streets of Milwaukee were concerned, but he had also made it to the point-of-no-return where the game was concerned. Any day now, he could be outside watering his grass and shots could be fired, or he could get in his car, stick his key in the ignition, and just like Danny Green, be blown to smithereens. To some, what they saw on the outside was making it, but behind the closed doors of the real mafia world, no one ever truly made it. Not Capone, not Gotti, not Escobar— no one truly makes it out the game. The thing that bothered him was he wasn't only risking his life, but the life of his entire family would be in jeopardy.

"I need you to take care of something for me, Mickey. I need two low-key rental cars, one for me and one for Cassie. Then I'm going to have you take and put all my cars away in storage for now," he said to his brother, looking in the bottom of his third shot glass. He threw the remainder of the liquid in the bar sink.

"Not a problem, Rico; I can do that," Mickey replied.

Rico wrote something on a piece of paper before handing it to his brother.

"Also, when that's finished, I need this address completely cleaned out and everything in there donated to the Goodwill."

Mickey loved Rico dearly, and he knew now something was really going on that there was no turning back from. He accepted the wad of bills his brother handed him to pay for whatever help he needed and the cost of the storage unit. Mickey left to handle what his brother had asked him to do. He knew no matter how many times growing up he had been there for Rico, Rico had tripled it in their adult life.

When Mickey left, Rico went inside his office area and relaxed for a second in his leather chair. When he turned on the television, the news was already on.

Two men gunned down in cold blood at a liquor store on 51st and Burleigh. Witnesses say a black Honda Accord fled the scene.

A seven-year-old girl was abducted on her way to school. Police have no leads and are asking the public for help. Anyone with any information is to call Crime Stoppers.

The news was the same, day in and day out. The city was getting worse by the day, with the murder rate soaring, taking Milwaukee above Chicago in the number of killings per capita. Rico hit the power button, wondering if and when he was also going to be on the news, with some reporter who didn't give-a-damn asking the city for help.

Rico knew he could go to war with Tito; he could have every thug in the city waiting with assault rifles and ready to die. He knew a bunch-of-niggas who would die for the godfather if he asked. But knowing what he knew, he also knew the mafia wouldn't rest until everyone in his bloodline, including women and children, were dead. He still had to wonder though, doing it the civil way and being the one who took the bullet, if it was all worth it. When he heard footsteps coming toward his office door, he didn't even turn to look at his security system. He just waited for the knock.

"Come in," Rico said. His youngest son walked through the door with his Kool-Aid smile plastered on his face.

"Hey, Pops; what cracking with ya, old man? You know I just knocked this dude off for a couple of stacks on the pool table at Romine's," Rickey Jr. said.

"I'm good, kid; your old man is good," Rico replied.

Rickey Jr. was the youngest of the two and was a barber by trade. Rico had helped him buy his first shop at seventeen and he was doing well in the business. When he wasn't running his business, he was at the pool hall playing his favorite pastime game and breaking anyone who thought they could play the game.

"You know something, son? The last time I watched you play, I saw you had a real steady hand."

"Man, Pops, my bank shot is up-top now. Shit, I sent a ball five rails on this cat today and watched him shit his pants," Rickey Jr. explained.

He noticed, for some reason, his father wasn't responding like he normally did when he told him his pool stories and he smelled like he'd been drinking. Rico was down for his boys, and making sure they were straight was one of his main priorities in life. He knew Dibiase really wanted to become the heir to the godfather's throne; he even knew he had a small clientele.

Rickey was the opposite of Dibiase. He was a hustler because it was in his bloodline, but he wanted to be a businessman. Rickey had dreams of owning not only a barbershop and beauty supply shop, but he wanted to own a flock of twenty-four-hour gyms, where the customers could use a key card and come and go as they pleased. He also swore, by the end of the year, he would have his own pool hall. Not just to hustle, but to give the youths somewhere they could go instead of getting in trouble.

Rico knew what he had to do when it came to his oldest son and his godson J.C. J.C. was a hustler, and at times, Rico had to think back to make sure he hadn't fucked some strange woman out there and left a baby behind, because J.C. reminded him so much of himself. Rico had done everything in his power to instill game in all three of his boys. He wasn't that fond of Don D., J.C.'s cousin, but he still treated him as proper as he could. He was sitting there listening to his youngest rant on about the pool game, when the only thing crossing his mind was the fact he was in a position to never seen any of his grandchildren.

Rico knew it was partly his fault, dating all the way back to Tito's father, Draco Hernandez. He knew he had been given specific instructions, and if he wasn't going to follow them to the letter, he shouldn't have taken the assignment. His boldness was what had him where he was today with the Colombian cartel family. He'd expected Dibiase to have a child, but he knew Rickey Junior wouldn't have a child until he was married and Rico commended him on his decision. It was crazy how close the two of his sons were even though their personalities were like night and day. Dibiase would kill for his brother in a minute if anyone tried to harm him. Rickey would have to be pushed to the limit to do harm to any human being.

"Pops, what's wrong with you? Did I catch you at a bad time? Are you all right?"

"Sit down, son; let me have a talk with you," Rico said.

Rickey Jr. took a seat in front of his father. He looked around the office at all his trophies he'd won playing pool and was glad his father kept them dusted off.

"Son, there are some things I need to tell you, and for some reason, I feel I can only tell you and only you—not your mother, uncle, or brother—nobody but you.

"You know something, kid, I have watched you since birth, and I see you've grown into a great decision maker. Actually, the world should be glad you chose to be on the right side of the law," Rico continued, cracking his first smile since Tito's private jet had landed.

"I know you know what I do for a living, and for some time, I was proud of what I did to make a way for my family. I've paid off politicians, judges, cops, and whoever I thought would take a bribe to make it this far."

"Pops, why are you telling me this stuff? I know what you do and I've never knocked you for it. Man, you gave us a good life, but if you're feeling remorseful, it's never too late to leave the dark side of the game."

"Yeah, son; I've always heard there was a thin line between God and the game, but in my case, son, it's too late."

"What's that supposed to mean?"

"Before you and your brother were born, I was in Colombia on a detail with some of my comrades. It was my last assignment before I was leaving the Navy for good. I didn't even want to take the assignment. Your mother was pregnant with Dibiase and I didn't want to be across the world when her water broke, but I had got a call from a Navy partner of mine who said it was imperative I make the mission because the team wasn't strong enough without me."

"You talking about that one crazy cat from the Chi?"

"Yeah, old Tango." Rico smiled again.

"I decided to go on the mission so I could get any extra earnings the Navy owed me. They promised, if your mother went in labor, they would send a chopper for me and fly me straight to Gary Memorial where she was, so I agreed. Colombia wasn't a tough detail at all; actually, the civilians there were happy to see American soldiers on their soil. When Friday came, like always, me and some of the crew stepped out to have a drink. We landed in a strip club. Son, if you ever want to see some fine women, visit Colombia."

Rickey was listening closely, trying to figure out where the conversation was going. He didn't like his father's last comment about it being too late. Rico opened the box of cigars on his desk and took out the last one. He thought it was ironic he was down to his last one; felt like he was having one last wish.

"Anyway, I was chilling, minding my own business, watching my team get it on with the ladies. I was too busy thinking about Cassie. Then this old guy walks over to me looking like he was from the Dos Equis beer commercial and buys me a couple of shots, making small talk. I saw he got offended when I seemed not to be listening to him. He went in his jacket pocket, removed ten thousand dollars, and sat it in front of me. That got my attention, at least made me listen to what he was saying. Son, to make a long story short, he knew I had a military clearance and he asked me to use it to transport something back to the

States. I thought it was dope, but when he said it wasn't dope and when I got it back if I'd delivered it safely to his son in Vegas, there would be another twenty-five bands waiting on me, I was very interested."

"Damn, Pops; so you did it, huh?"

"When we met up and he gave me a tube no bigger than a cigar case, you're damn-right I did it. Where I fucked-up is I broke his one rule."

"What was that, Pops?"

"He told me I wasn't to open the tube, just deliver it, take my money, and walk away."

"Son, all I had to do was keep the-fucking-tube sealed and deliver it, and I wouldn't be in this jam now. But with the birth of Dibiase, and me wanting to marry Cassie, I knew money was a stepping stone to financial freedom. What came along with that freedom was way more than I anticipated."

"Pops, what was in the tube?"

"It was a detailed map and layout of underground cities. The Colombians were building an actual trail way to transport drugs underground throughout the entire West Coast."

"That's deep, but that was years ago. Why are you stressing over it now? Can't bygones just be bygones?"

"I wish it was that easy. Not only did I take the money, I took my first package from his son. Years later, he told me he knew I'd opened the tube and I was forever in debt to the family."

"Seriously? That sounds like some-shit off television." Rickey Jr. sounded just like his father.

"I wish it was. I truly do."

Rico handed his son a piece of paper with some numbers on it. Rickey could tell the numbers were to a combination, but he didn't know what they were for.

"What's this, Pops?" he asked curiously.

"It's the combination to my safe. I want you to keep it in case of an emergency. I know when you have to open it, you'll know exactly what to do," Rico explained.

A tear formed in Little Rickey's eyes. He wasn't a fool and he could see the devil was at work. It was a situation he would have to pray on. He thought about it and couldn't wait for nightfall. Rickey grabbed Rico's hand and started to pray for his father and their whole family.

~ Seventeen ~

Even though the death of the godfather had shocked the city, J.C. wasn't stopping the flow. He already had things cracking and the product was moving in small packages as planned. He felt the small weight would keep them off the radar of the Feds and the DEA, and also the new group of agents out on the streets busting the hustlers.

Dibiase was in his rental heading for the projects. He prided himself for being a man of his word, so he knew he had to go straighten things out with Peanut like he'd said he would. He knew he had to try to stay focused, but he couldn't help thinking about his situation at home. Camille was having a baby. He'd hoped at first it would be a boy when he thought about how much his father had wanted a grandson. Now it didn't matter since he wouldn't be there to see the birth of the child. Dibiase had thought his little brother Rickey would be the first one to have a kid, but Rickey had gotten into his Bible. Even though he played pool in some of the raunchiest, rundown pool halls in the city, he still prided himself on two things: being a businessman and a man of God. Dibiase knew him having a kid first was out when he made his girl Regina get a separate apartment until they got married.

But it was Camille whose body had produced a child. The popular cliché said, when one life was taken, another one was birthed. Dibiase had started to believe it was true. He thought, because he'd never worn a condom before and Camille wasn't taking anything, now that she was having his child, he might as well take it to the next level. He thought he would finally face his little brother too and stop by the shop after he'd seen Peanut. Things were looking up for him and his click in just forty-eight hours, and he knew from here on, the money train would only get better. He wanted Rickey to know he had a niece or nephew coming, and he also wanted to see how his little brother was doing.

He pulled his rental into the project housing units from the Silver Spring side. He saw the black drop-top Peanut drove and pulled up next to it. He picked up his phone and scrolled through his contacts until he came to the entry that said Peanut.

"I'm outside your spot," Dibiase said.

"Come on in, bro; it's all good," Peanut replied.

"Yeah, but I'm sort of in a hurry. Come on out so we can holla and I can make my moves."

Shortly after Dibiase ended the call, he saw the young hustler emerge from the project door. Peanut was draped in gold pieces and his whole top row of teeth looked like he'd bought them at the Gold Emporium. Those things represented he was a street hustler, and that was a part of the game Dibiase wanted to remain far away from. His father wasn't big into all that and he knew it must have rubbed off on him. When Peanut entered the rental, Dibiase gave him four separate rubber bands, each containing a thousand dollars.

Peanut had known of Dibiase from the streets and knew he was Rico's son. There was once some slight animosity in his heart toward Rico, but he knew he was the one who was wrong. He had been hoping Dibiase would give him some work instead of cash. He was the re-rock king and he could have turned four stacks of work into about twelve grand.

"Say, playa, here is what's owed you," Dibiase said.

"I see," Peanut replied.

"All I ask of you is one small favor."

"What's that, D?"

"If my Uncle Mickey ever calls you for any more work, don't serve him. I'm going to straighten this out one time, and if there is another time, you know you have been warned already."

"Say, fam, I'm out here on this paper chase, and the only way I can promise you that is you make sure your people don't use my number."

"Well, do what you gotta do. I just won't be taking care of the bill any more, and if I do, it won't be with cash," Dibiase replied.

Peanut stood his ground, but he knew about J.C. and he didn't really want the trouble. Street wars were bad for business. Dibiase watched him as he climbed out the truck and walked back into his spot. He knew serving him would be a bad idea, so he'd left that one alone, but he also knew, if push came to shove, he would knock his neck off his shoulders.

He looked at the time on his Jacob and dialed Camille as he drove off. It was close to time for her to get off work and he wanted to hear her voice before he got to his brother's shop. He was only a couple miles from Rickey's and Camille's voice always seemed like the voice of reason, even when he didn't give her precise details. It was just the way the magic of love worked.

J.C. and Don D. were getting busy, making the paper flow like water. While Don D. was cranking small packages out of both spots, J.C. had taken his new recruit and worked the street, selling anything from an eight ball to a four-and-a-half split. Dibiase had given J.C. five kilos, which he'd turned into seven, and four of them were already gone. J.C. was pulled up in front of his favorite jewelry store to holla at his man Gino. All the playas spent a nice penny getting pieces customized with Gino, the jeweler. He was so popular people came from other cities, including basketball players and actors, to get his customized work. J.C. hadn't seen Gino in about six months, but he was now ready to get a slick piece made. He walked in and saw Gino was handling a Mexican dude who was having a cross sprayed with diamonds. Gino excused himself and came to greet J.C. right away.

"Hey, G, my man; how's business?" J.C. asked, making conversation.

"It's all good, James. You must be making some paper, you're on this side of town," Gino replied.

J.C. noticed Gino's conversation adapted to whoever he was working with at the time. He could stay Jew, go Rican, or get *niggafied* if he had to.

"Ain't-shit changed, G, but the weather. I stay on the grind." J.C. smiled as he noticed the Mexican customer checking him out.

"So what's it going to be for you, James? You looking for a platinum link, a Gucci bracelet, or maybe a nice watch? I got some new ones in today," Gino boasted, thinking about the new collection of Rolexes he'd just gotten in that morning.

"Let me see them watches, homie."

J.C. had a Tag, but it was just okay. He was thinking about trading it in and getting himself and Donna a couple of nice watches. Gino bought a tray of Presidential Rolex watches from underneath a nearby cabinet and sat them down in front of J.C. before walking off. Gino's respect and hospitality were what had earned him his reputation with the hustlers. Everyone use to shop at a store on the far east side until they'd locked the door and called the police on a NBA player, thinking he was there to rob them just because he was black. J.C. picked up a few of them before spotting the one he fell in love with. He called Gino back over and handed him the watch, not caring about the forty-grand price tag attached to it.

"Gino, spray this-bitch with some diamonds and get me a female one just like it," J.C. said, removing twenty grand from his pocket and handing it to Gino for a down payment.

"Sure thing, James. You'll have to give me about a week and I'll have them both ready. You're still with that same pretty lady, I take it?"

"Yeah, man; baby's still riding these waves with a-nigga," he replied to Gino's question, smiling.

J.C. walked out the store feeling satisfied about his new purchases. He was about to roll a blunt, but thought about it. He was too far out and he couldn't take the risk of getting pulled over driving a nice whip and being black. He knew it wasn't farfetched, knowing what side of town he was on. Instead, he called Donna and decided to check on her while he hit the freeway.

Don D. slumped back on the leather couch in the spot as he'd just moved the last five-thousand-dollar sack J.C. had bagged. He called over to the other spot they had working, and the young gunslinger they had running the new spot told him he was down to maybe about five-hundred-dollars-worth of work left. Don D. had known when he saw the work it would spark a flow of business like never before. He was placed in charge of both spots, and he was going to make sure he did his best to earn the favor of his cousin and Dibiase.

The new recruit, who was spending a lot of time with J.C., had proven to be an asset as well. He knew a lot of low-level dealers who bought small weight no matter how much money they made. Don had to admit he was a little jealous because he was stuck in the spots and Tyler got to run around with J.C., riding shotgun. J.C. told Don he had to make sure Tyler was properly groomed, and one day, none of them would be touching anything.

Don picked up his cell, knowing he was supposed to call J.C. and report the progress of the spots. Don was starting to feel himself though, sitting there counting the money over and over. He decided calling J.C. could wait and called his honey in Racine.

"Hey, baby girl; what's cracking with you?" Don asked.

"Hey, boo," Rakita said, sounding happy to hear from him. "A-bitch thought you'd forgotten about her," she said since he hadn't called her in almost two days.

"How can any-nigga forget about a fat-ass like that? Now come on, baby girl, you know you're the-shit," he stated, hoping his words of endearment would calm her down.

"Well, what-in-the-hell you been doing, boo? You know a-bitch misses her daddy," Rakita said, laying it on thick. She needed a few hundred to get her hair and nails done, and she knew Don would go for it if she talked sweet to him.

"Nothing much, baby; just laying back with a fat one, counting this paper the workers just checked in."

"Damn, baby, you're getting it in up, there ain't you?"

"Well, I'm claiming millionaire status, so I'd better act like it," Don replied, bragging to Rakita. "I'm that-nigga who went from crumbs to bricks," he said, laughing and lighting the blunt.

"That's what's up; I'm just glad to be wifey," she replied, making him grunt as he thought about the first time he'd fucked her.

Rakita had a fat-ass and a thin waistline. She was short and stacked in all the right places. Don D. loved her pigeon-toed, bowlegged walk, and every time he thought about it, his dick grew hard.

"Hell yeah, baby, you're wifey all day. That reminds me, a-nigga's horny-as-fuck, and I was thinking about coming down tonight. I've got to get the workers together since tomorrow is the first, but you think you wanna have some fun?" he asked, letting the thick cloud of smoke clear his lungs.

"That's what's up, boo. I've been horny myself. My hair and nails look like shit though. I know you want to sweat out something nice."

"Don't worry about that-bullshit. When I leave here, I'll stop and send you a few bucks Western Union. Then when I get there and fuck-the-shit outta you, I'll get that-shit redone," he said, bragging on his bedroom work.

"I hear you, boo; shit, I was damn-near ready to ride up there, my-pussy's been so wet," she said, keeping her routine going.

He grabbed his-dick, thinking about her mocha skin on top of him, riding him like a pony.

"Damn, ma, soon as I get-shit together, I'll be burning the highway up getting to you. I'll text you the reference number to pick up that bread," he said and ended the call.

Don D. sat back, finishing half the blunt and thinking about Rakita. He was crazy about her and she didn't remind him of his last situation. It was hard for him to get over what had happened in Baltimore, but he was finally over it and moving on with his life. He was making more paper now than he'd ever made and things were looking up for him. He knew he'd made the right decision not to go down south and come to the Midwest with his cousin.

Eighteen

Dibiase pulled up in front of R & R Hair Care for Kings and Queens, the shop his little brother owned. He saw the black Lexus parked outside and knew his brother was inside running his business. He got out the rental and tucked his heat in his waistband, knowing Rickey hated people packing heat in his place. Soon as he entered, Garland, Foxx, and Sylvester, who all worked their chairs for Rickey, spoke to Dibiase. He spoke back and surveyed the customers waiting to get a fresh line or a baldhead. He saw Ray-Ray, who had gone to school with him and supposedly had a scholarship to play ball. The word was he'd contracted some type of bone disease and couldn't get cleared to play. The two of them acknowledged each other as Dibiase kept heading toward the back office where he knew Rickey was.

Cyrena Johnson was the only female stylist there on Tuesdays, and she saw Dibiase and turned her nose up at him. She'd been his girl before he met Camille, and she swore up and down Dibiase had left her for Camille. That was only partially the reason, but he didn't need to explain he'd known she was cheating with some older cat who was her landlord now. He didn't even say anything to her, but took a quick sneak peek and noticed her ass had grown a little fatter.

Dibiase walked through to the back of the shop. It was set up with three chairs and a wash bowl. The back was Rickey's VIP section, where he cut his private clients. There was also a pool table that Dibiase could see had been recently re-clothed. The door to the office had a camera right above it, so Dibiase knew his brother had seen him coning before he even knocked. Dibiase waited for his brother to tell him to come in, and when he heard Rickey say the words, he opened the door.

Rickey stood up and came from around the desk to hug his big brother. The two of them hadn't chopped-it-up since their father's demise. Rickey still seemed to be taking things a lot better than Dibiase had anticipated he would.

"How you been, lil bro?" Dibiase asked.

"I'm good, bro; business as usual. What brings you to my neck of the woods?"

"My little brother, of course," Dibiase replied.

"Well, how has life been treating you since you're all grown up and paying your own bills?" Rickey asked, smiling.

"It's cool. You know I moved my girl in, so she keeps a-nigga grounded."

"WHAT?! You let her move in with you?"

"Of course; that's my lady and I feel like she's the only one in the world for me. So why not?"

"I could go to Scripture on you, but I'm not going to do that. I tell you this though, if you love it, put a ring on it," Rickey said.

Dibiase knew his brother read his Bible. Even though he hustled the pool table, he still followed God's word. They walked out the office as they continued talking so Rickey could observe what was going on. Today was the day he collected booth rent and he wanted to make sure everyone was busy so they could pay their dues. The shop was full and there were a few strangers who had to be walk-ins.

One of the strangers in the waiting area locked on to them as they strolled right by him toward the outside door. He admired how Rico's boys looked just like their father. He hadn't seen them in years and he was glad to see the men they'd become. Tango got up to leave, and one of the barbers tried to stop him to tell him he was next. Now wasn't the time to get with the boys since he was waiting on a phone call that would provide some pertinent information he needed. Tango looked at the barber, smiled, and walked out. He knew whoever had killed Rico was going to pay, one way or another.

Rickey saw the stranger walk past him and his brother as they stood next to Dibiase's rental. Something looked remotely familiar about the man, but Rickey couldn't put his finger on it. He was too busy preaching to his big brother.

"I'm telling you, bro, read your Bible, man. You need to read the book of Romans," Rickey said.

"Boy, you know you're going-to-hell, right?" Dibiase said.

"What do you mean?"

"You be knocking niggas' heads off on the pool table and now you don't want no live-in pussy until you're married. You know when you get to them pearly gates, God's going to ask you for His cut of that gambling money," Dibiase said, hitting his brother playfully on the shoulder.

"Ha ha ha, very funny. I'm just saying, you can't be fornicating, that's all I'm saying."

"Too late for all that," Dibiase replied.

"What is that supposed to mean? It's never too late."

"Well, for me and Camille, it's too late. You're going to be an uncle."

"Get-the-fuck outta here—oops, I mean heck," Rickey said, excited about the news. He was going to be a uncle finally. "You know they say, once a life is taken another one is born."

"I know exactly what they say," Dibiase replied, climbing into his rental.

He let the window down and told Rickey Jr. he loved him and he would be back soon to check on him. When Dibiase pulled off, he found it a little disturbing Rickey hadn't brought up the funeral or the death of their father. It was also disturbing that it seemed like nothing had changed in Rickey's life. Dibiase was worried his little brother might not be dealing with it and just might break down. He made a note to mention it to their mother to see how she felt.

෧ ✦ ෨

"You have a collect call from . . . *Pork Chop* . . . an inmate in the Baltimore City Jail. If you want to accept these charges, please press five. if you want to refuse these charges and any further charges, please press seven."

Pork Chop listened to see if the charges for the collect call were going to be accepted. He was in the Baltimore City Jail and knew he could have used another phone to get straight through since he was holding it down with the guards and the inmates. He was just in a rush before they called Rec Time and wanted to holla at his little cousin who he hadn't spoken to in quite some time. The call was taking a second to connect, so he knew she was accepting the charges.

"Hey, hey, what it do, little cuz?" Pork Chop asked, hearing her voice.

"Nothing much, big cuz. You know me, just doing what I do and staying beautiful as ever."

"Yo, check this out. I'm back in the county down here on some appeal shit. I think my lawyer's got these woods too, so I might be springing in a minute."

"For real? Ahhhhh shit, look out world."

"I heard that-nigga who got me in all this is supposed to be living in the same state as you're in, fam."

"What's the nigga's name?" Rakita asked.

"Donald Davis; they call this weak-ass-nigga Don D."

Rakita almost choked on the ice-cold Pepsi she was having with her blunt. She was sitting in her car, just leaving Walmart after picking up the money Don D. had wired her. She wondered if it was just a coincidence, or was it the same-nigga she'd been fucking. Her head told her it was because she remembered looking at her guy's driver license and it was a Maryland license. But she was blood over bankroll all day, so she had to tell Pork Chop what was going on.

"Damn, cuz, you aren't going to believe this: that's the same-nigga I've been fucking with. I'm actually at Walmart picking up some change he just sent me."

"You've got to be fucking-kidding! You mean this fool-ass-nigga is in Racine?"

"Not quite; he lives in Milwaukee with his cousin, and let me tell you, these niggas are balling out of control."

"This call is from a Baltimore correctional facility. This call and all other calls may be recorded," the voice said, letting them know they only had two minutes left on the call.

He rubbed his chin, wondering just how much Don D. was clocking. In his mind, Don owed him for the fucked-up-situation he was in. Didn't matter if was trying to take him off cash or not, the nigga had smoked his bottom-bitch and that was a crime punishable by death.

"So this coward-ass-nigga's really up there clocking, huh?"

"I talked to the nigga a few hours ago, and he told me he'd just counted a hundred twice and was getting his workers in position to clock another," Rakita replied, knowing her big cuzo was a killer for real.

Maybe she could get in on it and make her come up. She had a daughter who lived in Atlanta she would love to be able to really take care of, and if she helped bust a move, she knew her big cuz would break her off something proper.

"You know something else, big cuz?"

"What's that, lil mama?"

"This-nigga's cousin he's up here with is the real deal. The nigga just smoked some niggas up here in a club, left one of the niggas ten toes up."

"For real?"

"Yeah, and my-nigga is a pillow-talking-ass-nigga too. He's been telling me about some other-nigga named Dibiase, whose pops was supposed to be a kingpin but he just got merc'd," Rakita stated, giving her cousin as much detail as she had retained.

Pork Chop was twirling one of his freshly-done French braids like he always did when he was thinking hard. He hoped this appellate lawyer was as good as the money he'd spent to get him.

"Listen, baby girl,' Pork Chop said, as he'd heard enough, "do me a favor and keep this-nigga as close to you as possible. I don't care if you gotta suck this-nigga's-dick like your life depended on it. We gonna do this-nigga."

"I got you, fam. Let's do this square-ass-nigga," she said before the call disconnected.

She waited a few seconds to see if Pork Chop was going to call back but he didn't. Rakita knew he was probably twirling a braid and thinking about his next move.

Rakita Washington had moved to Racine, Wisconsin, a few years ago. She was once known as the baby queen from Baltimore. If you had a new-jack-nigga who was a mark, she was the marker. Her beauty was a force in itself, and not many playas she ran across could keep their eyes off the young tender who was stacked like a brick house. Her first lick came at the age of fourteen when she hooked up with a Cuban drug lord from Miami. She had him wrapped around her finger in just two weeks, and he forgot all the principals of the game when he was in her presence. When her older cousin Pork Chop found out what his favorite little cousin was doing, he'd insisted she set the drug lord up for a robbery.

Rakita was skeptical at first because the man she was sleeping with had brought her a Mazda, paid for her hair to be fresh every week, and kept her with enough pocket change to buy whatever she wanted. But after her cousin explained what he was giving her was what he was probably giving ten other women, she decided to go ahead and go with his plan. When the move was complete, her cousin gave her fifty thousand dollars in cash. It was more money than she'd ever seen other than on television. Rakita realized Pork Chop had murdered the man and she thought she would feel some type of way, but realized she didn't feel any type of remorse. Period! After that, they'd done several more licks, and each time, her payday had been good.

It wasn't until the last time, when the lick was supposed to happen to a local dealer who was doing big things, that things went afoul. Rakita had mistakenly got knocked up by the mark and she didn't believe in abortions. Instead of going on with the job, she'd alerted her baby-daddy to the whole move, and he'd left town, moving to Atlanta, only to return the day the child was born. Rakita felt she'd failed her cousin, and she fled to Wisconsin and vowed to change her life in certain ways.

After the first year of change, working a job six days a week and going to church on Sundays didn't seem to work for her. Rakita missed the thrill of taking marks down. It wasn't long before she hooked up with a gangsta from Chicago named Dickey. Dickey got his name from the pants he wore every day. He was her life, but Dickey was also as reckless as they come. She knew how much he loved her and knew he would do anything for her. On one of his runs to Atlanta to make a pickup, Dickey never made it. He was picked up after a routine traffic stop in Savannah, Georgia, and sentenced to thirty years for gun trafficking.

Rakita and her girls would come to Milwaukee to hang out because the population of ballers was much larger than Racine. She once again decided to change her life and get out the business of taking down marks. What she wanted now was just a sugar-daddy who had a bag and a bank roll, and didn't mind spending it on her. Her body was still up-top since her daughter's birth hadn't left any stretch marks, and her sex-game was so good it should have been branded and sold by Milton Bradley or the Parker Brothers. She prided herself on her million-dollar head-game.

She'd met Don D. in a club on 5th and Locust named Savoy. It was the spot where all the ballers went to get their Moet and chicken on, so it was the spot to be if a-bitch was looking. Rakita was sitting at the back bar with one of her homegirls when she heard a cork on a bottle pop behind them.

"Yo, Jimmy," the smooth-faced young playa called out. "Sit two more glasses in front of these beautiful ladies for me," Don D. continued as he was showing out for all that-ass he'd seen hanging off the barstool.

Rakita had already peeped him and the expensive chain he was wearing when he was standing by the DJ's booth chilling. She was contemplating approaching him, but she was making sure she wasn't going to stake a claim on another-bitch's-man. The Racine girls were all hated by the Milwaukee chicks anyway. She liked his cool and calm swag, and was glad she hadn't had to make the move; it had already been made for her.

Rakita had on a multi-colored Coogi dress that accented her thick frame. Her beautician had her hair in big curls and her Prada perfume had her area smelling like a suite at the Bunny Ranch. The DJ was playing Tupac's *America's Most Wanted* when Don D. stepped between her and her friend and filled their glasses.

"I guess they really let two of America's most-wanted in the same place at the same-muthafuckin-time," she said, smelling the scent of the Issey Miyake he was wearing.

"I guess you're right, baby," he replied. "I see you're a Pac fan?"

"I see you're a gentleman," she replied, not answering his question.

One thing about Rakita was she knew how to read any man and take control of the situation in just seconds after speaking.

"So, what's your name?" Don asked.

"Doll; they call me Baby Doll," Rakita replied, turning up the Moet and taking a sip.

"Damn, I ain't never seen a Barbie with an-ass like that."

"That's because you haven't been to the aisle with the black Barbies," she said, smiling.

"You're right. So, do you come here often?"

"Not really, boo; I'm from Racine. Me and my girl just came up to get away from Hicksville and have a little fun for the weekend."

"I see; maybe we could do breakfast after the club?"

"Maybe; it doesn't sound like a bad idea," she said, crossing her legs, giving Don D. a slight glimpse.

The three of them met up at Ma Fisher's, and enjoyed steak and eggs. Rakita's homegirl was upset when Don D. didn't invite one of his guys to join them, but he knew J.C. and Dibiase were home with their own girls. Don wasn't sure before meeting Rakita if he'd ever want to settle down, but he knew she could make the toughest playa change their mind. The conversation was good and Rakita sat on the same side of the booth with Don, rubbing him between the legs every chance she got. Don talked a little about his past and mentioned he was from Baltimore. Her friend almost blew it by saying something about Rakita being from the same place, but luckily, she caught the eye contact and knew it meant not to open her mouth.

Rakita now drove, heading to the hair shop, reminiscing on that first night. It all had begun to become clear to her now. Don was the one who'd killed the girl in the motel and her other cousin Worka, who'd worked for Pork Chop. She shed a tear knowing she had been laying up, fucking-and-sucking the-dick of the-nigga who'd murdered someone in her family.

~ Nineteen ~
The Meeting

Dibiase called J.C. and decided they all needed to meet. He knew things could get out of hand quickly with the kind of money flowing in already. He was the last one to make it to the spot where they were meeting. It was the second house J.C. had set up to keep the flow of traffic to a medium. J.C. was a smart hustler, and he knew, since they were now balling, a spot was only good for twenty-nine days at most. Every month, they would be relocating to two new spots in case one of the old ones was being watch and ready to be hit.

Dibiase pulled up in the rental, ready to get it on and over with. He felt a little restless, and needed to go home to think. When he walked in, J.C. was sitting at the wooden table with two bill counters counting the money from both spots. Dibiase didn't like that, but he guessed when they talked, they could discuss it. He didn't want that kind of money in a spot longer than it had to be.

"Look who's here! If it isn't the man of the hour," J.C. said.

"Nigga, don't let that bunk-ass-weed start making you act like Pooky," Dibiase responded.

Dibiase laughed at his joke. Everybody else laughed too, knowing Dibiase was referring to the way Chris Rock had acted out his role in the movie New Jack City.

"Nigga, we're 'bout to get rich out here. I mean Tony Montana-rich, playa," J.C. said.

"Well, that isn't all that bad," Dibiase replied. "But on the real, the money won't ever change me. I've been around this-shit since birth. I mean my baby crib cost a stack, and the milk I was drinking was probably from Janet Jackson's right titty."

"You're a fool, D; you're crazy, man," Don D. added, laughing at how cool his click was.

All he could think about was getting the day over with so he could go see his people. He wasn't even going to tell anybody, just get on the highway and go lay-up.

Dibiase looked at all the money that had been made off only five bricks and he knew J.C. was right. They were about to really get Scarface-rich with all-the-shit his father had left him. When they were finished with the count, the money was just shy of a quarter-million dollars. Dibiase took five thousand and slid it to Don D., and four more and handed them to Tyler, the new man.

"One thing for sure in this crew, if me and J. eat, we all eat," Dibiase said.

"You got that right," J.C. replied, liking the way his godbrother handled the money.

Dibiase had two duffle bags with him. One was empty and one had something in it. He unzipped the empty one and placed the rest of the currency inside it. Then he opened the filled one and dumped out five new bricks for the crew. He laid them side-by-side on the table, glancing at the logo. CCC was stamped on the top of each one. For a second, he thought about that alligator stamp and wondered who-the-hell was the CCC. He knew his father had never mentioned anything that sounded close to that to him.

"Well, I guess everyone's got their assignments down, so there's no need for me to say anything else," Dibiase stated.

"Y'all know we've only got a few more days in these spots, then we're moving both spots," J.C. added. "So don't get too relaxed."

"What about the clientele that's building?" Tyler asked.

"Don't worry about that. You'll see later tonight when we package this load up how we do it. I'm about to get on some *American Gangsta* shit and trademark our shit. If the work isn't in our seal, I bet no hype is going to buy it," J.C. stated.

"That's what's up . . . some new-millennium, Blue Magic-type shit," Don D. added.

"Nah, playa, Blue Magic won't have-shit on us," J.C. said, rolling a new blunt.

"Well, I'm about to bounce and let you-niggas do what y'all do," Dibiase said.

"Yo, bro, let me holla at you for a second," J.C. said, following Dibiase to the door and outside. They climbed back in the rental and J.C. sparked the blunt.

"Everything good?" Dibiase asked.

"I'm not sure."

"What do you mean?" Dibiase asked, not liking the response from J.C.

"Mickey, man; I think Unc is smoking."

"What?! Where'd you get that from?"

"You know that hype-bitch Sandra, the one use to look like Halle Berry?" J.C. asked.

Dibiase knew exactly who he was talking about because, when he'd first gotten in the streets, Sandra was still fine-as-hell. She was the first one to give him a blowjob good enough to make him bust. She was a sad waste of a pretty face.

"Of course I remember handy-Sandy," he replied.

"She was here and said she was partying with Unc over in the 'jects at one of Nut's spots. Said dude was running around naked-and-shit. I know this-shit is bothering you because it's fucking-me-up. Mickey is like my uncle as well," J.C. said, really not wanting to be the bearer of that bad news.

"That's fucked-up! I knew someone was going to be taking the-shit hard. I just had an eerie feeling it was going to be Little Rickey who did something stupid, not Unc."

"That-nigga Nut's out of order again though. He's really disrespectful," J.C. said.

"Don't worry, I'm going to look into it. I'm not just going to take a hype-bitch's word. She probably didn't have any money and wanted a free hit."

"I don't know, playa, but we need to follow up on this-shit," J.C. said, giving his godbrother some dap and exiting the truck.

Dibiase pulled off thinking about what J.C. had just said. He hoped-like-hell his Uncle Mickey hadn't wilded-out like he'd just heard. He made a mental note to find out the truth as soon as he made it home. He knew one phone call would get the truth. He picked up his phone and texted Camille, letting her know he was on his way home.

~ Twenty ~
Rico's Demise

Rico watched as his youngest son left his office in tears. He knew he had to talk to Cassie and tell her something so she didn't completely lose her mind. He felt he had less than twenty-four hours of life left. The CCC was serious about handling business and Tito liked things to be handled within a sufficient time frame; that was just how he was. Tomorrow, Rico had a wedding to attend for Slim, one of his partners, and he and Cassie were both supposed to be there. He couldn't let Cassie go because he felt it was coming. He couldn't be precise, but he was cool with being safe than sorry.

He locked his office and hoped his brother would hurry back with the rental cars. He had a very important run to make and needed to be on time and not in one of his own vehicles. When he walked upstairs, Cassie was lying across their king-size bed watching the Lifetime channel. Rico slipped off his gators and went and lay next to her, putting his arm around her. Cassie jumped when she felt his touch.

"You all right, honey?" he asked.

"Yes, baby; I was dozing off and you startled me. You seem to be feeling a little better since the trip," she said, hoping that was the case.

"Not really, baby. There's something I need to tell you."

"What's that, honey?"

"There is a serious war going on and I'm part of it, so I think it's best I go to the wedding alone. I also don't want you driving your car. I sent Mickey to get a couple of cars that should be here shortly in case you need to move around."

Cassie turned to face her husband and looked into his eyes with deep concern. She always knew, being the wife of the plug, these risks were possible. It seemed to have come at the worst time—when he was on his way out the game. Something about this war made her feel like Rico was deflated and defeated. She had never seen him like this before. Usually, he had ways of handling business that worked out in his best interests. Tears of fear formed in her eyes because she loved Rico so much and was so proud of his decision that she couldn't stand the thought of losing her soul mate.

Cassie thought about her life now. She thought about when she was a young girl and her affair with her best friend. She thought about Vegas, and what her and Julia had. And she thought about her marriage, which was her life. All she could do was hold him close to her, close her eyes, and say a prayer asking God to watch over her man.

Right before they dozed off, Rico heard a horn outside. He reached under his pillow and removed his nine, just in case it was some unwanted visitors. He knew he wasn't supposed to put up a challenge when Tito's people came for him, but they'd also agreed it would happen somewhere away from his home. When he peeped out the front curtain, he saw it was just Mickey returning with the cars he'd asked for. Mickey had picked up two Camrys, one blue and one tan that was perfect for Rico. Rico stepped outside and thanked his brother. He handed him some money and told Mickey he would talk to him soon.

A Few Hours Later . . .

Mickey was sitting in his car, parked on the corner of 12th and Vliet in front of the Welfare building. He had just done a few lines and was feeling wired. He was tripping when he looked in the rearview mirror and saw the all-black Chevy Impala that had pulled up behind him. The little antenna told him it was the boys. Two white men had gotten out and were quickly approaching his car.

"Good afternoon, Mr. Hammond," one of them said, leaning over, looking in his car.

"What's going on, Officer?" Mickey asked, wondering why they were sweating him. He saw the gold badges and realized they weren't the regular boys, but they was those real people.

"I'm just sitting here waiting on my friend-girl. She's inside seeing her case worker, making sure they don't cut her benefits next month. You know how it is. These-bitches want to make sure they're kids eat," Mickey said, wiping the excess powder from around his nose.

"First, let me advise you, Mickey, that anything you say can and will be used against you in a court of law. You do have the right to seek a lawyer before speaking with us if you feel it necessary," the partner said.

"You-muthafuckas here to arrest me? What's really going on?" Mickey asked.

He realized they knew his name, and being they were the Feds, they weren't there to speculate. Their conviction rate spoke for itself.

"Arrest? Now that all depends on you, Mickey. What we are going to do is take you somewhere besides a cell and talk to you about a few things. We both agreed that a guy like you shouldn't be behind bars," the first Fed said.

Mickey knew they was on some-bullshit, but he was smart enough to play along for now.

Agent Squales was a field agent who worked Colombian cases. He had taken down some major players and he was onto something once again. Mickey was advised to get out the car. He had to leave his friend so he could see what-the-hell these people wanted. They rode, stopping at a Starbucks, picking up lattes and brownies, and continued down to the lakefront to find a secluded area. They'd searched his car before they left and found a four-and-a-split he had copped from Peanut. He just shook his head, knowing if he'd listened to his nephew, at least he would have been clear of that. When they finally found their spot and parked, the smaller Fed turned to face Mickey in the back seat.

"Mr. Hammond, you could be in a lot of trouble, or you could help yourself and that-little-shit we found could disappear like it never was under your seat. But let me warn you, if I feel you're telling one little lie, I know this place called Milan I think you could get use to."

"Do you understand what my partner is saying to you, Mickey?"

Mickey felt that bad-cop/good-cop-shit coming on, but he had to play his cards to see exactly what these people were on.

"We can't be nothing but clear," Mickey responded.

Agents Squales and Hawk had been part of a raid on several cocaine factories in Colombia last year. Rico's name was attached to a board as one of the Midwest distributors, and he had been under investigation since the raids. When they ran his name, nothing came up for him until they'd used a special system and saw that Rico was Rickey Hammond with a first-class military clearance. The Feds felt Rico was the major reason this particular family was getting their dope in the country. They explained all this to Mickey, knowing he couldn't go back and say he was talking to the Feds about Colombia no matter what happened.

"You're the brother of Rickey Hammond, street name Rico, is that correct?" Squales asked.

"Come on now; if you-muthafuckas are going to interrogate me, at least let's not start out like we're in the first grade. You both know that's my little brother. Next question please."

"Is that dope we found in your car part of the product he pushes?"

"Naw, man; I got that-shit—" Mickey stopped in mid-sentence, almost mentioning Peanut's name.

"We know already. Peanut, the wannabe big shot in the projects." Hawk finished his sentence for him.

Mickey was sure now his world and a lot of others' worlds were about to come to an end.

"What we want to know is more about your brother; like, who is his connect?" Hawk asked.

They wanted Rico, but they wanted his testimony more. There was also some paperwork that implied the Colombians were on to something big, and whatever it was, most likely was the reason they traveled under the radar. Whatever the papers were, the Feds hadn't gotten to them before they'd been shredded. They had a specialist working on them, but so far, the high-tech shredder had done its job.

"I didn't know my brother sold dope, so I can assure you I don't know who he deals with if he is. Rico, as far as I know, is a family man," Mickey lied.

"Well, we just seized over a million-dollars-worth of cocaine from a house tied to your brother. Is that why you're buying from Peanut?" Hawk asked.

"I told you both, Rico don't sell no dope; that's the reason I buy from Peanut."

"Seems like you don't want that-shit to disappear. Maybe we should just book him. Should be enough of that mixed-up-shit to get him at least a dime. What do you think, partner?"

"Ten years? That's a long time for a fat-fuck like you not to get any-pussy," his partner replied.

Mickey wasn't buying anything they were saying. His high was wearing down and he really wanted another bump.

"Hold on a minute. You-muthafuckas asking me-shit and I'm cooperating, but you're acting like I know some-shit I don't know nothing about!" Mickey exclaimed.

He was starting to get a little worried because of the dope he had in his car. He knew he was out of order buying work from Peanut, even if he was getting it on the front side.

"You know more than you're telling us, Mickey. You think we were born yesterday? Look, we don't want you, and to show you how serious we are, here's a little proof."

Agent Hawk took the dope they'd found in Mickey's car and opened the bag. He used his empty Starbucks cup to scoop some of it and pour it out the window.

"Now answer our questions and the rest of this-shit can go bye-bye too," he said, smiling.

Mickey watched as it looked like it was snowing outside the car.

"Wait a-muthafuckin-minute, man! Y'all asking me-shit about my brother's connect and-shit. I don't know anything about that. All I know is it has something to do with a group that goes by CCC," he said, knowing he was in trouble now, not only with Peanut but also with Rico.

Hawk felt like they were getting somewhere now. The CCC was in the database and was known to be an organization run by Tito and his father, who still lived somewhere in Colombia. A few things were starting to make sense to the agents now. They knew the son lived in Las Vegas, but they had no idea where his father was. There were too many places to hide in Colombia.

"Okay, here's the deal, fat boy: You walk today, but you keep this here ink pen on you at all times," Squales said, handing Mickey what looked like a regular ballpoint pen.

"What-the-fuck is this? I see y'all trying to get me killed!" Mickey replied, knowing that carrying whatever it was, was his only way out of the car.

"This here is a wire recorder, camera, and GPS, so we will know exactly where your overweight-ass is at all times. You shit, we want to hear a toilet flush; you fuck one of them crackheads, we'll be right there cheering you on," Hawk said.

"If you lose this pen or tip anyone off, that little-shit that went out the window will resurface double, maybe triple, and you'll be charged as a kingpin," Hawk added, knowing they had him by the balls. They released Mickey and made him walk.

A few hours later, Mickey was home in his apartment, walking around naked. He felt like the heat was on ninety, as he was sweating profusely from head to toe. He had always been known as a playa in the streets, and up until now, he had managed to maintain that title even though he got high every blue moon. He sat on the couch and looked at the ink pen the Feds had given him laying on his marble coffee table. It was fucked-up that the Feds now had constant surveillance on him and he knew they were either watching him or listening to him.

He walked in the kitchen and removed a jar from the cabinet and the box of baking soda from the refrigerator. Turning on the flame on the gas stove, he went to work making himself a hit. He needed to be high right now to deal with what was going on. The knock on his door startled him as the dope was just about ready. He looked back at the pen and hoped the Feds hadn't come to arrest him again. When he opened the door, it was the-broad he had left at the welfare building.

"What you doing here, bitch?" he asked, mad she'd showed up.

"You left me, muthafucka! I had to suck a-nigga's-dick for a ride. So what-the-fuck you mean, what I'm doing here?" she replied, just about to go off until she smelled a familiar aroma that calmed her down instantly.

Before Mickey could say anything, she started taking off her clothes so they would look like Adam and Eve. Mickey loved her body, although her face could use a few doctors. The scar from her ear to lip had been acquired when she'd tried to rob a trick of his wallet.

She sat on the couch, rubbing her pussy, waiting on Mickey to return from the kitchen. She had her pearl tongue in one hand and her straight-shooter in the other.

"Say, bitch, there's an extra toothbrush in the bathroom closet. I know your-ass' planning on brushing your gums before fuckin'-with-my-shit," Mickey said, remembering she said she'd just sucked-a-dick for a ride. He watched her shapely-ass bounce as she got up mad, stomping to the bathroom to brush her teeth.

The drug soothed Mickey as he took the first pull, feeling the rush of the cocaine. It took him way up and slowly bought him down to a peaceful state of mind. He leaned back on the couch, rubbing on his-dick, now waiting for his-trick. When she came in, she smiled and scraped a piece of what he had just cooked, placing it in end of her straight-shooter. The two of them spent the first twenty minutes getting high on the cooked dope. She walked over to him and bent down, spreading his legs open. He leaned his head back as she took his-dick in her mouth.

~ Twenty-One ~
Tango

Charlie Oliver was sitting outside one of Dibiase's spots. He saw Rico's son hadn't wasted any time following in his father's footsteps. He had parked three cars down from the rental he had been following for the last couple of hours. Tango had made a U-turn when he left Little Rickey's salon and waited for Dibiase to leave. When he did, he'd trailed him, staying far enough back that he wasn't spotted. Dibiase's first stop was an apartment complex, which Tango figured was where he resided. When he finally emerged from his unit, there was a very pretty redbone who accompanied him to the vehicle. They talked for a second then kissed before she went back inside. Dibiase was carrying two duffle bags when he left.

Tango stayed close to his person of interest as Dibiase cruised at a slow pace. It didn't take long before they ended up in a rundown neighborhood that didn't look anything like the neighborhood where the complex was. Dibiase exited his car carrying the same duffle bags and went inside. Tango waited patiently while he was inside. He turned on the radio, listening to an old replay of Howard Stern, who wasn't one of his favorites.

Tango was worried about Rico's boys. They seemed okay, but he knew losing a father was a lot to deal with since he'd lost his own at such an early age. That was what had propelled him to take up life in the Navy. When he was born, his mother had passed away from complications on the table, so he'd never had a chance to know her. He had pictures of the woman they use to say looked like Dorothy Dandridge in his safety deposit box, but a photo was the only memory he had of her. Tango was always amazed when he looked at a troubled kid who had the luxury of having both parents under the same roof.

He shook off the thoughts about his mother when he saw the front door opening to the duplex. The house was a two-story home that had no grass and looked like it could stand a few coats of paint on the outside. He could only imagine what the inside looked like. The place was apparently a drug store for Dibiase's clientele. When Dibiase was outside the door, Tango removed his military binoculars and zoomed in as far as his lenses allowed. There was another guy about an inch shorter than Dibiase right by his side. Tango looked him over and could tell he was packing a gun by the way his shirt bulged on the left side.

He watched intently as Dibiase opened the trunk and placed the bags back inside. The two men began a conversation, but Tango wasn't close enough to read their lips to know what they were talking about. He opened a little notepad he had, looking at the description his girlfriend had given him of the civilians who'd come looking for him. When he looked back at J.C., his description fit the description of the one she said had done all the talking. Moments later, a third fellow emerged with a stick of illegal marijuana in his hand and stood on the porch. Tango took a quick look and right away knew he was the other man who'd showed up in Chicago. He didn't know Don D. and J.C. personally, but he knew if they were here right now with Rico's sons, they were friendlies.

The third man went back inside after yelling something to both Dibiase and his comrade. Tango watched and they finished up their conversation shaking hands. The second man looked up and down the block before he let Dibiase pull off, and soon as he signaled the coast was clear, the rental car slid out its parking spot. Tango waited for a second until the second man turned his back then proceeded to get behind Dibiase again.

In his profession, he knew one thing for sure: timing was everything. Some people who had a minute to spare found out they only had a second to die. It was always too late for those people. He'd learned his lesson well when Rico saved his life. Tango knew it was close to the time for him to reveal himself. He was at the point he was ready to let them know he was in town so he could find out what had happened to his friend.

When Don D. went back inside, he felt the anticipation growing in his pants. He couldn't wait for Dibiase and J.C. to get-the-fuck out of Dodge. He knew Dibiase was happy with the way things were rolling so soon, so he would be going home to his woman, while his cousin J.C. would be going home to play house with Donna.

He was sure, in moments, the coast would be clear for him to bust his own move. J.C. had given him his bread, so his pockets were fat and he could clown a little when he got to his destination. He was ready to execute his plan as he lifted one of the floorboards in the back bedroom were the hidden safe was installed. He put the rest of the work inside and turned the combination lock until he was sure it was sealed tight. He sat on the twin-size bed in the room and dialed his girl's number.

"Hey, Baby Doll, what you doing?" he asked, smiling before she even got a word out.

"I see you ain't left yet," she replied. "I was just about to step out for a minute to watch one of my girls perform."

"Perform, huh? She stripping?"

"No, silly, she does open-mic poetry every week. I told her I was going to come check her out. Don't worry your hard-dick soft, baby. I'm sure I'll be back before you arrive."

"That's cool. I'm just finishing up counting this paper and getting my people ready so I can bounce your way. I should be highway bound in about twenty minutes," Don D. said, still fronting.

"Don't be playing with me, boo. You'd better hurry up and get up here. This-pussy's been on fire all day and you're playing shot-caller a city away."

"Stop tripping, baby. You know ain't nothing in this world that would keep me from getting between them thighs but an STD," he said, laughing.

"Ugggh, Don; that ain't funny."

"I'm just playing, baby," Don said.

When they finally hung up, he pulled out all his cash and counted it. He had close to six bands on him and what he wanted to do was spread it all over her bed and make her come on Jackson's face.

Dibiase pulled the rental car back inside his apartment complex. When he saw the spot was empty, he remembered he'd forgotten to tell Camille to park her whip outside so he could use the underground parking for himself. He didn't want any nosy people seeing him hauling bags from the trunk to the house. He figured he should be okay for this one time and the sun had gone down, so that was to his advantage. He killed the engine and got out, walking to the trunk to get his paper.

Before he could close the trunk, he felt the cold steel on his neck and knew he was being jacked. In his mind, he felt it had to be a setup because no one even knew where he lived. His second mind was telling him to play hard and reach for his own heat, but the position he was in would have probably left him an automatic dead man.

"What-the-fuck is up?" Dibiase asked, not turning around. If the person jacking him wasn't wearing a mask and he looked him in the face, it was automatic death, so he didn't turn around.

"I want to know, besides jailbirds, what other kinds of birds can't fly?" the gunman asked.

"You robbing me, muthafucka, or you here to give me a pop quiz? If so, try do-do birds," Dibiase replied, still a little worried the man might take his paper and shoot him. That was what the jackers were doing nowadays. They would get what they came for and still leave you stinking.

"I knew you wouldn't get it right. I'm talking about those cocaine birds, white flamingos, baby, China pigeons. See, I've been watching you, blood, all day. Nope, don't try to turn around either. Just know I've been to both your spots. I know you've got a spot full of dope and let's see here, a couple of bags full of cash," the gunman said as he reached around Dibiase, taking one duffle bag at a time.

Dibiase was livid now. He really wanted to try the man since it was apparent he was on a solo mission. He tried to think what Rico would do in a situation like this. What he did realize was he had been carefree and careless to let someone get this close to him. It was a good lick for whoever because there was at least one-twenty-five in each bag. Some fool had just scored himself a quarter mil. He figured he couldn't think like his father because Rico would have never been caught in this position. He knew if this-fool decided to shoot him, it was his own fault. He said a quick prayer, knowing his mother and brother would be devastated, and Camille would be left to raise the baby on her own.

'This-shit can't be happening,' he thought.

Now he had to wonder if the gunman knew this was where he lay his head since he'd commented he'd been watching him all day. Dibiase had forty keys in the basement and not much money in the house. Just enough to make a fool angry and shoot his woman and unborn child. He had to think quickly.

"Say, man, what you want? You got my paper. I just moved in here, so there's nothing else for you to acquire," Dibiase said, still facing the inside of the trunk. The gunman could have forced him to get in the trunk and closed him in while he went in his house.

"Let's say, Mr. Hammond, that I know these bags are full of the D-boy money and that woman upstairs in 201 is having your baby, the pretty lady in the SUV. Nice truck; did your daddy buy that?"

Dibiase felt instant fear run through his blood. It wasn't that he was scared to die. He was more so scared of being the cause of someone else's death. He tried to reminisce and go back to another time in his life when he was scared to figure out what he'd done to overcome the fear. He thought about the time he'd gone head-to-head with a neighbor's crazy pit bull when he was twelve. The dog had run up on him, jumping at his neck. Dibiase was on his way to school and it was picture day. When he saw the paw prints on his white shirt, he'd lost it and scooped up a two-by-four, letting the dog have it on top of the head.

Dibiase knew the man must have followed him all day to know the things he knew, and right then and there, it dawned on him about the stranger in his little brother's shop. There was something familiar about the man's voice, something even before he recognized it from the shop when he'd spoken saying he would come back later. Dibiase began to wonder if this was the person responsible for Rico's death. If he wasn't the one who'd done it, he'd probably had something to do with it. Now Dibiase's will to live made him react to the gunman. He reached for the forty-five in his waistband, but as quickly as he moved, the gunman had disarmed him, sticking Dibiase's pistol in his own back waistband.

"Say, blood, I don't know who you are or what you're on, but if this-shit is about that haircut earlier, there's enough money in the bags to cut you and your great grandkids' grandkids' hair for a lifetime."

"Well, damn!" Tango laughed, not at Dibiase, but at the comeback line he'd chosen."

"Let's go, little-nigga. March your-ass up them stairs. One false move, like they say in the movies, you're a dead one."

This was exactly what Dibiase was afraid of. He could have died right there, but then he wouldn't have been able to see Camille one last time. But, maybe it was possible he wouldn't die at all. He didn't know what to think at that moment, so he followed the gunman's orders. When they got to the door, his Jahiem ring tone *Find My Way Back* started blaring; that was his ring tone for Camille.

She was in the bathroom, but when she heard the keys in the door, she hung up before Dibiase answered. She was so happy he was home, she came running out the bathroom still in her panties and bra. She stopped dead in her tracks when she realized her man wasn't alone. All she could think about when she saw the stranger with the gun was Rico's body in the coffin. She wondered what Dibiase had gotten himself into.

His body had lain there still, his hands crossed, his suit neatly pressed with matching tie. A thousand-dollar pair of alligator-skin shoes on his feet with a pedicure most living men didn't have. Rico's haircut was perfect, as the funeral parlor had allowed Little Rickey to cut his father's hair. For a split second, in her mind, Dibiase had just changed places—same outfit, same shoes, same haircut. The baby was crying out, "Daddy!" and she had fainted in Uncle Mickey's arms.

Tango realized Camille was hysterical and he didn't want her to lose the baby.

"Go put some clothes on," he said to Camille as he tossed Dibiase back the duffle bags with his money in them.

"Here's your money, kid," he continued.

"Young lady—it's Camille, right?" he asked and she nodded her head to his question. "After you're decent, would you please grab me some ice water."

"Now, you sit down; we really need to talk," he said to Dibiase.

Dibiase watched as the gunman put his pistol away. He first instinct was to rush him and kick off in his ass, but something told him he would still be fighting a losing battle. Tango removed a picture from his pocket and handed it to Dibiase. It was a picture of Dibiase, Little Rickey, and Rico on a Navy ship that had been taken one summer. Then he took out a second picture and placed it in front of Dibiase. That picture was of Rico and the man he'd thought was a robber, both in their uniforms receiving Purple Heart medals. When Dibiase looked at the name on the man's chest in the picture, it said Oliver.

He couldn't believe who he was sitting in front of. Charlie Oliver had aged a lot since the last time Dibiase had seen him. He didn't even look like the same person he remembered, but he sure was still crazy like Dibiase remembered. Dibiase grabbed him and hugged him, then he began to yell and shed tears. It was the first time he'd broken down since Rico's death.

Camille was on her way back into the living room with the glass of water she wished she had some poison for. When she saw Dibiase hugging the man who'd just had a gun on them, she was at a loss for words, not understanding what was transpiring. Something was going on, but one thing for sure, she was glad there was no more gunplay. When Dibiase finally settled down, Camille went and got him a glass of water also.

"I sent my people looking for you over in the city a few days ago. They wouldn't have ever found you because I didn't have an updated description of you," Dibiase said.

"I had colon cancer; I beat it," Tango said, thinking about how bad the radiation treatment had done him.

"When I heard about the two young men who came and the old-school car with Wisconsin plates, I thought about you and Rickey. When I heard about your father being killed, I was stunned. I know I wouldn't have been any good to anyone being at that funeral. Your father and me were beyond best friends. I know sometimes life takes people in different directions, but that didn't change a thing between us. We stayed in contact as much as we could, and I can never forget the time he saved my life."

The two of them talked for hours, catching up. Dibiase filled Tango in on family life and Tango talked about some of the crazy shit they'd done when he and Rico were in the service. Dibiase got a chance to flash a few smiles and grins with the stories he told, and he honestly knew Charlie Oliver loved his father like a brother. Tango explained Rico had made a big change from the man he was when he'd first left Gary, Indiana. He was a rough-neck-thug who'd toted a pistol and would use it if you looked at him wrong. The Navy had made a man out of a thug, and eventually, had turned a father into a kingpin.

Tango talked about the detail assignment in Colombia and how it was Rico's last mission. Dibiase knew Gary wasn't his father's original birthplace, but it was where his mother was born. Tango said, after the trip, it was a few years before he heard from Rico again. He knew he had moved to Milwaukee and was doing okay, but one day, he was mowing his lawn, heard a car pull up, and turned to see his best friend in a shining, brand-new Eldorado. When Rico got out, he'd tossed him the keys and told him Merry Christmas in July. Dibiase remembered seeing a picture of an '84 red convertible Cadillac.

"That wasn't the gift. Your father handed me a brown envelope with fifty large inside. He knew I'd always wanted to start a business and told me that was my start-up money," Tango said, sipping his water.

He had been talking so much his throat was dry. Tango explained he knew Rico had connected with a drug lord over in Colombia, and the two of them had done some business. Dibiase knew his father wasn't Frank Lucas, the man from Harlem bringing the dope back himself. He didn't see Rico being that bold.

"I think this was a hit," Dibiase said.

"I'm sure it was that, but why, I don't know, and frankly, I don't give-a-flying-fuck. They hit the wrong SEAL, that is what I do know," Tango replied. "When you're dealing with them type of folks, running them type of operations, they play it like the Mexicans—blood in, blood out. Too many people alive to tell, and eventually, someone is going to tell, so they don't take any chances."

"So you think my father was actually part of the Colombian mafia family?"

"I can't say for sure, but I've got some people who are deep on the inside doing some research, and when that phone call comes, I'll be able to say for sure," Tango said.

"You don't know how many times I've looked over that-damn-police report. They aren't trying to do-shit. To them, it doesn't matter that he fought for this country; he's just another nigga-dealer who got caught up."

"You got the report here? I would love to take a look at it," Tango insisted.

"One second."

Dibiase handed the report over to Charlie Oliver, telling him that what bothered him was the stolen car from Arizona. He said his father had dealt with somebody from Vegas and that he was sure of.

That was all the information he really had for Charlie to go on. Dibiase saw Charlie was in thought mode and didn't bother him. It must have been a Navy thing because the position he was in while thinking was the same position Rico use to be in.

"Where did you get these police reports from?" Tango asked with a serious look in his eyes.

"The homicide detective working the case," Dibiase said, confused. "Why do you ask?"

"Do you have his card or his name? I can assure you these papers aren't authentic. Someone fabricated this report," Tango said, knowing the report was false by the watermarks on the paper. "Look closely at the last page. You'll see watermarks, and also, there is no proof seal, which they know most civilians no nothing about."

There had been a lot of police shootings of black men all over the country. It was even happening in the Midwest and Dibiase had started to wonder if the police department had shot Rico because they couldn't catch him dirty. Maybe they wanted him off the streets, maybe they'd set up the hit themselves, but now it really wasn't making sense. Tango knew that was what Dibiase would think, but he knew it was bigger than that.

"The drug lords have money to burn, and most likely, they have people working for them in every city with badges. Whoever this officer was, he worked for the people who killed Rico and his job was to cover up the murder. I'm going to tell you like this, kid, the police here didn't kill Rico. One or two of them are dirty, and most likely knew the hit was going to take place. Their job had to be to watch out for the hitman or men, and make sure all the tracks are covered."

"So this Detective Torres is dirty? He's working for the mafia, huh?"

"Yes, but it's my guess Torres doesn't even know his boss. At some time, probably as a rookie, he was approached and offered a considerable amount of money to work for the mob. The mob always makes offers that can't be refused. That isn't just television, kid; that's some real-life-shit. But something else is strange."

"What's that?"

"There is still a piece of paper missing from the report. The pages are numbered and page three isn't here. That must be either one or two things: Torres is protecting himself, or he turned it in to his boss, but didn't want you to know what was on it."

Tango removed his cell from his back pocket to call another friend of his who he had on speed dial. When Glen Dixon left the SEALS, instead of doing like Rico, he'd followed the right path and taken a high-profile job with the NSA. They had all the intel on mafia families around the globe. Tango remembered when Dixon told him every nationality had a mob family, even the Jews.

"This is Alpha-1 ," Glen said, answering his phone.

"This is Alpha-00; did anything pop up yet?"

"Well, I was reduced to checking the federal database and nothing popped-up at first. Then I broke into the mainframe of the federal computer in Ohio and found a sealed report. What was fishy was, even though the file was in the system, it was protected with an encryption that only the secretary of defense and the acting president knew how to decipher," Alpha-1 stated.

"Speak in English, Alpha-1. I flunked Computer 101," Tango replied.

"It's like sending a new Windows file to an outdated computer. When any normal person tries to open it, they would be better off watching *The Twilight Zone*."

"So, somebody with a high clearance didn't want this file to be readily available?"

"You must didn't hear what I said in the beginning: the secretary of defense—my boss—and the president of the United States—my boss' boss."

"So, you weren't able to see it, huh?" Tango asked.

"Who do you think you're talking to? I'm smarter than every fifth grader put together in the country," he replied, smiling.

"That-a-boy."

"When I cracked the report, it was the second Black Hawk mission that took place in Colombia. Over two hundred people were killed trying to protect a drug lord and over six thousand kilos of cocaine were seized from a factory. Hey, I bet they put at least half that-shit back out on the streets too, dirty-motherfuckers," Alpha-1 said.

"Is that it? Nothing specific?" Tango asked.

"The mission was to seize a titanium tube that contained something undisclosed in the report. It was more important than the dope they seized, but the tube was never found and the drug lord they'd come for also escaped." He paused for a second.

"You might not want to hear this, but several Americans were killed and several escaped. The one thing they did confiscate was a list of Americans' names, and Alpha-23's name was on this list."

"Cool, cool, I figured that. Do me a favor. I just went over some phony-ass police report that Alpha-23's son has in his possession. It was given to him by a homicide detective whose last name is supposedly Torres. See what you can find out about this Torres guy. Phone records, financials, I even want to know what night he buys his-pussy. One more thing, see if there's an authentic report floating around in one of them-damn-computer systems."

"I'm on top of all that and I will be there as soon as possible. Did you make contact with Alpha-23's sons?"

"Yeah, I'm sitting with the oldest now. Son-of-a-bitch is just like his daddy too."

"Tell Dibiase to remain tight; the remainder of the Goon Squad's got this under control," the man on the other end of the phone said.

Dibiase sat patiently while his father's friend put in some work. He was always amazed how people who'd been in the military still had certain ways about them. Their body language was different than other people's—the way they moved and the way they spoke to each other in codes. A lot of it Dibiase didn't understand, but a lot of it he did from watching his father all those years. To Dibiase, it felt like he was reading a Clancy novel when he watched Tango in action. Charlie Oliver said, since they were a few hundred feet from a La Quinta, he was going to check in for the night, but Dibiase insisted he stay at his home with him and Camille. Even though Dibiase didn't know that much about Tango, as much as Rico had talked about him, he felt like he was an uncle. He had Camille search in some of the boxes stacked up on the far wall for some clean blankets.

Don D. was rolling, doing seventy-five miles per hour down I-94 toward Racine. He was smoking a stick of his favorite-shit and bumping his new Jeezy disc. *Trap or Die* was his shit and Jeezy was the man. The way he rapped his lyrics made Don D. bob his head to not only the music but also the lyrics he spit.

New paint job / get you a new blow job / 28, 36, I miss my blow job / I got it here, you get it back / niggas that's your problem / sounds like a snow job / you already know niggas won't starve / and you know nigga don't rob / don't make me change the grill / get a nose job / nigga, I'm still spending twenties from my old job / you nigga's get up off my dick / that's a ho's job / he said he want another one / I told him no prob / he just bring the quarter back like Brett Favre . . .

The exit was about a quarter mile ahead of him when Don D. started the track over he was listening to, thinking about what was about to go down in less than thirty minutes. Jeezy had a way with taking the game and mixing it with women and real life. Sometimes, it was like he was talking straight to Don D.

Don hit exit 20 onto Highway 333, putting him about nine minutes from his destination. He was a little hungry, but there weren't many places to eat in Racine this time of night besides Denny's, and their food always upset his stomach. He decided he could wait to eat, figuring he would have his tongue tonsil-deep inside some-pussy very shortly. He kept driving past the Denny's, turning left by the mall, getting closer and closer to fulfilling his desires.

It only took a few before he was pulling up and exiting the rental he was driving. He was dialing the number as he was walking up to the front door of Doll's house. For some strange reason, she wasn't answering her phone or his knocking. When he walked to the back, he noticed her black Avalon wasn't in its normal spot, which to him meant she was still out with her friend.

Don had stopped to pick up a bottle, but he decided to hit a small corner bar close to her crib. That way, he could kill two birds with one stone: get a drink and be close to her place when she called. Don rode down the street to a hole-in-the-wall called Smitty's. The bar was next to what the D-boys in her city called Hustlers' Circle. It was where most of them stood to get off their work to the hypes who used. It kind of reminded him of how-shit went down in Baltimore, but the caliber of niggas was a lot different than the ones back home. When he was parking, he saw a few of the diehards were still out there, clocking that late-night paper, and he admired the drive he saw in them. It still wasn't like back home though. He smiled, checking his phone to make sure he didn't have a missed call.

The bar on the inside reminded him of a juke-joint down south he use to go to when he visited his aunt. The only difference was the juke-joint had dirt floors and Smitty's had cheap tile. Other than that, it had the same atmosphere to it, making the niggas in Doll's city seem country-as-hell. Don D. looked around as he made his way to the bar. He could sense people looking at him like he was from Venus or Mars. He knew Racine was small and everybody there knew everybody else, so he knew that was why most of the guys were looking at him. Besides, he had on his bling chain, and most of the women were getting in their glance, wondering if he was fair game. It still made him feel a little uncomfortable to the point where he patted his waistline, making sure his trusty heat was right where it was supposed to be. It didn't help that the song on the jukebox was an R. Kelly song and Kell's was spitting he was a player and not to bring your girl to the club. He just smiled because, little did any of them know, he was in love with Doll already.

He eased up a little when he heard a familiar voice call his name. When he turned, he saw Doll's friend, the one who had gone out to eat with them when they'd first met. Cedilla was short and stacked, and Don knew if he'd met her first, he would have tried to knock her. He made his way over to where she was chilling.

"Is this seat taken?" he asked.

"You're so silly; have a seat," she said, telling the bartender to pour Don a drink on her.

Don watched as the fine, thick-ass-chick behind the bar poured him his double shot of Remy and coke on the rocks. When she turned to give him his drink, she made sure he got a glance at her double-D's resting inside the see-through lace shirt she was wearing. Cedilla noticed how the bartender was acting and just rolled her eyes.

"You have to excuse her," she said.

Don didn't reply to that comment; he just sipped his drink.

"So I guess you're in town to see your boo, huh?" she asked.

"You know it. I came up to see Baby, but she wasn't at the crib yet, so I decided to step out and have a quick one," he replied, watching the fat-ass jiggle on the bartender.

"Looks like she put too much coke in there if you ask me." Cedilla laughed.

Don was glad someone was there he knew. It seemed to take all the attention off the stranger, and the rest of the patrons continued doing what they were doing before he'd arrived. Cedilla seemed to have her head in the right place. They shared conversation about her and her future goals, and Don was shocked when he found out she didn't have any kids. Her body for a short woman was banging.

"No kids, huh? You a virgin?" he asked.

"I told you that you were silly. No, I'm not a virgin. I just want to finish my master's in nursing and get settled before I bring a child into the world," she replied, taking down half her Long Island.

"Can I ask you something?" she said, looking at him like she was sizing him up.

The two of them hadn't talked much to each other the first night because he and Doll had been so into each other. She had really been a third wheel, in the way.

"Of course, lil mama; you can ask me anything."

"I just wanted to know what a man like you sees in a fake-ass-bitch like Doll?" she asked, admiring his dimples.

Her comment threw him all the way off. He almost choked on his next sip of Remy.

"Run that by me again."

"I'm just asking. The girl ain't-shit in my opinion. She doesn't work, she won't go to school, and she's a big-ass-liar. She's from Baltimore too; you know that, right?"

"She's from Baltimore?" Don asked, wondering if that was true, why hadn't she told him. He figured she was born there and her family must have left when she was a baby.

"Yeah, that fake-ass-bitch is from your city. When I was about to say you two had something in common, she kicked me under the table," Cedilla said, showing Don the dark mark that looked like it was almost healed.

"Cheap-ass-Payless shoes that-bitch had on did this to my leg."

"Damn!" he said, looking at the bruise.

"That's why I changed it to Boston. It was obvious she didn't want you to know about her past. She doesn't really like to talk about her home city too much to anybody. I don't know what happened there, but it must have been something terrible. Shit, I've watched every episode of *The Wire*." She smiled.

The Long Island was starting to take effect on her. She started rubbing his leg while she talked, running her fingers up and down his True Religions until she was clutching his dick. She gave a smile of approval at what she was feeling as her touch had already aroused him. He had to do a double-take at her now and pay her a little closer attention. She had on a pair of white shorts that hugged her hips and showed her camel toe.

"Yeah, baby, that is a little strange and makes me wonder why she didn't share that information with me," he said, sliding his body a little so she could continue rubbing on him. "Might not mean-shit, but I gotta look into it."

"I just think it's fucked-up that-bitches like that get all the good men just 'cause they know how to wear expensive weave."

Don really sensed the haterism in Cedilla's words and figured the two of them must have had a really bad fight, or the Cedilla-bitch was bold-as-fuck. He knew if he wanted to have his way with her, he could take her outside and have her suck his-dick right in the parking lot. It sounded like a good idea, but he was just going to put it on the back burner for now. Don stood up, took a hundred-dollar bill out his pocket, and placed it on the bar. She asked him what it was for because she was paying for the drinks. He told her it was a tip for the bartender.

He turned, walked out, and headed to his car, thinking about what she'd said to him about Doll. Don wondered again, if she really was from Baltimore, why hadn't she just told him.

When he got back to her place, he could see her car was back and she was finally home. When Don D. knocked this time, she answered the door right away. She had on a pair of lime-green thong panties and a matching lime-green bra. Her hair was done nicely and she smelled better than the entire perfume section in the Boston Store. Don felt his-dick rise like it was the first time he'd seen a woman in her panties.

Baby Doll had the house all set up with the sensual scent of candles and exotic fruits in a bowl for him. She was playing some real smooth R&B and the lights were perfectly dim. Don removed his pistol and rested it on her coffee table, forgetting for the moment everything Cedilla had just revealed to him. It was the classic Don D.— letting his little head outthink his big head.

ے ✦ ﮺

Alpha-1 was waiting on his people to come through for him. He was very hurt his friend had been murdered in cold blood outside a church. He leaned back, thinking whoever had gotten Rico had to be well-trained professionals. All the time they'd spent together in the service, Alpha-1 knew firsthand Rickey Hammond was no joke. He heard his fax machine ring and knew he was about to receive an incoming fax. The government had a satellite that tracked cellphone calls and recorded certain calls by a program they'd input called Trigger Words. Each call was monitored in each language, and if certain words were used in a certain context, your call was automatically recorded.

There were quite a few calls that had been recorded from Alpha-23's cell records. There was also a heavy pattern-flow of calls to a California and an Arizona number, but the Las Vegas number was what had really caught Alpha-1's attention. He listened to the calls that had been trapped by the Trigger Words software and some things became clear to him. He tapped a few keys on his computer and checked on the last Black Hawk operation.

"Rico, what-in-the-hell did you get yourself into?" Alpha-1 asked quietly as he put two-and-two together.

He packed up the information and called for a private flight. He knew it would only take a couple of hours for him to arrive in Milwaukee.

~ Twenty-Two ~
The Church

Rickey 'Rico' Hammond, the godfather, was dressed to the nines for today's event. The triple-white Brooks Brothers suit looked tailor-cut the way it molded to his body. His black button-up Givenchy shirt had his initials engraved on each sleeve, and to complete his ensemble, he sported a custom Armani bow tie that matched his Muri big-block crocs. He was set to be the best man at his friend's wedding.

Cassie stood in the doorway, watching her husband get ready. She wished she was going, but she never questioned Rico on what or how he did things. He had proved to her over the years that his way was the best way. She walked up close to her husband, smelling his Burberry fragrance, and laid her head on his chest, telling him how much she loved him.

"Stop acting like this is the last time you'll see me, woman," Rico said, raising her head by her chin and kissing her lips.

"Something just doesn't feel right," Cassie replied.

"Everything is cool, honey. I shall see you in time for dinner," Rico assured her.

Cassie didn't want to put up too much of a fuss as she watched him finish putting on a few pieces of jewelry. He didn't pack a piece, which was a little unusual to her, but again, she didn't question him. Rico grabbed the matching diamond bracelets he'd had custom-made as a gift and headed to the rental car so he would be on time.

The church was crowded and people were still arriving by the bunches to see OG Slim tie the knot. The limo was outside with 'Just Married' signs in the windows and cans on strings hanging off the back bumper. Rico tucked his wedding gift under his arm, thinking back to how lovely his own wedding day had been. He had been married to

Cassie for a long time now and he'd never regretted one day. He hoped Slim's mind was in the right place, and that retiring from the game was next for his friend.

The church was set up nicely. The person who'd decorated had to be a professional the way everything seemed to be strategically placed with the white doves flying around. The sounds of the organ reverberated off the high ceilings as the man played the melody for Just the Two of Us. Rico had a quick glimpse of the bridesmaids, who all looked beautiful and ready. It was just an unbelievably-beautiful sight.

Rico felt a warm sensation flow through his heart when the music changed and his friend came down the aisle. Slim waved when he saw Rico motioning for him to come take his side as his best man. Now the song selection changed one more time from Surface's Shower Me With Your Love to Here Comes the Bride, and Rico looked to see his homie's bride being escorted down the aisle by her father. He was happy for them. Marriage was a huge commitment and a lot of responsibility for two people. He was enjoying the whole ceremony, but he wanted it to be over. For some reason, he felt like going to the lakefront and just thinking, like he did on early mornings when he didn't feel like being in his office.

The pastor did his thing and now Slim was a married man. On his way out, Rico handed Slim an envelope and whispered something in his ear. The two of them embraced and Slim watched as Rico, the godfather, exited the church. Outside, the sun was beaming as he looked up in the blue sky. He started taking the steps two at a time to get back to his rental. He didn't even notice the lady pushing the stroller with her face covered by a veil. He stepped between two parked cars, looking for the rental car, when he saw another lady pushing a stroller on the other side of the street heading his way. Before anyone realized what was transpiring, because people were exiting from the church, what was supposed to be babies in strollers turned out to be AK-47's, and what were supposed to be women pushing buggies were two Colombian hitmen who had come to take out the godfather.

The gunshots were constant; the hitmen weren't going to miss their target. People were running and screaming, and some of the street thugs at the wedding had their own pistols and started to return fire. They could see the bullets were directed at Rico, so they figured if they saved the godfather, they'd be set for life. However, it was too late. The first bullet caught him in the leg, sending his body slamming into a parked Pontiac. As he was falling to the ground, the next bullet caught him in the face, causing instant death and ripping his skin completely off the bone. It was over; it was finally over.

"RICO'S DEAD!"

"RICO'S DEAD!"

"THE GODFATHER!"

"HE'S DEAD!"

People were shouting Rico was dead. A lot of people were crying as sirens approached from fire trucks, police cars, and ambulances. Those who walked up on the body looking at the once-white Brooks Brothers suit knew it was over. Rico's faced had been torn from his body with the impact of the assault rifles' shells. Slim was one of the people who went running to him, falling to his knees at the sight of his best friend gunned down.

~ Twenty-Three ~
The Goon Squad

Tango was meeting Alpha-1 at a terminal at Mitchell Field Airport. Alpha-1 was on a private charter that was about twenty minutes late because of the bad weather the pilot had run into. Tango sat patiently, thinking about the mission at hand and waiting for his man to arrive. There were no announcements or flight boards that showed the arrival and departures of chartered private flights, so when the plane finally landed, he hoped Alpha-1 knew exactly where to find him— sitting in the closest Starbucks, sipping a coffee.

Alpha-1 walked along the concourse until he smelled the fresh coffee ground and saw the green-and-white sign of the famous franchise. A few seconds later as he stood there saying nothing, he waited. Tango didn't have to turn around to know his man was standing right behind him.

"I see, Alpha-1, that you made it safely."

"You old fart; I see you've still got eyes behind your head too."

"You're damn-right," Tango replied as he stood up and greeted his partner.

The three of them had been close. Even though there had been other guys on detail with them, Alpha-1, Alpha-00, and Alpha-23 were as one. There wasn't an assignment too big or too small for the Goon Squad to handle, and when they went in, they always came out 'mission accomplished'.

As the two of them left the airport, Dixon couldn't help talking a little about the good old days and how it felt to finally be reunited. Dixon discussed how Rico hadn't wanted to go on to take command when Oliver was discharged.

"Yeah, he didn't want to take over because he didn't even want to be part of the last detail," Tango said. "Rico wanted to raise a family," he continued.

"I understand, but we could have still been something, a real force to be reckoned with," Dixon said.

"We were always a force, then and now."

Charlie Oliver talked about Rico's family, letting Alpha-1 know what kind of people he could expect to meet. He told him the youngest one of the sons was into church and the oldest one was a hustler like his father. Alpha-1 started to paint his own picture of Rico's family in his mind. He pictured both of Rico's boys having a bit of their father deeply-rooted in them. Alpha-1 sensed the instinct in Dibiase to be smooth but lethal, which was the way Rico handled most situations.

"Have you spoken to Cassie yet?" Alpha-1 asked.

"Negative; haven't seen her as yet."

They pulled into a Motel Six, where Tango had checked in that morning, despite Dibiase wanting him to stay with him and Camille. They'd camped out for the morning in the hotel room, going over everything Tango had on paper and in his mind. Dixon asked about the trunk and Tango told him the one trunk found in the basement had been filled to the top with kilograms of cocaine. Each SEAL had had two trunks when they'd left service, one that contained personal belongings and one that contained personal weapons. Neither of them had any idea where Rico had put his second trunk.

Alpha-1, aka Glenn Dixon, thought about the trunk being filled with dope and it started making a little more sense to him. He hated Rico had chosen the lifestyle he'd chosen, but nevertheless, he was still his brother to the end. Tango got a chance to look over everything Dixon had brought along with him: phone records of all of

Rico's calls, the official FBI reports, and the original local police report. It was obvious the detective who went by Torres knew a little more than he was willing to write in the reports. As far as Tango was concerned, he had now become the number-one suspect. He had to be on someone's payroll in addition to the Milwaukee Police Department's.

"Hey, you know I found out there are a couple more agents supposedly doing some extensive investigating on this case?" Dixon said.

"I see the names you attached to the federal reports," Tango replied. "What-in-the-hell do you supposed they are investigating?"

"Well, apparently, they have an informant on the inside who is supposedly working to bring down the rest of Rico's people. They say Hammond was the cause of some street drug war where some innocent people lost their lives."

"Innocent people, huh?" Tango said, rubbing his chin.

"In this business, no one is innocent. But what we can get from this is that Dibiase and his people are in direct danger of an indictment if the information is correct?" Tango asked.

"That would seem to be correct."

"So, these two agents on the case, did you check their service jackets?"

"Of course; you think I forgot how to walk and chew gum?" Dixon laughed. "But they both have clean records, like they're on the up-and-up. Every take down on file has been by the book, and neither has ever been in front of IA for any sort of reprimand."

"A lot-of-shit isn't adding up, just too many damn-false reports floating around, which means either one or two things: some politics are involved here, or somebody has a bankroll bigger than Warren

Buffet's and is paying a lot of money to keep something secret!" Tango exclaimed.

"I agree, but I think we should follow up on Torres. At least we can get a handle on the getaway vehicle and shake him down for any other pertinent info he's withholding."

Oliver insisted Dixon get a little rest before they went any further. He said they would go see Rickey Jr. a little later and find a way to pay Torres a visit. Dixon had been up all night, researching a lot of confidential files, and the flight had him exhausted as well. He decided Tango had given him some good advice. Oliver left Dixon's room, which was right next door to his own room. Once inside, he poured himself a healthy shot of Jack and sat on the edge of his bed thinking. Oliver knew Rico well enough to know he had to have left a clue as to who his killer or killers were.

Another thing that bothered Oliver was that the Feds acted like they were still investigating. That sounded like more cover-up-bullshit because, after the death of Rico, they really shouldn't have anything left to investigate. That was if he really was the cause of a war. There was a lot going on upstairs in Tango's head—in particular, a wedding his partner had attended without any street security and without his wife, and that being the place where the hit had happened. The police report didn't state anything about Rico packing a weapon, which was unusual seeing he'd been packing at his own wedding. His property contents were just his bloodstained clothes, a set of rental car keys, a wallet with a few hundred dollars, and a small photo of his family.

The more he thought about it, the more Oliver thought Rico was aware of what was going to transpire. He knew if he wanted more information, Torres would most likely be the key. That was exactly where he and Dixon were going to begin. He picked up his cell and dialed Dibiase's phone. He wanted to know if Cassie was still in town so he could pay her a visit.

~ Twenty-Four ~
The Verdict

"Has the jury reached a verdict?" asked the appellate court judge.

Today was the day for Brock—known to the streets of Baltimore as the notorious Pork Chop—to find out his fate. His lawyer had gotten his case heard thirty days earlier than they had anticipated, which meant there was a possibility he could surface sooner than the haters were expecting. There were a lot of people he would love to surprise and he had high hopes things would go his way. The twenty-five grand he'd spent on his appeal had better have been well worth it. He knew the hotshot lawyer was good, but good wasn't good enough; Pork Chop wanted to walk.

His new mouthpiece assured him he would be doing just that since there was no murder weapon and the hotel cameras couldn't place him at the scene of the crime. Pork Chop felt he owed a lot to his baby cousin Doll, who he'd helped get out of Baltimore some time ago. She had moved to Wisconsin and had been putting her hustle down ever since her arrival. It was Doll who had tricked a few balling-niggas from the city of Chicago and some from Milwaukee out of their paper. That currency, in turn, had helped him get the new trial. He was going to do any and everything to make sure she was straight.

He remembered it like it was yesterday when they were both shorties how the two of them had become so close. Doll had gotten herself knocked-up by some west-side cat who was handling his business in the streets. When it came time to be a father, the nigga swore he wouldn't take care of a baby by an east-side bitch. Doll knew she was breaking code by dealing with a thug from across town, but what was done was already done. He remembered when he asked her

why, she'd said she'd gotten tired of dating niggas on her side of town. She said all they did was gang-bang and she wanted a different life. Pork Chop understood that because, at the time, he wasn't hustling yet. He was doing exactly what she had just said: robbing and killing people for a little of nothing.

Doll was very pretty with a banging body and she always wanted to be pampered, so she needed a-nigga who was about that D-boy life and could stand to foot the bill. She showed up one night to his spot, banging on the basement window and crying her eyes out. Doll knew her aunt was home because she'd seen her Volvo parked in the driveway and she didn't want her to know her situation. She also knew that meant Pork Chop was probably in the basement, smoking his weed and playing video games. When he heard the banging, he picked up his heater and went up the backstairs, ready for an ambush. When he opened the door, he saw Doll standing there, looking like she was auditioning to be a clown in a circus. Crying, her makeup had run down the side of her face. He had no choice, seeing she was family, and rushed her downstairs to see what was wrong with his cousin.

After hearing what went down, it had taken about a week to catch the-nigga Stacks slipping. If he wasn't going to take care of the baby or pay for the abortion, he had to be aborted. They devised a plan and Doll told Stacks she needed to see him. He invited her over, thinking at least he could fuck-her one more time before he canceled her, period. He even thought about feeding her some castor oil or punching her in her stomach to kill the baby.

When Doll got there, Stacks was chilling, counting his paper and smoking a blunt, still walking around in his boxers. She slipped off to the bathroom, giving herself a chance to unlock the side door before returning. Doll joined Stacks on his black leather sofa like everything was all good. He started kissing her, acting like he'd missed her, sliding his hand under her T-shirt. Doll felt sick to her stomach letting him touch her again and couldn't wait for her cousin to get there. She had never set anyone up before, but there was a first time for everything.

At first, she'd thought she loved Stacks. He'd pampered her just the way she had dreamed, took her shopping, paid for her hair to be done weekly, and wined and dined her at some of the city's premier spots. It had all ended when she told him she was carrying his child. Stacks had turned his back on her like she was a bum on the streets. It was time for her to get the revenge she felt she deserved. Doll returned his kiss, remembering how she use to love the softness of his lips. Stacks thought he heard something, but he was too busy trying to work his zipper so he could have Doll suck his dick. How fitting, he thought, if he could cum in her face and all over the last hairdo he'd paid for.

Just a few seconds later, a masked man was standing in front of them with a pistol pointed at them. Scared for his life, Stacks directed the killer to the kitchen, letting him know there were two bricks and fifty thousand there if he spared his life. It wasn't what Pork Chop had come for, but the bonus was going to be nice. He took his mask off and Stacks knew exactly who he was. It was too late for any more pleading as Stacks looked at Doll and knew he had been set up.

"Bitch, you did this to me?!"

"You-damn-right, you punk-muthafucka! You think you going to leave me with a baby and not fuck-with-me? I'm going to kill this baby and you too!" she replied.

Doll stood up, looking as his hard dick went soft and seemed to travel backwards into his stomach. She took the gun from her cousin and pointed it directly at her unborn child's sperm donor.

"Come on, bitch, you ain't serious! Do you have any idea who you're fucking with? I'm going to have you and this-nigga's heads!" Stacks exclaimed, knowing he was in no position to be issuing threats.

Pork Chop's gun went off and the silencer keep the noise to a minimum. Both bullets entered Stacks' forehead, killing him instantly. It felt good to Doll. The sight of the blood and his body falling backwards were something she felt she could get use to. The fifty thousand was *just throw off because Doll knew exactly where Stacks kept the real money, and it was the beginning of Doll and Pork Chops' Bonnie-and-Clyde relationship.*

"Yes, Your Honor, we have a verdict," the jury foreman said.

It was time for Pork Chop to finally hear what he had been waiting for. His palms were sweating and his legs were shaking as the judge directed the jury foreman to read the verdict.

"On the count of first degree murder, the jury finds the defendant NOT GUILTY.

"On the second count of reckless endangerment, the jury finds the defendant NOT GUILTY."

Pork Chop could see the district attorney was furious, but that didn't matter; he was now a free man. He turned and whispered to his attorney before the bailiffs came to take him back while the paperwork was being processed. All he could think about was the few haters he had to go pay a visit to in the city—the ones who'd played him, figuring he'd get a life bid and that would be the end of him.

A couple of hours later, Pork Chop was climbing off Alexis Green. He had spent his first few hours of freedom deep in her guts. He was ready to continue, but she was sore from the built-up tension in his loins and couldn't take it. While she pleaded for a break, he used her cell and dialed his cousin Doll in Racine. He knew a trip to the Midwest was in order.

Twenty-Five

Mickey was tired of driving since he had been up for two days. He was getting money and wasn't going to stop until his body shut him down. He had gone and copped a four-and-a-split from J.C., flipped that, and double-dipped, copping his re-up from Peanut. When he flipped the work he'd gotten from Peanut, he called J.C. back, who was busy and told Mickey to meet up with Don D. The whole time Mickey was busting these moves, the Feds were listening and recording everything he said, making notes on who the key players were since Rico had expired. Both officers knew Mickey Hammond was giving them the run around like they were a couple of fools. They weren't as dumb as he played them to be. They knew they would have to haul him in sooner or later, and it seemed sooner was better than later in their eyes.

Mickey had gotten close with Don D. over the last couple of days. Don D. talked a lot and that was what Mickey needed—good product and good information. The three of them had sat in the spot—Don D., Mickey, and Doll, who had talked Don into bringing her to Milwaukee. She was happy her cousin was free and they'd talked about him coming there to pull a major caper. She needed to make sure all her T's were crossed and her I's were dotted.

Don was feeling himself as Mickey was there to cop again. Mickey had stepped up his quantity and asked for double what he normally got. It was nothing for Mickey to be broke one day and on a hundred bands a few days later. He'd blown money like kids blew bubbles when Rico was alive. The fancy trips with the-bitches and the cars, then there were the rampages he went on getting high himself. But that was just who Mickey was and everyone knew his habits. Mickey asked Don D. to ride with him for a moment, but Don knew if he left Doll alone in the spot and J.C. found out, he would have a fit.

J.C. didn't trust any woman but his own. He figured they were all snakes, especially the Racine-chick his cousin called Doll. He didn't know her, but he did know she was the-chick who stayed in the city where he'd left a body behind. When Mickey questioned Don's manhood, he put Don D.—who had just said the world was his—on the spot in front of his girl. Mickey was old-school and knew exactly what he was doing.

"Say, man, you're your own man, right?"

"Yeah, man; of course, playa. It's only for a second anyway, right?"

"That's what I said."

Don D. had just been acting like he was the shot-caller and to bow down now in front of his girl would leave him shame-faced. Doll knew Don D. was clocking paper, but she also saw right through him. She had been around quite a few blocks and knew when the man was the man, or just a-nigga who was down with the man.

"So, you want me to hold it down. huh, baby?" she asked jokingly.

Don D. looked at her and smiled. He pecked her on the lips and told her to just chill, he was only going to be gone a second. She watched out the window as they got in Mickey's rental car and pulled off.

Doll now had a chance to see what was what. She was looking around and knew where they were was just a spot to hustle and only that. The place was still nice and clean, but there was nothing there to make it a home. She heard several knocks on the door and ignored them, figuring it was just the hypes coming to spend their money. The spot was a step up from the last-nigga she'd messed with. He'd only had empty milk crates and black-and-white televisions. Don D. had furniture, even a fridge and a stove in the kitchen. In the bedroom, she saw a new Ashley set and a curve television on the wall. This let Doll know whoever Don D. was down with had real taste in the way he did business. She had met J.C. and knew he had potential to be the man, but something told her the totem pole went higher than J.C. as well. One thing she told her cousin was Don D. worked with a guy who she knew was a real killer. It didn't scare him one bit though.

Doll continued searching the place quickly, not knowing how long Don was going to be gone. She looked in the bathroom and in the closets, when she got back to the kitchen, she found what she was looking for. Under the sink, she found a triple-beam scale and two bricks, broken down. She had been around enough cocaine to tell it was some good shit from what she knew about dope. There was a bag of money, too, which looked to be about fifty thousand, in thousand-dollar stacks.

She had to put her thinking cap on because her first instinct was to break Don D. off for the fifty and make a run for it. She knew several-niggas in Milwaukee who were dying to get in her-pussy. She could have hit it to a remote location, called either one of them, and they would have come running to her side. But her mind told her not to be so quick to use her damsel-in-distress routine. If these-niggas had fifty in a spot, there was a much bigger fish to fry, and that was what she and her cousin would want.

Doll had a new determination now that she knew Don was well-connected. She grabbed her phone out of her Coach bag and began dialing her cousin's new phone number. Pork Chop answered on the first ring and listened to the report she was giving him. His money was fucked-up but he agreed she should wait on taking the fifty. He licked his lips and told her he would be there as soon as possible.

Mickey had Don D. stop at McDonald's so he could grab a quick bite to eat.

"Damn, Unc, didn't you just eat a seven-piece chicken deal?"

"The two things I like to do is fuck-off and eat, young blood," Mickey replied.

They both laughed as Don pulled the rental in the parking lot of the Golden Arches. When Don looked at Mickey, he could tell something was bothering him because of the way he continued to sweat. It was actually making Don D. nervous seeing Mickey drip the way he was.

They rode back and Mickey continued making small talk. He talked about Peanut and how he was selling bad dope. Don already knew about the incident Dibiase had had to straighten out for his uncle. He had hoped-like-hell Mickey wasn't still fucking-around with Peanut. Mickey also threw in that he didn't want to call J.C. any more but get his work direct from Don D. Mickey swallowed down both double cheeseburgers while he was talking, washing them down with the large Coke he'd ordered.

Don D. felt Mickey was cool and he could learn something from the old head. He was glad he'd chosen to take the short ride with him so they could chop-it-up. Don began opening up a little, telling Mickey about how much work they were moving and how the cash was piling up quickly. In just a couple of weeks, they had easily done a million dollars.

Mickey raised an eyebrow when he heard the number. Mickey knew Dibiase was smart, but he was sure the product they were moving was product his brother had left. Mickey wondered if his nephew Dibiase had gotten to his father's plug. He felt something had been shaking good for his nephew because he'd been too eager to handle the situation with Peanut. He knew his primary motive was love of family, but something was up because Dibiase hadn't asked many questions. He thought again about the number Don D. said they'd made and he knew four stacks weren't shit for his nephew.

Dibiase had become the man overnight. Mickey didn't speak for the rest of the ride. He just thought about what his next move needed to be.

Something was going wrong as Agent Hawk tapped his transmitter. They were hoping to zero in on the conversation between Don D. and their CI, Mickey Hammond, but the signal had faded. The agents followed the rental car Mickey was in down 35th street. They wondered if it was a technical mishap or had Mickey Hammond done something on purpose. Hawk's partner insisted they pull the rental car over, but Hawk felt that would alert the players that they were on to them if they did that. He wanted to continue to play it safe.

Dibiase had just hung up the phone from talking with his man Oliver. Oliver had explained he had information to share with him and he wanted to meet up with him. Dibiase let him know he would be happy to meet up with him. He heard Oliver on another phone he carried talking to his boy Alpha-1, asking him if he was ready to roll. Dibiase knew he had done a good thing enlisting the help of Rico's old comrades. He knew they would stop at nothing to seek and destroy the people responsible for the death of his pops.

When he walked in the house, he could smell the aroma of a roast. Camille had prepared dinner after she'd gone shopping for their new apartment. He was glad she was happy to be there with him and he didn't know what he would do without her. She heard him come in and hurried to give him the biggest hug and kiss he'd ever had.

"Hey, lil momma; you must miss me," he said, returning her affection.

"Is the Pope Catholic?" Camille replied.

Camille worried about Dibiase. After they made love on the one hundred thousand dollars he had spread out over the bed, he'd commented there was plenty more where that had come from. She always knew he and J.C. played in the streets, but now she knew he had somehow just leveled up. He had expressed, while holding her close to his sweaty chest, that he was going to be bigger than Rico and that really worried her knowing his pops had been murdered for his lifestyle. When he made the comment he would make a billion dollars, she knew again he was seriously going to try and that worried her even more. Ever since she'd met him, he'd kept every promise he'd ever made to her. Before last night, that was something she had always admired about her man.

Twenty-Six

The huge 747 Boeing landed at San Jose Airport and Cassie departed her flight dressed in a cream-colored Louis Vuitton dress and matching Louis Vuitton wedges. She thought about the Mary J. song *Sunshine* as the heat beamed down on her, letting her know she would enjoy her little getaway. She wondered if Julia Hernandez would be on the concourse waiting for her; then again, she knew her friend would.

Julia had been a tad bit upset Cassie didn't want to fly straight into Las Vegas, but she let it go after hearing Cassie's reasoning. When she confided she didn't want to be in the same spot where she and her husband had vacationed, it made perfect sense to Julia. The only reason Julia wanted to stay back was because she'd booked Jennifer Lopez at her club and wanted to meet her in person. But nothing was more important than seeing Cassie.

With Cassie being first off the plane from first class, the two women spotted each other instantly. Cassie couldn't miss the pretty Julia Hernandez waiting there on the platform looking like new money. They hugged and Julia spun around, displaying her new hairstyle, wanting to see if Cassie approved.

"Wow, Jules! You make Susan Lucci look like Whoopi Goldberg. I just love it."

"Thank you," Julia replied with a shy grin. "I'm glad you approve."

Cassie really did think the new style fit her bone structure perfectly. The two of them walked through the airport to the valet, where Julia had parked her Bentley coupe. They made small talk about the club and what was going on back in Cassie's hometown. The trip was as usual: Cassie didn't bring any luggage, so their first stop would be all the stores to get whatever she needed. Cascade

Mall was a place where they frequently shopped and spent large sums of money on whatever they desired. Cassie had every dime her husband had left, which was enough for ten lifetimes. She enjoyed spending money but she only went all out when she was on vacation.

Cassie let her mind wander back to her early life. She thought about Tangela, her friend growing up, and how they'd established a relationship. She didn't really have deep emotions for Tangela, though she like the fact that she was very sexually-attracted to her and their very first interaction in the bed had been like magic. Cassie knew at that time, even though she was a virgin, she still wanted a man. She had always wondered if she would become a lesbian, liking the way the soft body of another woman felt. The two of them started having sex more frequently, but when she met Rico, her world changed around.

Things didn't change at first between Cassie and Tangela because the young Rico was still on details with the military and was away most of the time. Tangela filled the void of loneliness she'd felt only being able to talk to Rico on the phone every blue moon or read a letter he sent once a week. She wondered as they entered Cascade whatever had happened to Tangela, since they'd lost contact after her marriage.

Julia snapped her finger in front of Cassie, releasing her from the trance she'd fallen into.

"Are you okay?" Julia asked, hoping Cassie wasn't getting sick from the flight.

"Yes, girl; I'm perfectly fine," she replied as they headed into the Coach store.

"I thought you were getting sick the way you were looking."

"Not at all. I was just thinking about life and how the world can change for a person overnight," Cassie replied.

"I know exactly what you mean," Julia replied, with a quick thought about her own childhood and how it was before she'd come to the States.

"Well, I say we do some shopping like big girls," Julia said, knowing they were in their favorite place.

"You know something? I second that emotion," Cassie replied, giggling.

They left the Coach store with several handbags and hit Macy's, where Cassie picked up some jeans and perfume. She bought several shirts made by DKNY, a St. John pants suit, and something else sexy to wear when they went out. Her black-face credit card didn't come with a spending limit, and the cashiers always did a double-take, checking her out from head to toe when they took the card from her.

They made one more stop in Aldo's, which was Julia's favorite store to buy shoes, other than online. They sat in the cushioned seat and had the sales rep bring box after box filled with different designer shoes. The man helped them try on at least twelve pairs a piece, and he was now getting a little agitated as he'd had women before do this to him and not buy one pair. Before he could say anything, Julia stood up and told him they would take them all. It was a good day for commissions he thought as he went to the desk and gave them the total.

"I'm getting hungry," Julia said.

"Yes; all this walking has made me a little hungry too," Cassie replied.

"I'm not sure what I want though. Did you have anything particular in mind?"

"Not really; maybe a steak."

"Why didn't you shop much?" Cassie asked, changing the subject for a minute.

"I don't know, but I do know I was having so much fun watching you shop and try on different stuff. I always love it when I know you're having a good time," Julia replied.

There was something about her tone, the way she'd said it, that sent chills up Cassie's spin. Julia was a real friend and Cassie loved her very much.

"In my head, while I watched you, you reminded me of Shirley Temple."

"Shirley was white," Cassie joked. They both laughed.

"No, silly; I was thinking you were like a cute little girl in a candy shop. I was actually humming the tune when you were in the dressing room."

"You mean the song that went, *On the good ship Lollipop, it's a sweet trip to the candy shop . . .*"

Julia finished the song and they both laughed again as Julia touched Cassie's hand. Their friendship was very refreshing. The fact that Julia had been supportive of her when her husband was killed was also a plus. Her own parents, who'd never liked Rico for taking their little girl out of Gary, wouldn't drive up to support her during her grieving times. She felt all she had was her sons and Julia, which she felt was all she needed.

Cassie remembered her father telling her he didn't like men in the military. He use to say Rico was going to break her heart, that he probably had kids floating around, half-American/half-Colombian. Cassie's father's belief was all men in the service just wanted to be *serviced*. She was glad she hadn't listened to him or her mother about Rico. For once, they'd both been wrong.

Cassie had long ago stopped listening to her father anyway when she learned the real reason she didn't get the dress she'd wanted for the prom. Her father had gambled off all the money, including the money set aside for her to go to college. It was a funny thing though: the man he didn't like, the man he claimed only wanted to be serviced, had paid for her college and still spoke highly of her father. Rico had explained to her one day when he saw her crying that her father had only tried to provide for the family the best way he knew how.

They settled for Red Lobster and was glad it was still early so the restaurant wasn't that crowded. Julia chose a corner booth in the back where they were the only ones seated.

"You know it's crazy how our husbands have been friends for so many years and it took us this long to connect," Cassie said as they ordered two different wines.

"I agree. If it wasn't for the stupid boxing, you still might not be in my life," Julia said.

The words 'be in my life' played several times in Cassie's mind and she didn't hear Julia's next comment, but Cassie knew she liked the sound of being in her life.

"Really, Cassie, I'm tired of it all. I have managed to put away a lot of money for myself in offshore accounts. When I say a lot, I mean *a lot*."

"I can dig it."

"It's just that one can never walk away from the lifestyle once you get in so deep," Julia said.

Cassie understood exactly where she was coming from. Although Rico only owned a few pieces of real estate, he had still left her sitting pretty well-off. She knew she would never want for anything.

Finally, the food came and Julia sent the waiter back for extra melted butter and another two glasses of wine. As they ate in silence, they continuously looked into each other's eyes, seeing they each contained pain in their hearts. Cassie had always been a firm believer that the eyes were the true windows to the soul. Whatever pain one felt, it would show all right there.

After they ate, they headed to Julia's mansion. In the car, she made reference to how violent things had become with all the changes her husband had made. Cassie was a little lightheaded from all the wine and she was listening to her friend, but she was really ready to lie down and take a nap.

~ Twenty-Seven ~

Dibiase and his right-hand man J.C. had done it. They had moved more work in such a short period of time and had more money than they had ever imagined. They sat in Bernard Jason's office, smoking a blunt while he showed them two lakefront places. He was the same man who Rico had dealt with when he'd bought his two apartment buildings. Bernard didn't care for the smell of the drug, but he was only concerned about a nice commission. The side-by-side places he showed them required them each to come to the closing with one hundred and fifty thousand dollars, which had overnight become chump change to them. Since J.C.'s street-cred was impeccable, they had been moving the dope Rico had left behind like items on sale at a Family Dollar store.

Dibiase liked the places and assured Mr. Jason the money wasn't an issue. Bernard Jason licked his lips hearing those magic words. They could smoke all they wanted. He would just have his secretary fumigate the place after they left. When they left, they got in the new CLS J.C. had just purchased from the Benz dealership. Dibiase hadn't bought a new car yet. Beside the truck his father had given him, he seemed to like riding in rental cars for the time being. He told J.C. about his bottle-popping habits at the clubs and the five-grand shopping sprees he kept going on. He had watched *Goodfellas* enough times to know what brought heat to you when you were the man.

"Say, bro, I've been working on a new connect. You know we're going to need to do something soon," J.C. said.

"Sounds good; hope they ain't trying to rape a-nigga," Dibiase replied.

"Shit, seventeen ain't bad, and fifteen if we do more than twenty at a time."

"Now you're talking, but shit, who are these people? You know prices like that in the Midwest are almost unbelievable."

"I feel you, but these cats are from Miami. I've got a homie who messes with them."

"Okay; well, when all this-shit is over with my pops, we'll check them out. Try to set up a meeting and we will see what these boys have to offer. You know I ain't playing though. Any foul-shit and I'm going to kill me a-muthafucka. I think we cop another fifty and call it a day in the game—in and out."

"I feel that," J.C. replied.

He said he felt Dibiase, but he wasn't really sure if he wanted out so soon. The money they were making could easily put them in a category with Escobar in no time. Dibiase was different. To him, he already had enough money to invest and do something different. He knew his father was dead because he hadn't gotten out the game. What he didn't know was Rico had made several attempts to get out, but the people he was connected to wouldn't let him out—not with his head.

Oliver parked the rental he was in across the street from the Third District Police Station. He knew the intel he had on Torres was correct and that his shift was about to end in ten minutes. Oliver and Dixon focused their high-powered binoculars on the side entrance where they knew the off-duty police exited. It was ten minutes after midnight, and just like the information had said, Torres was out the door, heading to his personal car. He drove a silver Impala with black trim which wasn't much different from his on-duty car.

Oliver followed Torres and was careful not to get too close to him. Torres was a cop on the drug unit, so he knew Torres had training to tail and to spot a tail. He made a pit stop at a Shell gas station on North Avenue, and Oliver and Dixon pulled into the Checkers burger joint across the street, still watching patiently. The smell of the seasoned ground beef crept through the windows of the rental and reminded Oliver he was hungry.

Torres didn't go inside the station. He used his credit card and paid at the pump. Oliver noticed a woman walking up to him as he pumped his gas. The two of them said some words and the woman got inside.

"Ain't this a-bitch," Dixon said.

"He's buying pussy."

Oliver continued looking through the lenses at the short skirt the hooker was wearing. It was an inconvenience but he wasn't going to let the chance to get at Torres go. The route Torres was driving let Oliver know he was still heading home. His file said he was married, but it was odd for a married man to be taking a hooker to his home.

"Maybe his wife is on vacation," Dixon suggested.

"Just don't seem right still. But it doesn't matter if they're freaks or not, we're still finishing this mission."

"Hell yeah!" Dixon replied, seeing the look on his friend's face. "Look, man, please don't beat yourself up too much. You knew Rico better than anyone and you know no one could tell him shit."

"You're right, but it's always hard to lose one of your own."

It was about seven minutes later when Torres pulled the Impala into the driveway of his home. He and the hooker got out, and he used the remote to open the garage. Through the lenses, they could see he had a bed right inside the garage, which was what he most likely used for his hooker fetish. Oliver and Dixon figured his wife may have been ill, or she never used the garage. They scanned the rest of the house from the outside and it looked like he was having some work done. Ladders were on the side of the house and there was piles of boxes stacked containing roofing material. They waited until he closed the garage door and both sprang into action. Oliver popped the trunk on the Lincoln and removed a little black box, while Dixon pulled his mask over his face. The black jackets they wore had yellow letters on the side, G.S., which stood for Goon Squad. It had been a long time since the jackets had been worn. They fit a little snug on both men, but that didn't hinder what they stood for.

Oliver gave the signal using two fingers for Dixon to get ready to move in. Dixon knew exactly what each signal meant. He cocked his weapon, ready for any foul play that might occur. Oliver gave one more signal and Dixon kicked in the door that led to the garage. What a sight to see. Torres was dressed in a woman's nightgown. The hooker was now wearing one of his old uniforms from when he was a beat cop. She looked like she was just preparing to spank him with his nightstick.

"WHAT-THE-FUCK IS GOING ON?" she yelled.

"Get dressed, lady; this has nothing to do with you," Oliver instructed her.

Oliver looked closer at what he thought was a woman and noticed she had a lump the size of a small tangerine protruding from her throat.

"You're damn-skippy it has nothing to do with me," the trans said in a deep voice.

"I'm a-fucking-cop! You can't rob a cop," Torres said.

"Who said anything about a robbery?" Dixon spoke.

It actually worried Torres when he knew the two men weren't there to try to rob him. He was connected, but being connected had its worries. If the big people felt you were out of order, they would send someone to get you in order or complete your expiration date. He was racking his brain trying to figure out what he had done for them to come. His she-male friend dressed quickly and got-the-hell out of there, leaving him to deal with Oliver and Dixon on his own. Dixon didn't have to pat Torres down since he was wearing a see-through gown.

"I guess you're the true definition of blood on the badge," Dixon said.

"I've got sixty grand in my bedroom safe. Take the money and let me live."

"You think this is about money?" Dixon asked.

"No, he knows this isn't that," Oliver added.

They walked him through the door that led to the house. Inside, the kitchen was also being remodeled, like the outside of the house. They sat him at his table, leaving him uncuffed.

"So, I take it you boys aren't here to collect money or a ransom?"

"I'm sure you're well advised on MO's," Oliver said.

"Now that you've got your beams playing connect the dots with my forehead, why don't you tell me what-the-fuck you want? Did I bust somebody I wasn't supposed to?" Torres asked, thinking about his last three busts.

"I'm going to be direct. We are here strictly on the Hammond matter."

Dixon noticed when Oliver said Rico's name that Torres' eyebrows shot up, almost leaving his face. That said he knew a whole lot about what they were there for.

"Hammond? You mean Ricky Hammond, the drug dealer who got gunned down at the church?"

"Don't act like you don't know. We know it was your case," Dixon replied.

"I don't know what rock you boys climbed from under, but this might not be what you want. I want to give you both a little heads-up to get-the-fuck up out my house. I might just have the heart to overlook your little invasion," Torres spat, trying to use a reverse tactic and induce fear in his captors. He didn't scare either of them one bit, and by their tones and looks, he knew it.

"Man, who-the-fuck are you-niggas anyway?"

"I don't think *you* really have the slightest idea who *you're* dealing with," he continued.

Oliver was now getting irritated with Torres and his idle threats, and was ready to apply some pressure the old-school way. He walked around Torres' chair, placing a finger behind his ear.

"Ouch! That-shit hurts! What-the-fuck are you doing, man?" Torres shouted.

"You're done asking question, cop. Now it's my turn to do the questioning," Oliver said. "Yes, I think me and my partner will ask what we want to know, and each breath you take will decide if I believe your answer," he continued, placing his finger back in the same spot.

Torres was really unsure who he worked for. He received a brown envelope containing two grand once a month and any instructions he had to follow were always inside with the money. Usually, he would just be told to drive by a few places and make sure everything was okay. That was until the last brown sack had arrived with ten grand inside and a small note.

"Question one: What do you know outside the reports about Ricky Hammond's death?" Oliver asked.

Torres was quiet until he applied pressure to the same spot.

"WAIT, WAIT, MAN! All I know is he had a hit on him!" Torres exclaimed.

"Okay; we're getting somewhere," Oliver said.

"Keep going," Dixon ordered.

"Look, fellas, all my duty was, was to be a watchdog. I got a payday once a month to ride by certain places and make sure operations were running smooth. The money came once a month, placed in my mailbox. I would do a report, place it back in the same package, and put it back in my mailbox."

"That's it?" Oliver asked.

"It was, until a few weeks ago. When the package arrived, it was extra thick I thought when I felt it. Then I opened it and found ten grand and a note."

"What-the-fuck did the note say?" Dixon asked, getting tired of the runaround.

Torres felt Oliver about to apply pressure.

"Wait! Hold-the-fuck-up! There's no need for violence," he said, holding up his hands. "I scanned the note to my computer in the living room."

"I like you, Torres. We seem to be getting somewhere," Oliver said, standing him up and heading to the living room.

Dixon was a computer expert. He didn't even need Torres to give him his password as he sprayed something that looked like hairspray on the computer keys.

"You're a sick-bastard, Torres. No wonder crime is up in this-damn-city," Dixon said, entering the password he'd found. ILIKEBOYS1 was the password that opened Torres' outdated MacBook. Dixon knew he was going to hate looking through his pictures. He could already imagine what he would find waiting there.

"I'm telling you, I don't have a clue who ordered the hit. All I know was I was supposed to alter the reports. It was ten grand! I've got a daughter in college. What was I supposed to do?" Torres pleaded.

"Alpha-1, come take a look at this," Dixon said, remembering to use code names.

Torres paid attention. He figured these guys were military or CIA. He also remembered Hammond had served in the Navy. He still was unsure who they were, but he was sure they meant business.

Assassination of Rickey Hammond set for Sunday at 2 o'clock at Mt. Zion Baptist Church. My men will need a safe getaway to the highway. Enclosed is a large sum of cash. This is a vital assignment. Make sure it goes as planned.

The note was signed with a stamp, CCC. Oliver understood the position Torres had put himself in when he'd accepted the initial payment. It was clear they were dealing with an organized crime family. He knew Torres was damned if he did and damned if he didn't, but it was a choice he'd made.

Torres felt like things weren't going to end well now, either way. He had to figure out something.

"Wait; I've got something for you," he said, pleading.

"I'll give it to you in exchange for my life. I don't want to die! I didn't kill Ricky Hammond and I don't deserve to die for it!" he continued, pleading for his life.

Oliver hadn't planned on leaving Torres alive, but he wanted to know what he had that he thought would be worth his life.

"So what is it you have?" Oliver asked.

"Do I have your word you won't kill me?" Torres asked.

"My word? You don't know enough about me to think that-shit means anything, so let me see what you got and I'll make a decision."

Torres got up and went to a wall, removing a cheap painting that hid his safe. He entered the combination and removed a tape.

"This is the surveillance tape of the crime scene," he said, handing Dixon the tape that showed everything.

Dixon popped the disc in the side of Torres' computer, watching frame by frame. Oliver knew he was still going to kill Torres because he was in town strictly to avenge his friend's death. Anyone responsible, or had anything to do with it, had to pay.

"This better be good, Torres."

"I think you will find what you need," Torres responded, feeling somewhat relived he wasn't going to die.

Dixon went through the disc, getting to the church. He smiled as he saw Alpha-23 walking from the church dressed to the nines like he always had. The next frame showed two men dressed as nuns pushing baby carriages. They simultaneously dropped their veils to conceal their identities as Hammond came down the steps toward his car. It seemed like Rico was inattentive to his surroundings, which wasn't normal for a SEAL. Once he passed the second gunmen pushing his carriage, he caught on, but it was too late. AK-47 bullets tore his body to shreds right in front of a crowded church.

"I hope this will suffice. Please let me live." Torres continued begging for his life.

The two SEALS ignored him for the moment, watching the disc. Dixon removed a cord from his top pocket, plugged it into Torres' computer, then into his phone. He extracted the footage, saving it to a file on his iPhone.

"See, I told you this would help. I don't know the guys nor did I get a chance to talk to them. I was just ordered to give them an escort to get out of town after they were finished," Torres said.

Oliver still wasn't paying Torres much attention. He could hear him talking, but his words were mumble-jumble as the scene of Rico's murder played over and over. Something wasn't sitting right still, but it was clear Rico was really dead. Oliver kept picturing himself holding Rico's body, instructed him to breathe. He was wishing he'd been at the church that day.

Dixon sensed the anger growing inside Alpha-1 and knew what was about to happen as he watched him walk closer to Torres. As Torres stuck his hand out to shake hands, Oliver broke his wrist with one twist and pulled him close to him, spinning Torres around.

"YOU PROMISED NOT TO KILL ME!" Torres yelled.

Oliver took one more look at this man in a gown and his blood pressure shot through the roof. He wrapped Torres' neck in his arm and began cutting off his air.

"I never promised you-shit. Now, in six seconds, you will begin to lose consciousness, and in ten seconds, your brain will start shutting down your organs from loss of oxygen. At first, it's going to be painless, but in twelve seconds, it will be night-night," Oliver explained.

Things were happening just as he'd explained as Torres' arms reached for Oliver's face, but the seconds passed so quickly, his body went limp before he could attempt any type of self-defense. Oliver dropped Torres to the floor and picked up his home phone, dialing 9-1-1. He never spoke to the operator, just left the phone off the hook.

Dibiase met with his father's attorney to talk about the purchase of the houses on Lake Drive. Jimmy Toran had handled all Rico's affairs when he was alive, so Dibiase thought he was the person to see. They spent about an hour chopping-it-up, and Dibiase wondered why, when he brought up his father's demise, the lawyer changed subjects. He figured they were close and Toran was taking it hard like everyone else.

When he left there, he had a better understanding of buying property and knew he had to call J.C. to fill him in on what was what. When he got back in his rental, he called J.C. and told him both places had heated indoor pools and wine cellars. Dibiase laughed when J.C. asked him if they had greenhouses so he could grow his own bud.

"Look, man, the one you're getting's got a bar bigger than Club Escape in the basement, so your-ass can pop bottles at your own spot," Dibiase said.

"Now that's what a-muthafucka's talking about. I might name it Club Crib," he replied, laughing.

They talked for about five minutes and Dibiase started thinking about Camille, ready to get home.

"Well, my man, we will chop-it-up tomorrow. I need to call the boys since I haven't heard from them all day," Dibiase stated.

J.C. knew he was talking about Rico's partners since they had given them the nickname 'the boys'.

"Okay, one, bro," J.C. said before ending the call.

J.C. heard Don D. cough off the hit and reached for the blunt.

"You're getting old, my-nigga." He laughed.

"This-shit right here is that real-shit," Don D. said, covering up the fact he was a little upset Dibiase and J.C. were buying new cribs and no one had said anything to him.

By rights, he should be getting a third crib next door to them since he worked damn-near twenty-four hours a day moving the work. He wasn't really feeling the club scene now and wanted to go back to the spot to think. He knew J.C. was meeting with a few out-of-town players from Benton Harbor, but he figured, since his cousin was doing everything else on his own or with Dibiase, he could do the meet-and-greet as well.

"What, my-nigga, you want to go to the spot and miss out on all that-pussy that's going to be courtside tonight?" J.C. asked, puzzled.

He knew the place was going to be packed since the Bucks had just beat the Golden State Warriors. The players would be there and that would bring out the-bitches.

"Yeah; I'm just not feeling it tonight. Must be that Pizza Hut," Don D. lied.

"I got you, cuz," J.C. said, busting a quick left, heading to the spot.

Taking Don D. back would make him a little late, but he had VIP status and wouldn't have to wait in the long line that would be outside the club.

~ Twenty-Eight ~

Mickey was sitting in the spot with Don D. He was getting high every chance he got, trying to deal with his problems. The bruises on his face was from the Feds who had visited his apartment the night before. He'd lied to Don D., telling him he'd had a car accident on the freeway. He didn't have any idea what Hawk and his partner were really after. He'd given them enough information on Peanut to make a bust and they hadn't made a move. Hawk was hitting him, mentioning something about some blueprints, but with each blow Mickey took, he was losing consciousness.

They said something about Rico's personal belongings, wanting to know where they were kept, and if either of his sons had safes in their homes that may have contained anything their father had left behind. Dibiase was his blood and Little Ricky was square as could be. Mickey had no intention of telling them anything about either one of his nephews. If they had asked about J.C. or Don D., he might not have been so reluctant to say something, but neither one of them was their focus.

Mickey had been spending a little more time than usual with Don D., and Don really didn't mind. He knew Mickey was on that-shit, but he still felt Mickey was an old-school player. Besides that, he still wasn't cool with the way his pay scale was set up. He wasn't getting a new home or driving a new Benz, so he continued to let his friendship with Uncle Mickey blossom.

Mickey had a lot of old-time stories that Don D. liked listening to. He told him how he'd gotten in the game and how he'd pimped on the-bitches. Mickey had mingled in L.A. with porn stars, movie stars, and basketball players like they were normal people. Don loved to hear how they'd all get high and spend millions on dumb-shit. Don always paid close attention to every story. Now, he was feeling Uncle

Mickey was cool enough for him to open up to and tell him some things that were on his mind.

"You know something, School? I haven't really been feeling this-shit lately," Don D. said.

"What do you mean, young blood? You-bitching and you're clocking this paper like a human ATM machine? You're like Burger King, nigga. Ain't you having it your way?" Mickey asked.

"It's always a good look to a person on the outside looking in, but on the inside, the pay scale isn't matching the work scale."

"Elaborate, young blood," Mickey said, taking a hit of his laced joint.

"For starters, my cuz is busting out with new Benzes and both D. and J. went and put money down on beachfront cribs. I'm up here in a spot with enough dope to land me in a cell next to Pablo. I feel something is going to have to change, or I'm going to have to change. Shit, School, I could have stayed back at the crib for this-shit," he continued, smoking his own blunt that wasn't laced.

"You thinking about going back to Baltimore? The Wire is dead, nigga. That place is burned up."

"I feel you on that note, but this poker change a-nigga's letting me make ain't worth the risk." He paused for a second.

"If I hadn't left a few stankin'-bodies up there, I might have considered it, but it's a wrap for me up there," Don D. said, telling a little more than he should have.

"Damn, you had to merc a few-niggas, huh?" Mickey asked curiously.

"A-bitch tried to set me up for a one-eight-seven with some bangers, and shit, School, it was either them or me."

"Hell yeah, young blood, you did right considering the circumstances. It had to be them because you're right here with me, firing up this good-shit. Wanna hit mine?"

"I'm good, School. I knew the-bitch had a-nigga when I started fucking with her. The-nigga she was fucking-around with was a gang-banging-ass-nigga. He wasn't on no real paper, but she was really only sucking on my-dick trying to put me in the middle of a jack-move. I figured that-shit out though."

"You know these-bitches out here ain't to be trusted. From me to you, a-nigga's downfall in this street life has always been a-bitch."

"I know that's right. If it wasn't for my man, who was a rival banger, I might not be here right now, but when I got that dime he dropped, I was prepared, and when them-fools came knocking . . . pow, pow," Don D. said, making a gun symbol with his thumb and index finger.

"That's it, young blood. Always be prepared to peel a-nigga's cap."

Hawk and his partner were outside the spot, listening to the whole conversation, making notes about what they'd just heard. They figured the beating they'd put on Mickey Hammond was what he'd needed to get his fat-ass in gear. Squales was already prepared to run the name Pork Chop in the national database for gang members. If the man had ever been arrested on any charges, they would find out who he was.

Hawk was just happy they had the first insight on Dibiase and his crew. The word on the street was Rico's seed was moving a lot of dope. The dope they were moving had to be product Rico had left behind. Hawk and Squales were smart enough to know, if Rico had made a copy of some paperwork he wasn't supposed to, it was probably somewhere close to where that dope had been hidden. They had bosses to answer to and they knew they needed the information their bosses were requiring.

The CCC didn't play. If they wanted something, they got it. They both knew they needed to crack this thing wide open or they would be dead. They'd both overheard the dispatch from their homes last night about Detective Torres' horrible death. It wasn't a mistake Torres was dead, and if they didn't produce, it wouldn't be a mistake when their bodies were found.

~ Twenty-Nine ~
Rico's Last Phone Call

When Rico and Cassie returned from Vegas, he made a point to buy a burn phone. He knew the call he had to make was inevitable and had to be done. As soon as he got a chance, he went to his basement office and dialed the many numbers it took to reach Colombia. Draco Hernandez looked at the number and knew exactly who it was. He answered the call on the second ring.

"'Ello, me friend," he said in his heavy accent.

"Hello, Mr. Hernandez. By now I know you know what has transpired here. All I'm asking is that my family remain safe," Rico said.

"Mr. Hammond, I had high hopes for you, but I guess the American saying that every dog has their day is true," he replied.

"Well, your son has made his mind up, and I'm not even going to sweat it. I know the money I made the family doesn't matter, but as long as my family is safe, your secrets are safe. If anything happens to any member of my family, I have left certain papers with a certain person who will expose you and the whole organization."

"I see," Draco replied.

"You are a smart man, Mr. Hammond. I knew that when I first laid eyes on you. That was why I chose you in the first place. I can assure you, I'm giving you my word, nothing will happen to your family."

"Thank you."

They ended the call abruptly, both parties satisfied with the outcome.

Rico lay back in his chair, thinking about that moment many years ago, when Draco ha approached him with his offer. He'd figured Draco wanted to use his military clearance to move drugs, but that wasn't the case at all. When he offered him a large sum of cash, Rico was reluctant. He knew he could transport the kingpin's dope, but it wasn't what he really wanted to do. The fact that Cassie was pregnant made him listen to the offer more intently. When he found out all he had to transport back was a titanium tube, it was a done deal. What he didn't expect was his curiosity to get the best of him and his wanting to know what was in the tube worth that amount of currency.

When Rico arrived back in the States, instead of going to Vegas and just doing as he was paid to do, his first stop was St. Louis to see an old friend. Big Meech was his high school partner and owned a welding company that had been quite prosperous. When Meech agreed to open the tube, Rico couldn't believe his eyes at what was inside. Blueprints mapped out underground tunnels under California, Mexico, and Arizona that led to a hub underground city in Nevada. It was obvious, since the government had recently stopped letting the cartels transport by submarine, that the CCC had figured out a new way. The blueprints showed everything—plumbing schematics, lighting schematics, and plans to build sleeping corridors. It was top-flight planning that had to have cost hundreds of millions of dollars. Rico knew it would be manifested if the blueprints made it to Vegas. He had no choice but to deliver them.

When he made it to Vegas, he wasn't prepared for what Draco's son Tito had proposed to him. Rico accepted the money and accepted being the first black man made by a Colombian cartel. That was his entry into the game. Now the same entry was his exit. Tito was about to unmake Rico.

Thirty

J.C. sat with Don D., his cousin and right-hand man. He had made the call to his connect in Peoria, and the meet-and-greet was set. Dibiase was on his way so things could get situated and the final decision could be made. J.C. was confident the street player who went by the name Shorty Mac could provide what they needed to make their last and final run, according to Dibiase. The Peoria connect had shown up first, arriving before Dibiase made it. Shorty and two of his boys had made their way to the spot. They had their own weed, which they shared, and J.C. had to admit it was some quality-shit. They all sat back and chopped-it-up, waiting for Dibiase.

Ten minutes later, the rental pulled up with the boss man wanting to get it over with so he could call Oliver back. Oliver had said he had some important news for him and that was really more important to Dibiase than meeting a new connect. Dibiase left the money in the trunk, wanting to make sure there wasn't going to be any foul play. He knew J.C. had said the connect was on the level, but there was nothing like making sure on which level he was talking about.

Dibiase liked to remain low key, which was one reason he hadn't splurged on a new whip, or been seen in the mall with stacks of money buying clothes. The word was already on the street that Rico had risen from the dead, meaning the streets knew his product was moving even though he was gone. It was like the Blue Magic epidemic and it would be no time before it was linked back to him and J.C., so he had to be extra careful.

Dibiase entered his spot and the smoke was thick and the weed smelled good. He observed the new connect and his crew, and they seemed normal—but seeming and being were two different things. It was a lot of money they were spending. Hell, Denzel Washington could act normal for that kind of loot. When Dibiase walked in, J.C.

introduced him and Shorty to each other. The two shook hands and Shorty offered Dibiase his personal blunt. Dibiase accepted, liking the way it smelled, and the two of them hit it off right away. They talked for a second and Shorty sent one of his men out to their rental. When he came back inside, he was carrying two duffle bags.

"This-shit here is like that-shit you've already been slanging. It can stand a double-up," Shorty said.

He busted open a brick and showed Dibiase the work.

"Looks like fiyah and desire," Dibiase replied.

He looked at Don D. and tossed Don the keys to his rental. J.C. removed his Tech-9 and followed Don to the door. Don went outside and returned with a duffle bag too. Shorty saw the money and smiled.

"Now I see you're a straight-up businessman and I like that," Shorty said, removing a counting machine from under the dope.

They plugged it in and went to work while Dibiase and his crew opened every brick on each corner. It was something he had seen his father do on many occasions. When he asked Rico why he did that, his father had said people always open the center, and if someone was out to gank you, the real would be in the center surrounded by the drywall, or whatever they used.

"Hey, Dibiase," Shorty said, wrapping back up the last bundle.

"What it do?"

"No disrespect, but the machines were to make sure we were all on the same page. Your money wasn't short even a dollar, and to me, that speaks volumes."

"I don't play any games, brother," Dibiase replied.

"I see. I heard about your father too. I met him once in Detroit at a Players Ball; real stand-up dude. Sorry for your loss."

"Thanks, Shorty."

He meant that. It was real cool Shorty had met Rico, and it seemed the two of them had respect for each other.

"They find out what happened?" Shorty asked, knowing it had probably been a hit.

"I never expected the police to do any police work, but I got the-shit handled," Dibiase replied, sealing the last Ziploc bag with the dope.

"Cool, yeah, cool. Please let me know if there is anything me and my people can do. I feel we're family now and a family that prays together sprays together," Shorty said, standing up.

"We have to be getting back. Hate to count and run, but I've got some folks flying in from Atlanta tomorrow and I need to be there."

"One, man. Drive safely, or slap a Brinks' magnet on the side of the car," J.C. said, laughing.

They all shook hands, and J.C. and Don D. retrieved their semiautomatic weapons, making sure their new friends got to their vehicle safely.

Dibiase made sure J.C. and Don D. were straight before he left. He told Don D. he wanted to talk to him soon before he finally walked out the door.

J.C. was in the mood to club-hop and asked Don D. if he wanted to roll. Don declined; he had something else on his mind and didn't have to go to no cheesy club to get it.

☙ ✿ ❧

It took Don D. about forty minutes and he was off the exit in Racine, heading to his baby's crib. He had helped Doll move into a single-family home off Washington Street and helped her furnish the place. His only requirement was she get cable and he would do everything else. He pulled up in front of the house and took his heater from under the seat, placing it in his waistband. He actually hated the neighborhood, but the whole little city was a ghetto. It reminded him of his hometown. He had a key and let himself in.

Doll was sitting on the new leather couch naked, smoking a blunt, waiting on him. Her hair was pulled back in a ponytail hanging past her shoulders and her shaved-pussy was exposed for his attention.

"Hey, baby; that was quick. Are you hungry?" she asked.

"Yeah, I'm starving, but if you think I want some food, that-shit ain't got the nourishment I'm looking for," he replied, smiling.

Don walked over to her and hit her blunt before kissing her.

"Well, damn, should I show you to the bedroom?"

"I think I can beat you there," he playfully said, running toward her room.

By time she'd hit the blunt one more time and met him in the room, he was already stripped down and waiting. Doll didn't waste any time. She wanted the-dick just as bad as Don D. wanted the-pussy. She was already soaked from his kiss.

"Oh shit, baby; you're deep in this-pussy. Come on, big daddy, keep it in me . . ."

"Damn, this-pussy's good!"

"I LOVE THE WAY YOU FUCK-ME, BIG DADDY. COME ON, HIT THIS PUSSY!" she cried out.

Doll always acted like she was losing her mind when they had sex. It wasn't just an act. He was the only man who had ever hit her G-spot and he made her body do things no other man had done before. She felt really bad knowing it was going to be over soon for him, but she wanted all the-dick she could get before that moment arrived.

"You like that stroke, huh? That-pussy's like an Ethiopian kid, hungry for that-dick. Tell me, baby, is this my-pussy? Is this daddy's-pussy or what?"

Doll liked to play tough when he questioned her. She knew when she didn't answer his questions he would squeeze her hips and pound her guts like a vigilante. She loved it rough and he loved to give it to her that way. The curve that bent to the right made his enormous head massage the right walls, and after about twenty strokes, she would squirt all over the place, leaving the sheets and mattress soaked, having to be flipped over.

"You ain't answering daddy, huh," he asked, long-stroking her, making her clench the sheets tightly.

He was making her savor every inch now, hitting it hard on the way in, holding it for a second on the in-stroke. It was what she was waiting on.

"Come on, daddy. Yeah, this-pussy's yours, it's all yours, now give it to me."

The grand finale followed and her juices exploded, wetting the bed and his torso. Don fell to her side as she slid her face onto his chest, enjoying the smell of the Issey Miyake he always sported.

'Shame, shame, shame,' she thought, 'that all that good-dick would be six-feet deep soon, fucking the top of his casket.'

Don didn't know how it had happened, he just knew he had fallen in love with Doll. She was a bad-bitch, but it didn't have anything to do with her looks or how good her-pussy felt to him. She was a challenge. She wasn't like any-other-chick he had fucked-around with. Doll's feisty ways drove him crazy. He figured now was as good a time as any to fill her in on the bar incident.

"Doll Baby," he said, leaning over to check his phone.

She loved when he called her that.

"Yes, honey," she replied, stroking the thin hairs on his chest.

"I forgot to tell you something. Last time I was here and waiting for you at the one bar you go to sometimes, your little homegirl was there as well," he said, thinking it might not be a good idea after all.

"What about it?" she asked, knowing that hoes could be backstabbers.

Her mind was already set to whup her friend's ass if she'd tried to backdoor her for the paper. The-dick she could have, but the paper was off limits.

"Just that ol' girl seemed adamant on trying to make me believe you were from B-more, where I'm from, not Boston."

Don D. had her attention more so now than when he'd been stroking her with his nine inches. Her friend was on some-bullshit that could have fucked-up all the plans. Doll knew she would kill the-bitch if she fucked-anything-up.

"You mean that baldheaded-bitch-Cedilla? She's up to her old tricks again, I see, trying to go behind a-bitch and fuck-with my-nigga."

"Listen, Doll Baby, none of that matters. You know I've only got eyes for you. I'm in love with you," he confessed.

'This is fucked-up,' Doll Baby thought. 'Here this-nigga is in love, my homegirl's trying to fuck-my-future-up, and neither one of them means a-fuckin'-thing to me.'

Bringing down his empire was going to be like taking candy from a baby with a group of fat kids as your back up. She wondered where that cliché had come from because, every baby she'd known with some candy, you damn-near had to pry their little fingers apart until you broke them to get the candy.

"You listen. I'm going to tell you this and it's something I really don't like to talk about. Don, I really am from Baltimore, true enough. I was born there, but I left at the age of fourteen," Doll said as she paused, getting her acting together.

"I was raped by a man who didn't use a condom, and when I got sick, I thought he had given me AIDS. I had no idea he had gotten me knocked-up because I was born with a disease that didn't allow my eggs to be fertilized," she continued, making her eyes start to tear up.

"Damn, baby, I didn't know." he replied, listening and feeling her pain.

"I moved to Boston because my parents tried to make me keep the baby, saying it must be a blessing from God. That was bullshit! I knew since I was the only child that they wanted a grandchild. I wasn't having a baby by a rapist, no matter what, so I went to live with my Aunt Glory. When I got there, she agreed to help me with the abortion," Doll claimed now, letting the tears actually roll down her cheeks.

She was good; so good, she could have been nominated for an Academy Award for her performance.

"After that whole little episode, I tried to disown the city and didn't ever want anybody to know I was from that dreadful-ass-place."

"I feel ya, baby; it is a fucked-up city," Don replied, mad at himself for bringing up any of it.

Doll knew she had him right where she wanted him.

"Can we just go to sleep, baby?" she asked as she nestled in his arms.

Don D. woke up earlier than usual and saw Doll was still asleep. He thought about last night and all the things she had told him. He knew she'd had a rough life and was mad he'd pushed her to relive the terrible tragedy she'd been through. He kissed her on the forehead and slipped on his jeans. Before he left to head back to Milwaukee, he left her a stack of bills on the nightstand. He knew she would do some shopping since she always made sure to let him know shopping was a woman's therapy.

Doll opened her eyes as soon as she heard his car pull off. She hadn't been sleep at all. She was very upset at Cedilla and had decided to handle it. She looked at the clock and knew she still had time. She slipped on an Ecko fitted jogging suit and tied her hair in a ponytail. She looked out her front window to make sure the coast was clear then made her way to her car. It only took ten minutes to make it to Henry Street where Cedilla lived. Doll figured she would still be sleeping since she knew Cedilla was a last-minute-chick. She was late to her job at the hospital at least four times a week.

When she got to the door, she knew Cedilla kept her spare key under the mat like she lived in Beverly Hills. Doll removed the key and walked in. She saw Cedilla had her work uniform on the ironing board pressed and neat, ready for when her alarm clock went off. Doll walked in her bedroom and there she was, sleeping soundly. Her naked body was sprawled across her bed with the fan in the window on high. Cedilla must have felt the presence of someone there because she opened her eyes.

It was too late. Doll had removed her twenty-five automatic and let off two rounds, piercing Cedilla's chest. It was a done deal as her life slipped away instantly. Her eyes remained open and still as Doll turned and left.

~ Thirty-One ~

Dibiase didn't hear from Oliver until the next morning. He and Dixon called him from the Denny's a few blocks from his house and asked him to come there. Dibiase hurried out of bed, kissing Camille and letting her know he would be back shortly.

Oliver and Dixon had been up all night, pooling all their resources to help them with what they needed. They found out who the car the hitmen were in belonged to and traced that back to an address in Arizona. When they pulled the city tax records, they found out the same owner of the car also had a residence in Las Vegas. When they zeroed in on the disc, they were able to get a pinpoint facial shot of the driver, who was also one of the shooters, and he also came back as residing in Arizona with a second home in Vegas. The National Security database gave them a name when they forwarded the picture on the driver.

When Dibiase walked in, a server approached him trying to seat him, but he told her he was good when he saw Oliver and Dixon at a corner booth sipping coffee. He walked over the booth where they were.

"Top of the mornin', fellas."

"Good mornin', youngin'," Oliver said.

"Top of the mornin' to you," Dixon replied.

"We called you because we wanted you to know what we have," Oliver said, adding another sugar to his cup. The coffee was almost gone, but he needed the rush.

"Okay, shoot," Dibiase instructed.

"First of all, there is something you need to hear from Dixon," Oliver suggested.

"We checked you out as well," Dixon said. "Now don't trip. It's just a precaution since we know you took over where Rico left off. It benefits us to know what we're up against. Whatever goes on out here in the world, you can trust and believe satellites are set up to capture everything. The government can't act on certain issues because it's a violation of civilians' constitutional rights to eavesdrop. But they have the information and it's all in a huge database. Like the O.J. shit; you think he's doing time now for that-bullshit in Vegas? Well, it was a ploy because they knew what really happened and couldn't provide proof."

"Damn, that's some serious-shit. So, what did you find out about me? I'm just curious to know," Dibiase asked.

"For starters, the Feds are on to you. There are two agents, a Hawk and a Squales, who have been investigating you. They penned you in the system as a kingpin. When we cross-referenced the agents, we found out they were on a countrywide sting that ended in Colombia. They were supposed to be there to extract a drug lord by the name of Draco Hernandez. The thing that had us baffled was, at that time was when our whole SEALS unit, including your father, was in Colombia as well. We were on some Black Hawk mission that was bogus."

Dibiase was trying to bring his memory up to par to see if he remembered his father ever mentioning the name Draco. He couldn't remember, but he knew for sure he had heard the last name Hernandez before, from his mother and his father.

"One thing we found out is the Feds have an informant who's working on you and your crew. It's obvious they have enough information to move on you and some other player from some projects, but the informant wasn't named in the article and that was puzzling as well. For some odd reason, the Feds haven't moved," Dixon explained.

Dibiase was feeling a little paranoid knowing that, as careful as he was, he still wasn't under the radar. He wondered if it had anything to do with the way J.C. was handling business and running around being so flamboyant and frugal with the proceeds. He knew he would retain a lawyer sometime this afternoon, just as a precautionary measure.

"I see it this way, Dibiase," Oliver began speaking now. "These people are searching for something, and in my opinion, it's more than a few frickin' kilos of cocaine. Otherwise, you and your crew would already be looking to post bond. So my thought is, whoever this informant is, has to be someone close to you, someone who can get you to open up about personal conversations to help them locate what they are looking for," Oliver continued.

Dibiase ran his fingers through his hair, wondering who-in-the-hell could be dropping-the-dime on him. Who would be close to him and set him up at the same time with the Feds? He knew J.C. and Don D. were going to take it hard, but he had to shut down the operation right after this meeting concluded. It was too detrimental. He couldn't risk spending his life in the joint, leaving his mother, brother, and his future wife and child. Dibiase couldn't believe it was just his second shipment and he was hot already. He really needed to know who this confidential informant was.

"We can't figure out what the Feds are looking for, but what is apparent is, whatever they're looking for, it's the reason your father was killed," Oliver said.

"Quick question," Dixon said. "Did you and your father discuss anything before his demise? We know he knew the hit was issued, so we wondered if he gave any last instructions to you?"

"No; I didn't even know about the dope he left. He said he was going to St. Louis to see a friend and he was getting out the game soon. That was all he said to me!" Dibiase exclaimed. "Wait a second.

He did spend some time with his brother, my Uncle Mickey. The two of them were close. Unc was the one who gave me the dog tags and the key to where the dope was kept."

"You mentioned something about the CCC?" Dibiase asked. "What exactly does that stand for?"

"CCC stands for the Colombian Cocaine Cartel, which is headed by Draco and run by his son in Las Vegas. It is rumored they are the biggest family in the world and that ninety percent of the families buy from them," Dixon said, scrolling through his text messages at the same time.

"We still can't figure out what they want, but in the meantime, we need you and your crew to put a lid on the business. I don't think they're looking to pick you guys up—at least not right now," Oliver said.

Dibiase was smart. He wasn't a new jack to the game, as he had watched his father move and remain safe for many years. He understood some of what was going on and what his father's friends were saying to him. He really needed to talk to his mother. He hadn't really talked to her since she'd returned from her vacation. He stood up and told Oliver and Dixon he would call them in a few hours.

When Dibiase left, he headed straight to his old home to visit his mother. He loved her very much and hoped her life was getting back on track. He knew his father had been her first and only love, and losing him was a tough pill to swallow. He parked his rental in the driveway, not getting out yet. He sat and stared at the Jag his father had last driven. He figured, when it was all over, maybe instead of buying a car, he would just drive Rico's old car. It was still in tiptop shape. Sometimes when he woke up in the morning, it seemed like he could walk downstairs and his father would be sitting at the kitchen table with his normal bowl of oatmeal, reading the stock section of the paper. But he knew that was never going to happen again.

He still had his key and was glad to see his mother hadn't changed the locks. He let himself in and heard the sounds of Sade playing. The smell of food saturated the house like she was in the kitchen cooking a feast for an army. He didn't stop in the kitchen first. He took the flight of stairs up to go check on his old room. He didn't know if he wanted the memory or not, but he figured he might as well go see it one more time. He stood in the doorway, looking at the last poster he'd hung. It was a life-size poster of Jordan hitting the game winner over Russell. He felt a hand on his shoulder and turned to see his beautiful mother standing there. They gave each other a tight embrace and she kissed him on the cheek. It was the first time since he left the funeral that he'd actually cried. Cassie embraced him and let him know it was perfectly okay to release his buried pain.

"Let it out, son. I know you miss him; so do I," she said, wiping a tear of her own.

"I just can't believe he's gone. I can't for the life of me believe someone shot my father."

"I know, baby; I know how you feel."

"Come downstairs; I've got something for you," she insisted.

Cassie had baked a caramel apple pie she knew was his favorite. For some reason, she had sensed this moment was coming. Maybe it was a mother's intuition, but she was prepared as always. Dibiase washed his hands in the kitchen sink, using a little of the Dawn dish soap.

"So, you never told me how your trip was," he said, making small talk.

"It was okay. Not the same without your father, but I had a nice time," she replied, putting a slice of warm pie in front of him. "Now, enough about me. How are things coming with Camille and the new place?"

"Things are going great," he replied. His answer was kind of short.

"Dibiase, look at me. I don't have any hard feelings about you moving out. I understand probably better than anyone. You're so much like him and I know Rico probably would have done the same thing, needing his space."

"I knew you would understand," he replied, cutting a second slice. "Momma, there's something I need to tell you. I feel like this family doesn't need any more surprises.

"First off, let me start by telling you I have been hustling in the streets. Pops left me something and I decided to move it. I know, financially, you're good, but if there is anything you need, let me know. I've got it."

"That's another thing, son."

"What's that?"

"I always knew you would do this—follow in his footsteps—more so than your brother. I could tell by the way, when you saw him counting money, your eyes would light up like the Fourth of July. But you can plainly see where the lifestyle leaves you. I personally think it's selfish, especially since you have a person like Camille by your side. His death was one incident and I'm glad we didn't suffer any other casualties. I'm sure he had us protected—God rest his soul—but, son, it doesn't mean you'll end up as lucky as he did."

Dibiase respected his mother's opinion. He knew she was speaking from her heart, not being judgmental of him. He truly loved her for her wisdom.

"Another thing—the Feds are on to me already," he confessed.

"What? The Feds already? How can you be so sure?" she asked.

She wasn't lame to the game. She had been married to one of the biggest kingpins in the Midwest and knew how a lot of it went.

"Two of Pops friends are here investigating his demise—"

"Wait, wait a minute," Cassie stopped her son in midsentence. She needed to make sure she had just heard what she had heard.

"Yeah; Charlie Oliver and Glen Dixon, a couple of his SEAL partners. They're taking this really hard and wanted to come make sure there was no foul play on anyone's part."

They both paused and looked at the television screen on the side of the fridge. The news had done a newsbreak to talk about two murders that had happened in the last twenty-four hours. One was a Milwaukee detective found with his neck broken and the other was a young girl shot to death in her Racine home.

Cassie knew who both men were her son had mentioned. Charlie was a close friend and she hadn't really seen him since Dibiase was young. She had thought the service had turned him into a mental patient and he was locked up in some crazy home. But one thing she knew for sure: if he found out anything about someone being responsible, they would wish he was in some mental home somewhere. He loved Rico like a brother, and she was most certain Glen Dixon did too. They'd had a pact: once a SEAL always a SEAL.

"That's how I know the Feds are on to me; Pops' friends found out. They said the Feds have a CI who is dropping a dime, but they can't figure out why the Feds aren't moving in."

"Did they say who the informant was?" she asked.

Cassie had a pretty good idea who the informant was. She had a gut feeling and hoped-like-hell she was wrong.

"No, but they think Pops was gunned down because he had some type of leverage on the cartel family. They are still trying to figure out what that leverage was."

"Son, these streets are no joke. I think your father realized the game was changing, or should I say the players in the game were changing, for the worst. Honor among thieves doesn't exist. No matter how many people he helped or made their dreams come true, there is no loyalty out there in the underworld," Cassie insisted.

It was the first time he had ever heard his mother talk like she was hood. She saw the way he raised his eyebrows and smiled.

"Hey, I wasn't always a mother, you know. I am still Cassie Hammond, first lady to Kingpin Rico Hammond." She smiled again.

"You know we need to plan a family getaway, go on a cruise or something. Me, you, and Camille, and Little Rickey if we can pry him away from that-damn-barbershop for a day," Dibiase said, feeling better now that he had spent this time with his mother.

Dibiase had a lot on his plate, but talking to her made him feel like he could deal with anything that came his way. He stood, kissed her, and told her to seriously think about where she wanted to go for their next vacation.

"Okay, I will, but be careful out there, son, and if you or that beautiful woman of yours needs anything, call me."

"Okay, Mother. I love you."

"I love you more," she said, wiping the lipstick smudge from the side of his face.

Soon as she saw he had cleared the driveway, she retreated to Rico's office in the basement. She hadn't really been down there since he died. She didn't even wash clothes because the washer and dryer were too close to his office, so she used Jack's pick-up service to avoid the memory. But his office was where he'd had a private, secured line installed that ran off a separate server. It was completely untraceable. When she pushed the redial button, just as she suspected, his brother Mickey answered. Cassie just hung up the phone.

J.C. was sitting in the kitchen with Donna and her daughter. He was finishing his omelet and glass of rose Moet she had fixed him. Donna was at the sink, washing her baby girl's hair, while J.C. made call after call and smoked blunt after blunt. She had never seen him so busy but she never got involved when he worked. He had told her they were moving soon and she was happy about that. She was hoping a ring would be coming as well, but she didn't push the marriage thing. Sometimes, when something wasn't broke, you didn't have any business trying to fix it.

"Yo, my man, I need to see you and Fatz at nine a.m. sharp!" J.C. spat into the phone.

He hadn't spoken with Dibiase yet and had no idea the Feds were in arms-length of their operation. He made several more phone calls, talking to people with names Donna wasn't familiar with, and gave each person on the other end thirty-minute gaps between meeting times. She listened as she wrapped the towel around her daughter's hair like a turban. She kissed her baby and told her to go in the living room and get under the dryer.

J.C. had love for only two females and both were the females he lived with. It had taken years for the nightmares of what his mother had done to him to stop invading his sleep. Every once in a while, he'd still have one about the incident that had taken place in his kitchen when he was a teenager. He hated to have them because not once did he ever come out victorious.

He remembered that one because his mother Teresa had held him down while Tim groped his body, searching for the money he had saved. He was on the floor screaming and kicking, begging her to stop helping Tim. At the time, he'd felt he was going to die because he knew his mother was the same-bitch who'd let his sister die. She was so engrossed in giving some-cracker a head-job for a measly twenty bucks to feed her habit, and now she was letting him be violated by her crackhead-pimp-boyfriend. The words she said kept jogging in circles in his mind.

"James, stop fighting it! It will be over in a second. All you have to do is give us the money."

"STOP IT! STOP IT!" he screamed, *"I NEED MY MONEY FOR COLLEGE!"* J.C. remembered saying.

College and playing ball had been his dream, but he knew that monkey on their backs didn't care if he made it out the eighth grade.

"So, you want to be a smart-nigga, huh? You want an ed-u-ma-cation, huh, lil nigga?" Tim said, putting his hands down the front of J.C.'s pants.

"Well, where I'm from, a smart-nigga is a dead-nigga," Tim continued, groping his frail body for the money.

For years, the dreams had haunted him, and sometimes made him wonder how he'd chosen the life of being the monkey-provider for people like Teresa and Tim. He felt it was payback for the way his life had turned out, or that the streets owed him the money they'd taken from him when he was a kid. Maybe a smart-nigga was a dead-nigga; just maybe Tim was right. It didn't matter now because he was in the game. He'd been raised in the game and the game owed him. It was his mother, his father, his cousin, and friend; the streets were family for him. James was dead, he was the smart-nigga, and J.C. was the rebirth—the nigga with money, a bad-bitch, and a fly Benz, who'd just put a down payment on a mansion. He felt with the new connect the sky was the limit. Nothing was going to stop him and Dibiase from being the-baddest-muthafuckas ever to push product.

He had a quick thought about Tim and thought about how they'd found his body in three separate garbage cans. They were piecing him back together like a Mr. Potato Head for months. They never found his right leg, but they had enough to identify his body. He knew his mother was in prison for what had happened to Tim. He hadn't wanted to know the details of her arrest, but he was glad he'd never had to see her face again. She was nothing like Cassie. That James-shit was over; it was all about J.C. Hammond now.

Donna had gone in the bedroom, hoping he would come join her for some extracurricular activity in their king-size bed. J.C. had been so busy, it had been three days since he'd given her some-dick. When she called him in, he didn't want to have sex. Sex wasn't on his mind at the moment. All he could think about was their future and getting paid.

"I'm good, baby," he said, looking at her naked body.

Donna didn't know how to take the 'I'm good' comment. J.C. had never turned down her-pussy.

"You okay, bae?" she asked.

"Yeah, I'm straight; just got a lot on my mind. Nothing more, nothing less."

"Okay, bae; just relax," she replied, getting up and slipping her clothes back on to go check on her daughter under the dryer.

~ Thirty-Two ~

Cassie had thought long and hard, and her mind was made up. She jumped in her car to take a ride, knowing exactly where her destination was taking her. She picked up her phone knowing it was late, but the West Coast was two hours behind, so it wouldn't be that bad there. She needed to speak to someone, and Julia was actually the only real friend she had. Being the wife of a kingpin didn't allow much time for friends. Of course people wanted to be friends, but she could never trust their intentions. She was glad Julia picked up the phone right away.

"Did I wake you?" Cassie asked, hearing the muffled sound in her friend's tone.

"It's okay, mamacita; is everything okay? It's got to be late-as-heck there," Julia responded.

"Not really, girl, but it's going to be shortly . . ." Cassie paused. "You know how I get down and something has me on a little mission tonight."

The two of them had talked for a while on the phone and Cassie had become more comfortable with her friend. They had discussed a lot of personal things they'd both gone through since her last visit there. Cassie knew some of Julia's deepest secrets and vice versa. They had made plans, but Cassie's call now was to let Julia know there might be a short delay.

She didn't want to talk over the phone about what her son was going through, but Julia knew her well enough now to know something major was going on. One thing Cassie was going to do was make sure her sons were okay. Their plan to buy a private island was still going to go down. She just had to make sure her priorities were in order. When they ended the call, Cassie promised to keep her posted. She thought about the stories Julia had shared with her when they'd spent the night together. Her husband, Tito Hernandez, wasn't her husband at all. They were legally married, but Tito was actually her brother.

Julia had been kidnapped by Colombian refugees when she was just four years old. Her mother had been murdered on the spot, right in front of her, and Julia had been removed from her home and taken to the States. Her father, Draco, and her brother, Tito, had been out in the cocoa fields, working for the bosses at the time, and couldn't do anything about it. The Hernandez family had taken over after one of the bosses died of cancer and Tito had been sent to the States to get an education.

In the States, Julia had been raised in a home that had many young girls from different countries. Most of them were under fourteen, and the clientele paid thousands of dollars to be with the young girls. They seemed to really like the extremely young ones. Cassie was heartbroken hearing the details of what had happened to her friend. She was glad she'd been rescued by Tito, but sad he didn't know he was rescuing his younger sister. The worst part of it was Julia could never expose the truth. She knew her father thought she was dead and that was the way she had to leave it.

Cassie heard everything Julia said and that was when she opened up and told her about her and Tangela's love tryst. It wasn't that bad she'd been with a girl; what happened later as they got older was what had made Cassie feel bad. Her best friend had ended up sleeping with her father. Tangela had become jealous of Cassie in high school when she met Rico. She'd tried to carry on their relationship, but Cassie wasn't having it. Even though she missed the touch of a woman, she was dedicated to the young Navy man who was giving her everything she'd ever dreamed of. What Tangela did had been one of the main reasons Cassie had never trusted women or made friends with any of them outside her family. Cassie smiled thinking about her last night with Julia.

ൟ ✿ ൙

Cassie had finally made it to her destination. The night air was cool and it was later than she thought it was. She wasn't sure if she'd taken the scenic route by mistake but, nevertheless, she was there. She checked her purse to make sure her heat was still there. Her solid-gold nine millimeter had been given the nickname Nina Simone by Rico. He had loved taking her to the gun range, teaching her how to properly shoot, and she had become an excellent shot.

When she got out the car, she looked up at the street lamp and saw some kids had busted out the cover. The phone wires in the hood where she was had tennis shoes thrown over them and trash littered almost every front lawn. It was a drug-infested environment and that was one reason why she never came down to that side of town.

There were two buildings, side-by-side, and the one on the right was where she was headed. Between the buildings, she heard a woman moaning and knew exactly what was going on. Before she made it to the front door, another crackhead cut her off, claiming he had what she was looking for. She informed him he didn't have what she wanted, and when he insisted, he came nose-to-barrel with her friend Nina Simone. He backed up and quickly agreed he didn't have what she wanted.

"Damn, this-bitch is crazy!" he said, running back through the gangway where his comrade was performing doggie-style on a woman.

When she made it through the unlocked, unsecured front door of the building, she walked to the apartment and listened at the door. She could hear Harold Melvin and The Blue Notes song *Wake Up Everybody* playing loudly. She fiddled with the door, and to her surprise, it was unlocked. It was almost like whoever was behind the door was expecting somebody. When she walked in the place, she smelled cooked dope, like someone had smoked half a brick or more.

Besides the annoying smell, the apartment was very clean, almost like it didn't belong in the same building.

The upscale furniture and new paint on the wall told her someone had spent a pretty penny on the place. She'd never wanted anything to do with the building and had told Rico she didn't like the investment when he'd bought both buildings. She walked on an expensive soft, bear-skin rug that she remembered her husband shipping home from one of their vacations. The thickness of the fur muffled the noise as she headed to the kitchen area.

When she pushed the swinging door, she witnessed Mickey with the glass-dick in his mouth, and a young naked girl, who looked to be about seventeen, at the most. Cassie had a quick flashback of Tangela and her father, then Julia and her captors making her turn tricks. She looked at the young girl who had burn marks on her body like she'd been in a hotel room with Rick James, trapped for two months. Disgusted, Cassie instructed the young crackhead to get dressed and make her way home. Cassie had done everything with hand signals.

Mickey was so busy getting high, he didn't notice his sister-in-law standing there with her pistol in hand. He turned to get a look at his bipolar crackhead friend, then saw what had her so distraught. The scent of her perfume danced with his nostrils, right before he noticed the beam from her pistol finding a spot between his chin and stomach.

"Sis, what-the-fuck is this all about?" he asked.

"Why, Mickey? Just tell me why before I send you on a camping trip."

Cassie had always felt Mickey was jealous of Rico—jealous of the way he worked and the way people loved him. Mickey use to call him the reincarnation of Bumpy. She'd never trusted Mickey because of his night-and-day personality changes. That to her made him untrustworthy. She knew he used, liked tricking, and was a potential time bomb. There was no reason Mickey wasn't a millionaire himself. The only thing that stopped him was he was a fuck-off artist.

He threw his hands up, telling her she would never understand.

"Try me," she replied. "You think because your brother is dead that you're going to break up the rest of my family? I'm his wife, motherfucker, and the second set of ears on the streets. You need to start running your mouth like you've been doing."

The girl had gathered up her clothes and held them in a bunch. It wasn't her problem and she wasn't getting involved. She excused herself, taking Cassie up on her offer to get-the-fuck out of there.

"Excuse me, Mrs. Killer Lady. I got my things. I'm just going to leave now. I didn't hear nothing or see nothing," she said, grabbing about a half ounce of blow off the counter before she left.

"Cassie, this isn't what you think," Mickey pleaded. "I have been trying to spin the Feds, directing the heat to Peanut, not to Dibiase. I think the Feds want something besides the dope and money. They got to be looking for something Rico had and I'm almost one hundred it ain't dope," he continued, pulling his boxers over his nuts. "I don't know what else to do, sis."

"Well, I do," she replied.

The first bullet struck Mickey in the head. There was almost no blood from the hollow point. She walked up to his lifeless body and emptied her clip, watching his body jerk with every shell that penetrated his flesh. She reached for a paper towel and wiped the blood from her face that had splattered. She took one more look at Mickey's dead body, and before leaving, she said, "Nobody fucks-with my family!"

Cassie left and rode to a park to sit and think for a moment. She had killed a man, and not just any man. She had filled her brother-in-law with seventeen shots. She thought about something Mickey had said before he went to make his Maker. The Feds were looking for something, and it wasn't dope and money. She knew exactly what he was talking about. It was the blueprint to the underground cities. It was obvious, whoever the police were, they were working for the cartels and this couldn't be good.

She remembered thinking Rico was crazy sitting next to her in the delivery room, talking about an underground railroad and city where people lived and moved dope from city to city. That was until he showed her the money and the tube. She knew it would bring future danger when he divulged he wasn't supposed to know. Nevertheless, she would always stand behind Rico.

So many years had passed and nothing had come of it. Now Cassie wondered how much Julia knew about the blueprint, or if she knew anything at all. What Cassie did know was Rico had had two copies, and the second copy was with her and always had been. Cassie couldn't get rid of it if she wanted to. She wondered now where Rico had kept the other copy, then it dawned on her. If Dibiase had the dope, her youngest son—the one no one suspected—had to have the first copy. She touched the back of her neck under her long, lengthy hair where the tat of the blueprint was. She needed a long, hot bath and a cup of tea now. She put the car in drive and headed home.

~ Thirty-Three ~

Don woke up extra early because he knew he had to be at the spot to relieve the third-shift crew he and J.C. had finally hired. He looked at Doll as she lay there, her neatly-shaved pussy still dripping wet from the three rounds of hardcore-fucking they'd done the night before. She was awake, watching him dress, thinking about how good he'd been to her. Since she'd made the move to Milwaukee, Don had taken extra precautions to make sure she was straight and had everything her sexy heart desired. Doll recognized Don's true love for her. It was really a shame his days on earth were numbered. She'd even spent the night comforting him since he'd found out his friend Mickey Hammond had been found dead in his apartment. When Don left, she decided to get up and shower. She knew she had to make an important call.

When Doll stepped out the shower, she halfway dried off, leaving the huge towel wrapped around her body. She sat on the edge of the bed and dialed her old home phone number back in Racine. Another one of her friends answered on the third ring. Tiffany was her homegirl, and she had hit it off with Doll's cousin right away and elected to keep him company.

"Where's my cuz, Tiff?" Doll asked.

"Well, damn, I didn't sleep with you last night," Tiffany replied, not liking the fact Doll hadn't even said good morning.

"Bitch, ain't nobody got time for that-shit this morning." Doll laughed.

When Pork Chop had decided to come, Doll had originally decided to let Cedilla kick it with him. But that was a no-can-do now that she too was dead. Tiffany put Pork Chop on the phone and went into the kitchen to make them both a bacon sandwich.

Pork was ready to roll. He was going to handle this mission solo and get the retribution on Don D. he'd sat back in his cell and dreamed about. He knew he didn't look the same as he did before he'd gotten locked up. The constant pumping of iron had added muscle mass to his frame, and he now wore a full beard and his hair in braids.

Doll had been doing her part to gather all the information she could. It was easy now that she was residing in the same home with Don. He told her everything that happened and how much money he made every day. When she repeated it all word-for-word to her cousin, Pork knew Don D. was major now and he was really moving some big-shit. None of that worried him since he had always been heartless when it came to ending a person's life. Nothing about him screamed new jack and killing to him was second nature.

He listened to Doll tell him about a new plug and that the leader of Don's crew was talking about early retirement. She told him they'd made a bunch of money over the last few days and some of it was there at the house with her. Pork assured her she didn't need to touch that small amount, she didn't have anything to worry about, and Don D. was soon to be a ghost. They ended the call and Doll really wasn't sure she was making the right decision, but what she was sure of was, no matter what, blood was thicker than water and she couldn't turn back if she wanted to.

Pork Chop sat on the edge of the bed thinking about the grand finale. He couldn't believe he had finally had some luck fall his way. He thought about the days he'd sat on the edge of a cot in Baltimore State Pen, swearing to get revenge on the person responsible for his unwanted vacation. The word on the street was Don D. was nowhere to be found, but he'd always had faith he would eventually find him. Tiffany walked in the room with his food and a glass of orange juice.

"What are you making for dinner tonight?" he asked.

"I'm not sure. I was thinking about tacos," she replied.

"Tacos? Bitch, do I look like a Mexican? Shit, is that all bitches cook nowadays? I ate enough of them-muthafuckas back in B-more to shit-out a whole Taco Bell," he said, sitting his food on the nightstand. "In fact, come here and put this-dick in your mouth while you decide."

Tiffany didn't hesitate to do as she was told. She liked the roughness Pork Chop came with. They would-fuck maybe six times a day, and every time she let him inside her, it seemed like he was exploring, staking his claim to new territory. It was the first time she'd been choked doing it doggie style, and the harder he'd applied pressure, the more juices her pussy had made. She took all ten inches of his manhood in her mouth, relaxing her throat muscles.

Pork Chop lay back and let her work. He knew no matter how good her-pussy and head were, when he was ready to go, he couldn't leave any loose ends behind. He had learned his lesson about trusting a-bitch. Doll was the only woman in the world he'd ever trusted. If she weren't his blood, she would surely have been his woman.

~ Thirty-Four ~

Dibiase stepped out by the pool at his new mansion. He was happy to be able to put Camille in a place so beautiful and was ecstatic she loved the new home. He watched the early morning robins fly by and a few female squirrels as they gathered food for their young. It was still early, and he was expecting Oliver and Dixon to be there shortly. Since Mickey was dead, it was time to escalate the plan and take out whoever was responsible for his father's demise. There was going to be a war on the streets and Dibiase wasn't planning on losing.

His phone rang and he took it out of his robe pocket. It was Shorty Mac letting him know he was in town and wanted to meet up with him. The two of them had gotten close, even though Dibiase's love for the game had died down. It was basically all on J.C. now, which was cool with J.C. Dibiase knew no matter what he said, J.C. was going to continue to roll. It was just becoming too much for Dibiase, knowing the Feds were hot on him and now his uncle was dead. He had enough money to figure out something. He wasn't sure what type of business he wanted, but something had to give. His father's will had left him several properties and his real estate agent had talked about Dibiase going into flipping houses. A buyer's market were the words he'd used. But cocaine was always a buyer's market. He knew he had a lot of thinking to do.

When he walked back inside, he looked at a monitor and saw the car outside at the gate. He knew it was Oliver and Dixon waiting to get in. That was one thing about Navy men: when they had a time to be somewhere, they were always on time. His father had been the same way. J.C. was right behind them and Don D. was about ten minutes late, which had become the norm for him lately. Dibiase left everyone in the kitchen while he went in the bedroom where Camille was and changed. He kissed her and her mouth tasted nasty. She saw him frown and smiled.

"That's called morning sickness. That's what happens when you get knocked up," she said, still smiling.

"Damn! Don't throw my son up," Dibiase playfully said, kissing her again despite the aftertaste on her lips.

"Baby?"

"Yes..."

"I'll be glad when whatever you're on is over," she said, rolling back over and closing her eyes.

Dibiase didn't even respond. He knew she was right. He was about to become a family man in the near months to come, and he needed to follow in his father's footsteps and be a good daddy.

When Dibiase came out, he saw on the cameras that Don D. had finally parked. He couldn't believe his eyes at what he was seeing. Don D. had elected to bring his girlfriend to a meeting, which was a disrespectful gesture. Even Camille knew not to come out when they were meeting. Dibiase felt the less a woman knew, the less she could tell if she was ever sweated. There was something dark about Doll as well. Dibiase couldn't put his finger on it, but he sure-as-hell didn't trust her. He felt maybe he was a little biased because Donna was the only other woman he liked and she was J.C.'s ride-or-die. She had proven herself many years ago when he'd caught a weed case. But he also knew a little back story about Don D. that had been told to him by J.C. Dibiase knew a juicy-pussy was like cloud nine hanging over Don D. and that wasn't good for business.

Dibiase acted fast as he picked up the two-way radio. Mike-Mike was his security and watched his house for him. He'd once worked third shift and Dibiase had taken a quick liking to Mike-Mike.

"Yeah, boss," he said, clicking the radio.

"Make sure Don D.'s-bitch remains in the library when they come in."

"Roger that."

After Mike-Mike escorted Doll to the proper place, Don D. joined the meeting that was about to start. He saw the look on Dibiase's face and knew he had fucked-up by bringing Doll. Dibiase took everyone into a separate room off to the side. It was his office that he was having remodeled to mimic his father's old office.

"Let's get started here. There are a lot of things we are going to say, show you, and let you hear," Dixon said, removing his laptop from his bag.

"Uncle Mickey is where I want to start," Oliver said, looking back at Dixon, giving him the floor.

"This might be a hard pill to swallow, God rest his soul, but Mickey was a CI. Yes, he was working with *them* people," Dixon said, watching Dibiase closely. He and Oliver knew that news would hit him hard.

"My uncle was a snitch? Come on, man, what proof do you have to back that up?" Dibiase asked, knowing how he use to look up to his uncle, despite his fucked-up ways.

"Listen to this," Dixon said as he inserted a USB drive in the side of his computer.

There was no mistaking the voice talking to the Feds. It was Mickey and he was talking mostly about Peanut. Then it switched to a conversation he was having with Don D. Don knew what was about to be said and he knew it wasn't good. He was jacking about not being happy with the crew and how they seemed to be eating better than he was. Don D.'s stomach fell to the floor because he knew he was just talking-shit. He'd been a little upset, but since Shorty Mac had come on the set, J.C. had made things a lot better for him. His money was stacking and he was eating.

J.C. was hot as a pepper listening to Don D. talk-shit. He wanted to reach over and clock him one. Don saw the frustration on both J.C. and Dibiase's faces, and knew this wasn't going to be the end of it. He wished Mickey was still alive so he could kill him.

"Man, you get down like that? You fucking-put everyone in jeopardy with this-bullshit you're on!" J.C. said.

"My bad, cuz," Don replied.

"*My bad*?! Niggah, are you serious? *My bad* is all you have to say?"

"Hold up, wait a minute, J.C.," Oliver said, trying to keep him calm.

"Man, fuck-that! I bring this-nigga down here so he can eat and eat safely, and not only does he put me under the gun, but my brother as well? That-shit ain't cool at all!" J.C. blurted out.

All Don could do was hang his head, because even though he wanted to recant his words, they'd already been said. Dibiase was mad-as-hell too, but he needed to finish hearing what else Oliver and Dixon had.

"Well, Dibiase, we paid one Detective Torres a special visit to his home," Dixon said.

"Boy, was it special," Oliver added, thinking about the tranny they'd caught him with.

"Go ahead," Dibiase said, remembering the news about a Detective Torres who'd been found dead. He now knew how his death had come about.

"Seems he was the inside man for a cartel family that goes by the name CCC."

Dibiase and J.C. looked at each other when Dixon said the name. They remembered the batch of work their pops had left was stamped with those same initials.

"We found out Torres' job was to keep an eye on Rico once the hit on his life was issued," Oliver said, stepping in.

"So, the CCC put the hit out on my father? The same-muthafuckas he was working for wanted him taken out?" Dibiase asked, wondering why they would do that. He knew Rico had most likely been on the level with them, so it didn't make sense why they would want him dead.

"This is what's weird," Oliver said, looking at Dixon and nodding his head to play the next recording.

"Stop beating me, man. I told you all I know. I don't know what else there is. You keep asking me about my brother and he's dead."

"You think we're looking for cocaine, you stupid, fat-fuck? We knew about the fifty kilos."

It was clearly a conversation between Mickey and the Feds. Dibiase wondered, why now? If they knew about the dope, why hadn't they issued indictments? The whole conversation seemed as if they were trying to lead him to say something he clearly had no idea about. Dibiase felt a little sorry for his uncle. He could tell Mickey was stuck between a rock and a hard place, but still, he shouldn't have cracked. That was probably what had made him flip his bad habits.

"The leader of this family is a woman known as Julia Hernandez. The Feds have been on to her for some time. They haven't been able to get anything solid on her, and right now, they think she's hiding in a mountain-side home in Vegas."

"This-bitch ain't Bin Laden. Let's go get this heiffa." J.C. stood up.

"You're right, she isn't Bin Laden, but when you have the type of money she has, you're the next best thing," Oliver said.

"We're still puzzled about what the Feds are looking for. She has them on a mission and it's obvious she doesn't want any of you in jail until she gets what she's after," Dixon commented.

Dibiase was stunned. He couldn't believe any woman could have so much power—enough to have his daddy killed, enough to control the federal government. Rico was loyal but, if Dibiase knew his father, he knew Rico must have had a trump card—but he didn't have any idea what the card was. Mickey was on his mind as well. He felt his uncle had been ungrateful by putting him in harm's way. Dibiase knew if the cartel wanted them dead, they would have tried by now, so whatever Rico had on them had been keeping everybody alive. It was time for them to strike before they got it first. That was next to come out everyone's mouth, at the same time.

"Wait, there's one more thing you need to hear before we wrap up and put plan B into action," Dixon said, moving his mouse on his computer.

Dibiase didn't know how much more he could listen to. He felt he had enough to get on the first plane headed to Nevada and blow up the whole state. Dixon pushed the play button.

"Come on, baby girl, you want to get high. I've got enough dope upstairs to wake up Chris Farley. Besides, this might be my last time getting high, so I want to do it big."

"Last time? Why you talking like that, Mick? What's that?"

"This is a wire, baby. If Nina Simone finds out, I'm dead!"

The recording stopped.

~ Thirty-Five ~

After everyone had left, Dibiase sat back in his chair, thinking about his life and what was to become of it. He was about to be a father in about six months, and yet, he had to put his life on the line on some revenge-shit—his father was dead, his uncle was dead because of it, and he couldn't live with not handling his business. He knew there was something he had to do first. Dibiase picked up his cell and dialed Don D.'s number. He had to talk with him to let him know how he felt and that everything was going to be okay.

Don saw the number come across his caller display screen and was reluctant to answer it. He had just dropped Doll off and was headed back to the spot to put in some work.

"Hello," he said, worried about what Dibiase was about to say.

"Hey, lil homie; what's up?"

"Driving to the spot to put it in," Don replied.

"That's cool.. I called because I need you to lay low for a minute. Don't even open the spot for a couple of days."

"D., I'm sorry about all that-shit I said to Unc, man. I was just in my feelings, seeing you and cuz buying mansions, and I'm just now getting my own little one-bedroom."

"Look, man, I understand that; this isn't what this call is about. I don't want to look like we're slapping them people in the face. So its best we take care of this big fish before you get back to work," Dibiase explained.

Don understood that and he could tell by the tone of Dibiase's voice he'd calmed down. What he was saying made sense and would give him time to spend some extra time with Doll. Don agreed to what Dibiase was saying and busted a U-turn to head back to his crib.

He was eating now and J.C. was his blood. He should have known before he ran his mouth he was going to eat. He felt really stupid. Back home, he was a worker, and when he left, he'd sworn he didn't want that feeling any more. He knew that was what had him on edge—things had gotten to feeling too close to what he didn't want.

When Don D. walked back in the house, he didn't even pay attention to Doll and how quickly she ended the call she was on. His mind was preoccupied with the conversation he'd just had with Dibiase.

"Baby, is everything okay?" she asked, almost busted on her call with her cousin.

"I hope so; come give me a hug," Don D. replied.

Doll could hear a slight frustration in his voice, and for a second, she felt worried for him. She knew she had to snap out of her emotions and keep her heart off her sleeves. Don D. was a mark now and marks were business.

"Well, what's going on?" she asked.

"You remember Uncle Mickey? Dude was a snitch."

"Damn, that's fucked-up!"

"Dibiase's people had some recorded conversations of me and him talking, I had said some-shit about not being totally content. You know, same-shit I be running by you. My people didn't take that-shit too well."

"Well, you were just speaking your mind to a homie. Shit, you didn't know he was working for the Feds. Hopefully, that woke their-asses up and they gave you credit for all you do," Doll replied.

She knew all he was doing for the organization because Don hadn't missed one detail when he ran his mouth to her about it. She even knew who the new connect was and where he was from.

"I've got like one-twenty put up, like twenty bands in the kitchen under the sink, and another hundred in the basement. Shit, we should just run off and leave this-muthafucka," he said playfully.

That actually wouldn't have been a bad idea if she didn't already have plans to get the money without him.

"Boy, that little poker change won't be enough to get my hair done for a year," she replied in her own playful tone.

"Shit, I'd better get on my grind then." He smiled, swooped her off her feet, and carried her to the bedroom.

J.C. pulled up to the Hyatt Hotel downtown where he knew his man was staying. He was really upset, and since he had to make a money drop, he figured he might as well unload some of the-shit he'd just gone through to his new plug. Shorty Mac was already downstairs waiting in the lounge for J.C. The two of them sat in the bar and Shorty had the bartender sit the whole bottle of Hennessey down for them. He put five hundred dollars on the bar, knowing the bottle didn't cost more than fifty bucks.

"So, what was that-shit you were saying on the phone, homie? That-shit sounded serious," Shorty Mac asked

"Serious ain't even the word. Imagine your uncle being a snitch and your cousin being a stupid-muthafucka," J.C. replied. "Well, that's what I've been dealing with. My Uncle Mickey was working for them people. They were sweating him and my cousin's been jacking, speaking to the-nigga about what we do. He didn't know Mickey was wired for sound."

"That-shit is foul, homie." Shorty replied, tossing back his first shot.

"Tell me about it. Somebody already fucked-around and peeled Unc's cap back. Shot that-nigga up."

"Damn, man, these streets aren't for everybody. I always said selling this-shit is like taking the Forrest Gump chance."

"What do you mean?"

"This hustling, man, is like a box of chocolates. You never know who you're fucking-with."

They both laughed.

"But seriously, lil homie, you gotta walk lightly for a minute. I know you're a stand-up-nigga, but them-Feds, they're lay-me-down people for stand-up-niggas. They got that impossible-to-beat conviction rate that I know I don't want to fuck-with; feel me?"

"I know exactly what you're saying," J.C. replied, knowing there was some merit to what Shorty was spitting.

J.C. had known the Feds to indict whole crews at a time, and the only-nigga who had a chance at seeing daylight again was the weakest link, the one who told it all.

"That-shit about your cousin's crazy though, man. What type of cloth is dude cut from? He sure ain't from silk because that ain't smooth at all."

"I know. I can almost guarantee you Don was jacking for that gutter-ass-bitch he done moved up here."

"That's weak. All I can say is be careful."

"Shorty, I ain't running, man. I gets down like a champ. I ain't no snitch and I sure ain't no-bitch, so I'm going to get this paper like Frank Lucas!" J.C. stated.

"I like that in you, bro, but remember one thing: when you don't know better, you can't do better. So don't make the bed hard then complain when you have to go lie in that bed."

J.C. respected everything Shorty was saying. He knew Shorty was only a couple of years older than him, but he had been raised up by some OG-niggas from Chicago who were straight-up real and kept it real with him. He had plenty money and plenty game. He didn't even serve niggas in his own city any more. He had walked J.C. out to his whip, standing right by his side as he popped the trunk and handed him a duffle bag full of cash.

"I love the way you boys are getting it in. Tell your man Dibiase, if there is anything I can do for him, don't hesitate to call."

"Word. I'll be sure to pass along that message," J.C. replied.

J.C. knew his new plug meant every word he'd just said. He really liked Shorty and it really helped that Shorty was pushing that straight fire. Rico had told him a long time ago, the quality of a man's dope was equivalent to the quality of his heart.

J.C. jumped in his Benz and headed home. He knew Donna was waiting on him to get there. She had been packing for two days, ready to move into the new mansion next door to Dibiase and Camille.

~ Thirty-Six ~

Dixon pulled up in the driveway at the home of his old comrade. He knew Rico's wife was home because he had been following her for the last couple of days off and on. Glen Dixon didn't know how it felt to lose a personal loved one because all his life he had been connected directly to his job and had never found time to marry. Rico was probably the closest thing to that and they were like brothers. He knew Cassie should be overly distraught from not only losing her husband, but now losing her only brother-in-law.

Dixon reached to ring the bell, but before he could, Cassie opened the door. She had been being a little more cautious than she normally was, and she stayed packing, knowing the streets were going to be in an uproar. She now kept her pistol in the front of her apron.

"Hello, Mrs. Hammond. You don't know me, but allow me to introduce myself," Dixon said, looking Cassie up and down.

She looked stressed out but not worried. Her hair was pulled back, and he could tell and smell she was cooking. He was wondering if she was expecting anyone. Cassie stared and waited for the man on her porch to say who he was and what he wanted. She knew already, but figured she would let him go.

"I'm Dixon, Glenn Dixon."

"So Glenn it is, the man who has been following me the last couple days. How does it feel going grocery shopping and shopping for dresses?" she asked, knowing from his stance he wasn't the police but military. She'd also heard her husband talk about him often.

Dixon thought he'd done well as a tail and wondered when she'd made him.

"Come in, Mr. Dixon, or should I say Alpha-1? Don't see any use in leaving you outside."

"Thank you, Mrs. Hammond."

"Cassie will do just fine. Anyone ever tell you trailing a kingpin's wife could get you killed?" she asked, knowing she was a little out of her league.

Dixon was having a hard time believing what he was seeing. Cassie was Rico, just in a woman's body with a much prettier face. But there was no mistaking where she'd gotten her banter from.

"Now, why are you staring so hard? I'm real. Want to pinch me?" She laughed.

"I'm just amazed, Mrs. Hammond—I mean Cassie."

"Amazed at what? Just have a seat; let me get you something to drink."

"Thanks, Cassie."

"In fact, stay for a bite. You look like a homeless Navy guy who hasn't eaten in years. Go downstairs to the right. You'll find my husband's bathroom. There are razors and everything you boys use to get right."

"Thanks again, Cassie," Dixon replied, not putting up an argument. He figured it wasn't worth arguing because he knew he couldn't win.

Dixon went downstairs and found the bathroom. He looked at the razors, chose one, and lathered his face. He could smell the catfish in the hot grease and couldn't wait to dive in. He finished shaving and looked around the office, knowing his SEAL brother had spent a lot of time in the office he was in. When he lifted the phone off the receiver and listened to the broken dial tone, he could tell it was a private secure line that had now been tapped. He dialed a wrong number purposely, making sure to be on the phone for at least sixty seconds.

He continued looking around the office and smiled when he saw a large picture of the whole crew. Their names were underneath each of them and he now knew how Cassie knew who he was. He stood there staring at the picture, thinking about the last detail they'd shared in Colombia. Dixon didn't turn around until he felt a hand on his shoulder. When he did turn to see Cassie, she wore a slight smile, letting him know his food was ready.

"Okay, Cassie, I'll be right up," he said, taking his sleeve and dusting off all three of the pictures in Rico's office.

He left the office thinking about all the memories he was leaving behind. Dixon let his nose guide him back to the kitchen where he took a seat and watched his SEAL brother's wife prepare his plate and pour him a cup of coffee.

"I know this all has to be tough on you," Dixon said as she sat his food down.

"Tough isn't even the word, Mr. Dixon—"

He didn't let her finish her sentence before stopping her to tell her to please call him Glenn.

"Okay, Glenn. I can say I was physically prepared for anything, but mentally, I only thought I was," she continued, knowing how hard it really was. "My husband always talked about life from beginning to end and what could possibly happen living it the way he'd chosen."

"That sounds like Hammond."

"Yes, and he refused to have people around him with the title of security. He said he didn't feel invincible, but he also wasn't a coward," Cassie explained, fixing herself a cup of coffee now.

"Would you like another cup of coffee?" she asked.

"That would be fine," Dixon replied, pushing his cup to the edge of the table. "I know that's how he thought. I remember a detail in the Soviet when we were sent to guard our president. Hammond looked at all the different branches of security and said, when he became powerful, he would never need so many men around him."

"My husband was something else, may God rest his soul," she replied, putting the coffee pot back on the stove.

"At times, you couldn't tell he was a kingpin. He was a great husband, father, and all-around family man. He did for everyone in need. That's why it hurt my heart to find out about his brother Mickey. How dare he become an informant! And against his own family?!" she exclaimed, almost wanting to shed a tear.

"I know for a fact my husband's probably turning over in his grave knowing his brother tried to ruin his son. It hurt so bad I couldn't even see him laid to rest. By the way," she said, looking directly at Glenn, "did they finally get a lead?"

"Not really. The report says they're looking for a woman—well, actually two. Some young crack addict and another woman they think is the shooter. All they have is a street name on her though—Nina Simone," Dixon said, watching her closely.

Cassie knew he was watching her for tell signs in her body language. Her husband use to use his special training on her all the time until she'd learned to defy the training the government had taught him.

"Well, either way, I wouldn't be honest if I said I felt any sympathy for him. Rico was good to Mickey—hell, Mickey was his only brother—so I say bless this Nina Simone's heart, whoever she may be."

"I understand totally. We're just hoping it doesn't complicate things. A dead CI might make them start to move in on Dibiase. We don't want anything to happen to your son. We felt Mickey being alive was keeping them at bay; maybe they were trying to build a bigger case, or maybe they were looking for something else. It isn't all clear to us yet."

Glenn Dixon was making a lot of sense to Cassie. She hadn't even thought about it that way when she'd pulled the trigger. She just knew she wasn't going to let her brother-in-law say one more word to the Feds about her baby. She had been driving by Dibiase's new home twice a day to check to see if anyone suspicious was lurking. She knew much more than anybody knew she knew. The real estate agent had called the moment Dibiase left his office. He'd told her about the two new homes. The car lot owner had called her and told her about J.C. and the money he was spending. Every connection her husband had, she surely had as well.

"Cassie, I need to be honest with you why I'm here," Dixon said, bringing her out of her train of thought.

"Go ahead; say or ask what you want," she replied, sipping the hot liquid.

"The Feds are looking for something. I sat up all night with Charlie Oliver trying to figure out what-the-fuck they're after. They mentioned five thousand kilos of pure, uncut dope in one of their reports, so all we came up with is the transfer route. How are the Colombians moving so much dope unnoticed?"

"That's a lot of dope."

"Yes, especially when we're talking a week. We think Rico had some type of intel on the cartel family's manifest. He met with this leader back years ago when we were in Colombia on an extract mission. He wasn't a dummy for sure. If he got involved, I'm sure he had himself an escape plan."

"I can vouch that he wasn't a dummy, but he is dead, so escape plan or not, it didn't work out," she replied as she rubbed the back of her neck where the map was tatted.

She flashbacked to that day when Rico had made her get the tat, telling her it was for the good of the family. For three months, she'd had to wear a wig until her hair grew back to cover it up. Now she thought about the day her husband had left to go to his friend's wedding. His words all made sense to her now. "Use your head, baby. It will always keep you safe." Those were the words he'd left her with. Her head would always keep her safe. When he'd kissed her that day, for some odd reason, it had felt like a kiss of no return.

"I can't imagine, Glenn, what they're looking for," she said, getting up and walking to the sink.

"With my husband gone and my son following in his footsteps, I just don't know how much more I can take. You know, look at me, I'm no spring chicken any more. I don't have time to be running up to no prisons," she continued, being as simple as she could be.

"I truly understand, Cassie, but you can rest assured that whoever killed Rico isn't safe anywhere on earth. They took one of ours and we will take all of theirs until the repayment is fulfilled," Glenn explained as seriously as he could.

"I don't doubt you men at all. I know wholeheartedly Rico would have done the same for either of you. I have never seen a group as loyal as you men are. Just please be safe; I don't want any more casualties on our side."

Cassie knew firsthand who and what they were up against. Hernandez had people trained to die, trained to blow themselves up, if it was going to take necessary lives. The SEALs were in a dogfight. It was German shepherds against pit bulls, and Cassie was sure Dixon and his crew would find out who and go barking for the fight. She knew you could only send a killer to catch a killer, and only the most-vicious killer came out victorious. It was destined to be a war of bloodshed, she knew this. What scared her was she knew her son. She knew her firstborn son would be right there in the thick of it. Cassie knew if Dibiase knew anything about the CCC, he would have already been there. She was glad she'd been able to hold back this long. For some odd reason, she'd known the Goon Squad would come.

~ Thirty-Seven ~
Rico, Jr.

"Rickey, come on, man; it's your shot," Jabo said, trying to force the game.

"I know it's my-muthafuckin-shot. Soon as I down this here Remy, I'm going to sink the nine ball in the side pocket," Rickey replied.

"You think you're the-shit, nigga?"

"I don't get paid to think, and I know I'm the-shit," Rickey said, making Jabo even more upset that he was about to lose his paper.

Rickey was a sharp shooter on the pool table. He'd grown up playing with his father, learning everything Rico knew. Now, besides running his business, he would head to the pool hall three times a week and break all the niggas who thought they had a slick stick.

"Nine ball, side pocket," Rickey declared as he powdered his hand and chalked his stick.

He was showing off because he knew, in a game of nine ball, you didn't need to call the last pocket. Once the ball fell, Jabo pouted, called him a show-off, and counted out the five grand they were playing for.

"Show off? My game's just that tight. In fact, I've got a stack to any-nigga in here's hundred that I'll beat that-ass," Rickey boasted.

Nobody wanted to go against him even though he was giving ten-to-one odds. Jabo's friends were all laughing at him because he had lost his second game to Rickey. Everyone at the Ebony Cue Pool Hall had already learned their lesson about battling Rickey. Jabo was just a hardheaded-nigga who couldn't accept losing his paper. He had something else in mind as he looked at his two friends who accompanied him.

What made Rickey a great player was he always thought three shots ahead of his opponent, and nine out of ten times, if he got the break, the other player never got a shot. His cue control was a force to be reckoned with. When he saw his action was over for the night, he unscrewed his stick, ready to head home to see what his mother had made for dinner. He looked around for Jabo, but saw he and his friends had disappeared. He figured that was his loss. Rickey knew Jabo could be a good player with a few pointers, but he wasn't going to give lessons until he had won enough off him. Rickey finished one more double shot and headed for his Range Rover.

Rickey was a little tipsy now. He had forgotten where he'd parked, so he chirped the alarm to find his truck. He didn't realize he had drank enough for the alcohol to take effect, so he started walking. When he made it to the driver's side of his truck, he felt a gun being pushed in his side.

"What's this, a joke or something?" he said as he tried to turn around to see who was pulling a heater on him.

"Maybe you think this a joke, muthafucka," Jezzy replied.

Jabo and his other friend were two cars down as he watched his cousin put in the work.

"On the real, homie, the joke's on you. You think you can go around hustling people out their paper and get away with it?"

He reached his hand in Rickey Jr.'s pockets, making sure he'd relieved him of all the cash he had on him.

"How's it feel?" Jezzy asked.

"How's what feel?"

"To have everything taken from your corner pockets?"

"Yeah, my-nigga, you got jokes for real. Take this little-shit; it's yours," Rickey Jr. said, raising his hands.

"I've got ten grand in the back hatch. You can have it all, just don't shoot me."

"That's what I like: a-nigga who knows when he can't win and just surrenders," Jezzy replied, escorting him to the back of the truck, licking his lips about the extra cash. He knew Jabo didn't know anything about that and he was going to be real happy.

Rickey Jr. had a forty-cal. taped to the inside of his back hatch and he knew the robber would be too distracted with the money to see it. Jezzy had instructions not to hurt Rickey, just rob and scare him. Hopefully, that would deter him from coming around the pool hall, and Jabo and his crew could take back over their money-making territory.

It was just as Rickey figured when he popped the trunk. Jezzy's eyes got big looking at the paper, never noticing the pistol taped to the hatch. Rickey took the money from where it sat and purposely dropped a bundle. Jezzy wasn't thinking one bit as he'd never done a robbery before. When he bent down to pick up the fallen money, it was the biggest mistake of his life. The shot was loud, and Jabo and his other cousin saw the flames from the gun. The bullet had busted Jezzy's head wide open, spilling his brains all over the pavement.

Rickey heard the roar of an engine and the tires peeling rubber. He looked in the direction and caught the tail end of Jabo's ride, sending six shots in the direction. He'd known Jabo was behind it all anyway. His first mind was to call his brothers Dibiase and J.C., but he knew they had enough on their plates and J.C. was a fool who would kill whole families. He decided to take care of Jabo on his own.

He drove around for hours looking for Jabo, hitting up two known hoods where he hung out and came up empty. He questioned all Jabo's workers and no one had seen him. They didn't have any idea what was going on. They were oblivious to the robbery that had taken place. They were so dumbfounded, they even asked Rickey, if he saw him, to have him phone them. Rickey's first mind was to rob his spots, but he didn't want to alert Jabo that he wanted revenge.

The Next Morning ~

Rickey hadn't slept last night, so he got out early and hit the streets, looking for Jabo again. He turned right off King Drive, heading toward downtown, where the best hotels were located. He just so happened to turn his head right and couldn't believe his eyes. Jabo's truck was parked outside a church on Garfield Street. He didn't know what Jabo was doing at a church, but it didn't really matter. He had taken something from him and that wasn't going to fly. Nobody robbed a Hammond and lived to tell about it. Jabo wasn't going to be the exception to the rule.

Rickey saw there were only a few cars in the church lot and a hearse with the light flashing on top. It was someone's funeral, and by the looks of it, whoever the deceased was, wasn't that popular. He got out, putting his strap in his waistband, covering it up with his North Face jacket. When he entered the hallway, he saw a cute little girl in a white dress with a white flower in her hair. A little boy escorted the girl, and the kids couldn't have been more than ten years old. He slowly approached the glass doors that led directly inside the church and could see the people gathered around the coffin. He saw Jabo in his suit. His back was to Rickey, so Jabo had no idea what was about to happen to him. He was just about to reach for his pistol when the little girl and her brother reappeared.

"Did you see our Uncle Milton in there?" she asked, wondering if he had gone in and viewed the body already.

Rickey didn't answer.

"That's our uncle. He got killed and now he's going home to be with God," the little boy said.

"But we're okay because God left us one uncle, Uncle Jabo; that's all we got left," the little boy continued, touching a soft spot in Rickey Jr.

Rickey started to feel a little guilty about killing a man in a church in front of his family who were suffering from another death already. He had been in some battles before, but Jezzy was his first real body, and he felt he had to do what was necessary. He decided now wasn't the time or place, but he wasn't going to leave without saying something to Jabo.

He got close to the casket, standing right next to Jabo. The look on Jabo's face made it look like he'd just seen a ghost. Rickey Jr. tried not to look, but couldn't help noticing the body in the casket was that of a young man no older than sixteen. When he stared for a second, Rickey saw himself in the casket instead of Uncle Milton. He turned to Jabo to speak and noticed his face didn't have any color. It looked like he was dead already. He didn't even look like the same thug that had been gambling and setting up a robbery less than twenty-four hours ago.

"You owe me," Rickey Jr. said before turning and walking away.

He looked at the little girl and her brother and smiled before exiting the church. Jabo had no idea his niece and nephew had just saved the family from suffering from a double funeral.

Driving back home, Rickey decided the streets were too dangerous and decided to hang his hustling stick up. He knew if he played again, it would be in tournaments and leagues. No more street-shit for him. There was entirely too much drama in the streets.

Rickey met up with Jabo once again and reminded him that he owed him. Jabo knew he couldn't deny the fact and hoped he hadn't bitten off more than he could chew.

ॐ ✹ ॐ

It had been a few years since the robbery and Jabo had apparently gotten his weight up. But after meeting with his father, Rickey Jr. knew it was time to call in that favor Jabo owed.

Rickey wondered why his father would give him a letter and ask him not to open it unless something happened to him. Everyone always thought Rickey was a momma's boy, which he was, but he loved Rico more than anything in the world. It had been a long time since Rickey Jr. had felt fear. The last time was when Jabo had set him up to get robbed. He had visited church since then, changed his life, and gotten saved. Now his killer instinct was being called upon again.

He pulled over at the little café called Sherman Perk, which was on Roosevelt Street. He took a seat and couldn't resist reading the letter Rico asked him not to read unless it was necessary.

Son,

I know many things have changed for you in your life being a Christian. I also know you are still my son and have my blood. It's hard for me to say what I'm about to say, but I feel you're the one who needs to hear it. For different reasons I need not say, I'd rather tell you than Dibiase what is going on. Remember I told you, what goes up must come down. Well, that is what is happening.

I once took something from some powerful people and I had my reasons for doing what I did. I knew this day would eventually come, so what I took was my leverage for keeping my family safe. There is a safety deposit box with some important contents inside in a platinum tube. If you ever get contacted about this tube, you know what to do. It is the tube that has kept this family alive.

Rickey had to read the letter two more times to really get the full understanding of what his father was talking about. A tear fell from his eye as he adjusted his mind to what was being said. Rickey finished his smoothie and sped to the bank were the box was. He needed this tube. He needed to know what was so important that it had led to his father's demise.

Dibiase sat at the dinner table with his girl Camille. Stuffed pork chops and Rice-A-Roni were one of his favorite dishes, and he loved the way she melted extra butter on his biscuits. He had barely left the house over the last few days and she enjoyed him being there. He had spent countless hours on the phone with J.C. and the men she knew were friends of his father. She also knew she didn't like or trust the young female Don D. had brought to their home. She looked across the table and asked Dibiase what was wrong since he wasn't smashing his chops like he usually did.

"It seems like something is bothering you, honey," she said, pouring more soda in her glass.

"I know what you mean, baby. It's just that I didn't think it would be so hard. Running this operation and trying to figure out who killed my father is really wearing on me."

"I understand, honey."

"I mean, look at us. Just a few months ago, we both were living at home. Now we're about to have a baby and we live in a mansion on Lake Drive. We've got security guards and swimming pools."

Camille came around the table and kissed him on the forehead. She started massaging his back, trying to relax him. He turned to face her and wrapped her in his arms. The hug was so tight it felt like it was going to be the last hug she received.

"Whatever you've decided to do, baby, just know I will always be by your side. I mean that as your girlfriend or your wifey. I'm there for the long haul."

"I know, baby; trust me, I know," he replied sincerely.

He knew she meant every word she'd spoken. He had always felt God had broken the mold when He created her. The only two women in the world Dibiase would ever die for was his girl and his mother. They had that special spot in his heart. Soon as it was over with, he was going to make it a priority to make her wifey. That girlfriend title was for kids.

J.C. picked his cousin Don D. up. He had finally calmed down from what had been said at the meeting. J.C. knew he was spending a lot of money and he hadn't filled Don D. in on how the money was supposed to be divided. Don D. was family and had been loyal since he had come to town. J.C. knew Don deserved a better explanation. The one thing he hated was that Don had decided to share his feelings with Mickey since Mickey had turned out to be a rat. He had said enough that, if Mickey had told it, the Feds would be knocking soon. J.C. had talked to Dibiase, and they'd both concluded Don D. hadn't intentionally meant any harm. Don hadn't had any idea he was speaking to a man who was wired.

"Man, we can't ever let shit come between us," J.C. said, passing the blunt.

"I know, cuz. I was tripping and I apologize for that weak-shit, but you of all people know what I came from, being up there and being treated unfairly in the game." Don D. replied.

"You're right, cuz, I do know. That's why I had something for you. You think I'm just doing all this and not keeping you and your best interests at heart? There's plenty paper, man; enough for all of us," J.C. continued.

"You're right, man. I can't take-shit-back, but I can amend it. I know shit's about to change with Dibiase laying low, so I figured I step up and hustle twice as hard, get that paper for real."

"D. ain't wrong, man. He's my brother and all, but he really ain't cut out for this hustling-shit like we are. We live by the sword, so we die by the sword. I know the information them-people got has him shook, but I know if they had something solid, they would be on our asses."

"I ain't really worried about that-shit either. Mickey spent most of our conversation time talking about that one-nigga y'all can't stand; you know, ol' boy from the projects."

"Who, Peanut?" J.C. asked, puzzled.

"Yeah, that's the nigga's name, Peanut."

"Well, I don't know what that was all about, but it's like this: The plug's leaving soon and I cut a deal; I mean, the deal of the century. So, if we're going to do this-shit, we're going to do this-shit. No more of one person feeling left out," J.C. said, grabbing a duffle bag off the back seat and handing it to his cousin.

They were now back in front of Don D.'s house and he was anxious to get inside to see his piece-of-ass. He knew the bag was filled with money and that was his part of the take from last week, which had to be a nice chunk of change.

"We've got this, cuz," Don said, giving him five and getting out the car.

Don couldn't wait to get in the house to tell Doll about his new role. He figured they too were going to get them a mansion on the lake real soon. Also, since everybody else in the click was talking about marriage, he was thinking he should pop the question to Doll. He loved her so much he no longer went to clubs and bars and popped bottles with J.C. His mind was made up: She was the one; she was his queen.

When Don D. exited J.C.'s Benz, he saw Doll was still home. He had recently got her a little Passat since her car was a hoopty. She hadn't left all the day. He noticed it was parked in the same spot. He knew his cousin would be back later on. They'd made plans to go meet with the plug and Don knew he had enough time to talk with his baby before they left. When he entered, she didn't hear him at first because she was in the kitchen cooking and on the phone.

"Damn, Don, you startled me! You can't be sneaking up on a girl when she's holding the sharpest knife in the bundle," she said, letting the person on the phone know she would call back.

He walked over to her, putting his arms around her waist, kissing her ear.

"You wouldn't cut your man now, would you?" he replied, smiling. He started rubbing her ass and her breast, rubbing her pussy through her jeans.

"What's got into you, love monkey?" she asked.

"Nothing much; let's just say I had a real good meeting with my cousin. He ain't on that-bullshit no more and said he's making some transitions so we can really eat."

"That's wonderful. Now go shower and get ready to eat. We can discuss it over dinner," she replied, wanting to hear every detail.

"I'm going back out tonight. We've got some stuff to handle, but I do need a quick shower and a meal."

"I don't want you out in them streets too late tonight. I want my teddy bear home."

"You're just horny, girl," he said, hoping that was the reason.

"Well, if you aren't here, you'll never know," Doll replied, winking.

Doll had to keep her focus. She didn't know now if she was gathering information for her cousin, or if she wanted to know more because she was falling for Don. He was sweet and considerate, and he got her anything she asked for without questioning her. On the real side of things, she knew no matter what her personal feelings had grown to become, she had to stick to the script. There wasn't a shadow of a doubt in her mind that, if she fucked up, Pork Chop would put a bullet in both of them. She also knew, after talking to Pork Chop and getting all the details, that the money was just the bonus. He wanted to avenge the death of the girl Don D. had killed.

~ Thirty-Eight ~

Dixon was lying across his bed in his hotel room staring at the ceiling. He couldn't stop thinking about his encounter with Cassie and how much she reminded him of her husband. It also made him think about his old life, reminding him how much he missed Destiny. Destiny was going to be his wife as soon as he returned back to Minnesota, but that hadn't happened. It was years ago, when he was pulling a detail in Japan. Oliver had just resigned and Hammond had left with an honorable discharge to take care of his expecting wife. He had made plans to move her from St. Paul to Canton, Ohio, where he was going to take a position with the federal government. He had already gotten the rings and was going to pop the question before she gave birth to his first child.

His life had taken a drastic turn for the worst two days before he was set to pull out of Japan. Dixon had been summoned by one of the captains, and he was hoping they weren't going to ask him to stay longer. He was happy about leaving and getting his life together. When he entered the office and saw the look on his captain's face, he knew instantly something else was going on. The cap asked him to have a seat, he had something to tell him.

Glenn Dixon had not cried in years, but hearing that a drunk driver had killed his future wife and unborn child was too much. He broke down on the captain's desk and the SEALs had allowed him to leave ASAP to be with her family. Destiny was a sweet woman. She was his second breath, his second heartbeat. He'd figured in two months, he would be with his old crew, smoking cigars and celebrating, not with pallbearers, carrying her body to a deep hole in a graveyard.

Dixon heard the notification that he was receiving an email from someone. He raised up to get his computer to see who it had come from. He wiggled the mouse and the screen came to life so he could punch in his secure password. It was from one of his comrades in Ohio—the only man who wasn't a SEAL but still had his trust. He opened the file to see it was a complete layout of everything any branch of law enforcement had on the Colombian Cocaine Cartel family and it's known leader, Draco Hernandez. He continued reading and scrolling, and it was apparent the CCC was the largest family left in the business. Their ties had been leaked—Escobar, El Chapo, the families in New York and Chicago. They had been in business for two decades and were still running.

The report said it was suspected that the CCC was responsible for over twenty-five thousand pounds of cocaine a month coming into the United States, and over four hundred murders of men, women, children, and even politicians. A picture of Draco Hernandez came across the screen. He didn't look like much in his dingy robe and flip-flops, but that didn't mean anything. He was in Colombia living like a king and virtually untouchable. The file on the kingpin amazed Dixon. He was a smart man, a biochemist with two master's degrees, one in chemistry and one in political science. He also held high paperwork for engineering.

The file was very interesting as Dixon read. Draco had two children. The son was Tito Hernandez, who resided in Las Vegas, and the daughter was unnamed but was said to be deceased along with her mother, who was reported as Draco's second wife. There was another section of the file that really interested Dixon. It contained a picture of Rico and stated he was under investigation for running the Midwest region for the family. It also said he was rumored to be close to Draco and footage had him speaking with Draco in a bar in Colombia.

Dixon looked at the fuzzy footage and smiled because Rico was young and ready back then, but there was still a piece of the puzzle missing. He kept reading, hoping to find something useful to help them. A special agent had been working undercover in Colombia for the last ten years. Draco had reportedly engineered plans to build underground cities to move the cocaine. It sounded crazy, but the cartels had used airplanes; they had surgically operated on women to have them transport drugs in their stomachs; they had even gotten high-tech and built lightning-fast submarines to carry their drugs—so it wasn't impossible. He had worked his way into Draco's camp and had been reporting that the plans were nowhere to be found.

Dixon knew now they needed to move fast as he continued reading. Indictments were underway and he knew the Bush Administration had made it possible for our government to bring drug lords back to stand trial if they had evidence their product was moving in the United States. He closed the file, but not before watching the footage of Rico and Draco again. One thing he had under his belt was he was a master at lip reading. He studied and zoomed in, but couldn't make out much of what either man was saying. The footage was too old and the place too dark. That probably was Draco's intentions all along.

Finally, he decided to call Oliver. He knew he had to relay this information to him and get his take on what he'd just read and seen. He used his cell to call Oliver's cell instead of using the room phone. Oliver answered and told him he would be right over. When he got there, all Dixon did was point to his computer and Oliver sat down to read what was on the screen. Dixon sat on the edge of his bed, quiet so Oliver could think as he read. He knew whatever skills he had, Charlie Oliver's skills were ten times sharper.

"Hammond has the map, or should I say, had the map," Oliver said.

"I was thinking that, but I couldn't make out anything from the video footage," Dixon replied.

"Come here for a second," Oliver ordered as he pulled the scene back to seconds before the end. "Now look there at what Draco was saying."

"Damn, you're right! He just mentioned the blueprint. But what-in-the-hell would Hammond want it for now, this far in the game?" Dixon asked.

"It was a safety net; apparently, it wasn't enough to save his life," Oliver declared.

"Okay, so you think Hammond made copies of the map, blueprint, or whatever-the-hell it was, to save his life?"

"Not *his* life. At the time, he was popping them babies out, and he most-likely was thinking about his family. I think he made a copy and kept it for leverage to save his family's lives in case things went bad. Why things went bad, I don't know, but it's obvious now that the CCC is responsible for his death."

"Well, nobody kills a-fucking-SEAL brother of mine and walks this earth to tell about. It's time these drug-dealing-bastards learned what war really is about," Dixon replied, slamming his fist into the wall. "Playtime is over!"

They slapped hands and Dixon shut down his computer. Oliver went and used the bathroom, and came out and called Dibiase right away. When Dibiase answered, Oliver didn't even wait for a greeting, he just said, "Nine a.m., your office," and hung up the phone.

Dibiase didn't have to respond. He knew the nature of the call Oliver had just made. He knew how his father's friends got down. It was obvious they had what they needed to proceed on getting revenge. Dibiase hung up and texted the parties he needed to text.

Dixon looked at Oliver who had another puzzling look on his face. "Oliver, what is it?" he asked.

"It's got to be Rickey Jr. He has to have the map. He's the only one missing in action in all this," Oliver replied, leaving Dixon to ponder on that.

~ Thirty-Nine ~

The next blow he landed sent Tiffany falling backwards. Pork Chop was finally ready. He was feeling like Charles Bronson in *Death Wish* as he waited on his package. Don D. was about to pay and he was for-damn-sure not going to leave behind any witnesses. Jail wasn't an option for him.

Tiffany's face was swollen three times the normal size, her right arm was broken, and Pork Chop didn't show any signs of stopping until she was done breathing. She was lost, not even understanding where all the abuse had come from. He had been so sweet to her, especially the last few days. She could tell now he didn't feel any remorse for beating her the way he was doing. She was a friend of his cousin's and she had done everything he'd asked her. All she'd wanted was to be loved by a man.

Tiffany lay almost void of life on the kitchen floor. As she felt everything coming to an end, she still couldn't figure out why he had done it. She was going to tell him she was having his baby when they finished making love tonight. She had the test in her purse and couldn't wait to show him the results. He had confided in her he wanted a son and she was set to give him just that. He looked at her gasping, blood coming from her nose and mouth. One last kick in the head and her lights turned out for good.

"Night-night, bitch," he said, landing the kick flush to her head.

He could now move forward with the plans he and his cousin had put together. Pork Chop knew Doll was going off to Texas and he was going back to Baltimore to handle some additional unfinished business. Pork Chop looked at the dead body of the girl and just smiled. He was back; she had been practice just to make sure he still had his old killer instincts. He went into the bedroom to get dressed, throwing on all-black with his steel-toe boots.

Tiffany's purse was on the nightstand on her side of the bed. He knew he had to get it so he could get her car keys. Her Impala would keep him low-key. Pork Chop rambled through her purse, taking her cellphone and the couple hundred dollars she had in her wallet. He saw an EPT box and wondered why she had that. When he picked it up, the box was open but still had the test inside. Pork removed the test and dropped it to the floor when he saw the positive results. He knew he had just killed his first child and its mother.

"How could this be?" he thought out loud.

He was supposed to be sterile and not be able to produce a child. Pork Chop was blaming his bad luck on Don D. It was like all this was his fault and that meant more he had to pay for. He grabbed the keys and headed out the door. Milwaukee was only a twenty-minute ride.

"Soon this-shit will be all over with," Pork Chop said, looking in the rearview, plucking a gray hair from his beard. He lit a blunt, turned on Tiffany's Future disc, and hit the highway.

The black-on-black CLS pulled into the driveway entrance of Dibiase's mini-mansion. J.C. could have walked over, but he had left to get Don D. before arriving. He could see Oliver and Dixon's rental car was already there patiently waiting, and there was also an unfamiliar ride parked, waiting as well. J.C. didn't park where everyone else had parked. He pulled into the six-car garage since he had his own personal parking spot at Dibiase's crib and Dibiase had the same at his. This way, he and Don D. were able to enter through the garage and go inside through the kitchen, which is exactly what they did.

Camille had already left for work and J.C. wondered how long his brother was going to allow his future wife to punch a clock. He would be-damned if his Donna was going to be taking orders from some white person who undercover hated niggas.

They headed straight for Dibiase's office, where once inside, all the men began to greet each other. J.C. stayed focused on Dibiase because he had never seen the look on his face before. The eyes told it all, and right now, his were saying it was time to go to war. J.C. knew his premonition was super-correct when he looked over at the security cameras and saw a U-Haul pulling up and T-Glaze getting out. Dibiase wasn't paying much attention because his mind was so stunned with all he had just taken in from the Goon Squad. J.C. looked at the new man sitting there who was speaking to no one.

It was Mitch Peterson, the old pilot who flew for Oliver and his crew. Mitch was the best at getting a plane anywhere he wanted underneath anyone's radar. They were going to Nevada and it was going to be hard. The Air Force highly-protected the state of Nevada for various reasons. That didn't matter to Mitch; his expertise would suffice. When he left the SEALs, he'd flown Air Force One for six years under the Clinton Administration. He knew secrets about Nevada's air space few other pilots knew. He had to because he had become the best of friends with President Clinton, who used Las Vegas as one of his many meeting spots for his extramarital affairs.

While everyone was talking and looking at the guns T-Glaze had brought in, Dibiase couldn't help thinking about his little brother and what Oliver had suggested. He wondered if Rickey Jr. had some map that had gotten their father killed and was that the same map or blueprint that had stopped the mafia from coming after the family. The two of them were close even though his brother had gotten involved in the church and was dating a new girl.

Dibiase also knew Rickey Jr. had spent a lot of time with their father. He'd trained Rickey in martial arts and explosives control. Dibiase had always been into the girls and hadn't want to learn any of that stuff, especially when the family adopted J.C. The two of them had become inseparable, while Rickey Jr. learned how to protect himself and kill with his bare hands if he had to.

Dibiase came out of his trance and started paying attention. T-Glaze was handing out AK-47's and AR-15's like a ghetto Santa in Capitol Court Mall.

"Since I see you fellas are on your way to war, I brought nothing but the best for you-niggas," T-Glaze said, catching a cold look from Mitch Peterson.

Mitch hated the word and more so hated to be referred to as a-nigga.

"Ahhhhh! I see I rubbed someone the wrong way. My bad, old-school—oops, I mean, partner. Let me make it up to you. Old T-Glaze's got something special for you," he said, snapping his fingers.

His little guy grabbed the quilt that held his special-shit. They all watched, wanting to know what he had that was so special. The AK-47 was a bad-motherfucker and could cut through anything to get to its target. The AR-15 was what they'd all originally trained with and knew that weapon like the back of their hands.

"Now feast your eyes on this baby," T-Glaze said, unwrapping the guns.

"What is it?" Dixon asked.

"This here, school—oops, I mean, partner—is what you call the GA tactical shotgun. It comes fully-equipped with a pistol-grip stock and a supercell recoil pad," he explained.

"Not bad," Oliver said. "What's that other thing there?" he asked, pointing at the second weapon in the blanket.

"You mean Spider? That's the name I gave him, but the proper name is the Tantal 5. Yes, it does look a lot like the AK-47 with the glossy finish and folding-wire stock, but its power is not to be fucked-with. This is the one the government keeps a secret." He smiled, knowing he was dealing with some men who knew their-shit as well.

"We'll take everything," Dibiase said, handing T-Glaze a briefcase full of currency.

"Now that's what I'm talking about. Businessmen at our finest. I'm telling you, fellas, y'all got enough-shit to knock out a whole military base."

Oliver, Mitch, and Dixon all looked his way, letting him know how tasteless his joke really was.

"Just kidding, partners. Lighten up and go kick some-ass," he replied.

"That's what we plan on doing," Dibiase stated, showing T-Glaze and his homie the way out.

When he returned to his office, they set the meeting time at seven. It was about a four-hour flight and Peterson had their private plane ready and waiting at Timmerman Field. J.C. was ready. He wanted to avenge Rico's death just as much as anybody in the room. Don D. was excited about going up against a cartel family and he couldn't wait to get home to tell Doll what was about to happen. He hadn't gotten the chance to know Rico like his cousin had, but he knew how J.C. felt about the man and that was enough for him.

Pork Chop exited the highway on the North Avenue ramp. Doll had given him instructions on how to get there, but he had taken Tiffany's phone and used her mobile GPS to make sure he was heading in the right direction. He had been on the phone with Doll since Don D. had left that morning. She told him he had a meeting with his crew and she felt something major was about to go down.

Pork Chop figured it was his time to act, before things got out of hand and he couldn't get to Don D.

He was licking his lips as he got closer to the place where they stayed. He was going to take Don's cash and take his life, all within an hour. He knew better than anyone about how serious karma was, and everybody who had it coming had to face her one day. He also knew he wasn't exempt from karma, but now it was his turn to wait. Don D. was going to face karma today.

Pork Chop had to admit it, he was proud of his little cousin. He hadn't seen her since he'd gone away, but the pictures she'd sent him while he was down showed she had filled out and become a beautiful queen. He knew they shared the same blood, so she was just a beautiful killer waiting for the right opportunity to present itself. One thing he knew about a woman was, she couldn't lie around, get-fucked all day and shop all night, and not grow some type of feelings for the nigga who'd positioned her to do so. He heard the shimmer in her voice, but it was too late. He was going through with it; Don D. had it coming.

He thought about what had happened back in B-more and how Don D. had had the ups on him and his plan. Something had gone mysteriously wrong, and to this day, Pork Chop hadn't figured it out. That could have been him going through that hotel room door and taking them bullets from Don D.'s pistol. Fate had kept him down in the car and now it was returning to avenge itself. Payback was going to feel like fresh honey to a bee. He could taste it on the top of his stinger, ready to kill at will.

He looked up at the houses and followed the addresses until he was at the right home. He circled the block a couple of times, making sure everything looked safe. He didn't want to be hoodwinked like the last time. He saw his cousin Doll's car was the only car in the driveway, so he pulled down a couple more houses, blending in with the other parked cars. He checked his waistband for his nine, and she was right there ready and willing. He jogged back to the house where Don and Doll stayed and knocked on the back door. Doll knew the knock and let him in.

"I see you made it. Now get in here before someone sees you," Doll said, closing the door behind him.

Two more bodies were being tagged and bagged in the wee hours of the morning. Agents Hawk and Squales were found headless in a tenement building on Locust that use to be used to dispose of old rubber tires. The coroner said they had been there at least forty-eight hours. Whoever had killed them had switched their severed heads as a joke. Their captain was on the scene, wondering how-in-the-hell that was possible when the system showed them clocking in and out for their shifts. It was supposedly impossible, but the proof was right in front of him. There had to be someone dirty on the inside.

Captain Hernandez was the senior officer and he only reported to the mayor. He knew he had to cover this up right away. If anyone knew what was happening, he knew. Channel 58 was the first on the scene and he couldn't deny the interview. He said the bodies of two males had been found, but he neglected to say they were agents. That was all he had to say for the cameras before making his men get the camera crew away from the crime scene.

That night at home, Captain Hernandez lit up a fat cigar and relaxed his feet in his La-Z-Boy recliner his wife had gotten him last Christmas. He dumped the ashes on his Colombian tobacco stick and removed a key to his safe. He took out a special phone that was secure and dialed his cousin overseas.

"Well, how is *dings* in the land of *da* free?" Draco asked, knowing the number.

"There has been a serious screw-up."

"I've seen you already on the CNN news channel, but I tell you one *ding*: I send you my men to do a simple job—kill one-nigger in a small city—and now I see there is much commotion," Draco replied.

"I don't understand why my men did that. I haven't seen your men, Draco. I used Chino and his brother, but removing the heads and switching them wasn't protocol. I'm going to handle them when I hear from them. I won't pay them, and also, the next job is free."

"This is why I stay in Colombia. Your civilization has no idea what it takes to run this. I don't know where my men are either, but when they return, they will surely get a serious reprimand for their insubordination as well. It was a simple assignment. Kill Hammond and find out where any copies of the map may be hidden. Let me think about this for a while," Draco insisted.

Not long after they hung up, the captain got a call on his service phone. He looked at the number and was glad it wasn't the mayor calling. It was his office and he wondered what they wanted. He had explained he was going home for the night and he didn't want to be disturbed.

"Cap here."

"This is Santos. We found two more bodies in that same building. One of them was ID'ed as Chino," Santos said. Santos was his eyes and ears, and he knew what was going on.

"Okay; I'll be right down.'

The captain hung up the phone and knew in his gut things weren't right. Someone had killed Chino and his brother. They must have ambushed them when they were killing Hawks and Squales. He wondered if Draco's men were there and had been ordered to kill anyone who knew anything. He figured that might not be, because without all the copies of the blueprint, Draco's whole organization was at risk.

Captain Hernandez had flown under the radar his whole career. He knew the money and power his family possessed, along with the political contributions, had propelled him to his prominent position. He wouldn't let anything stop that—not his cousin in Colombia and not his cousin's son in Vegas. He'd learned long ago to trust none and suspect all.

Dibiase sat in the kitchen talking with his mother. She tried to do her normal thing and fix him something to eat, but he assured her he wasn't hungry. He really didn't have an appetite at all. He knew he had way too much on his mind, but he knew he needed to talk with her and keep her abreast of what was going on since she was the only parent he had left.

Cassie already believed Tito Hernandez, her husband's plug, was responsible for his death. She'd once wanted Nina Simone to avenge the death of Rico, but she understood the code of honor. She was reluctant for her eldest son to take on the responsibility. She knew just how powerful the Vegas mafia family really was. She did more listening than talking because there was so much she couldn't go into detail about without exposing herself or the map.

"Mom, I have a question to ask you."

"Go ahead, son. What is it you want to know?"

"My people mentioned something to me about a blueprint or some type of map Pops was supposed to be in possession of. They say it might be what got him killed and kept us alive. Did he ever mention anything about it to you?"

"Listen, Dibiase; your father was a good dad and a great husband, despite his lifestyle. Not many men could have handled his power and money the way he did. I do believe the map is what got him killed and saved us for now," she responded, trying not to lie to her son.

He shot her a look when she said now. He wasn't going to let anything happen to another member of his family if he could help it.

"The map, my son, is a passage way. It's a long story, but let me tell you this: it's the corner where at least five thousand kilos of cocaine makes its way to the United States once a week. It is basically a three-state underground city," she said, sipping her hot tea.

"I heard something about that. I also heard the Feds are looking for the map and Mickey was used as a scapegoat because they figured he could lead them to any copies Pops may have hidden."

"Copies, huh? That's what they're looking for?" She laughed.

"Oliver and Dixon came to some notion that Rickey Jr. may have the only remaining copy, and that Pops left me the dope and left him the secret, to keep things separate," he stated.

"Well, those military dudes are pretty smart, but they are wrong with that assumption. Come here, son, let me show you something," she said, taking her long hair and pulling it over her head.

When she turned around, she exposed a tattoo that he knew was the map. It was unbelievable, but it was safe. No one would have suspected that, many years ago, his pops had had the blueprint to the mafia's passageway tatted on the back of his wife's neck. It was surely a brilliant move.

"Rico had this done when you were first born. He regretted it at first, Now, I'm sure he's in heaven, knowing he saved us. So you can tell Oliver and that nice fella Dixon that Little Rickey doesn't know anything."

It was hard for him to imagine now that all this killing going on was for a map that was tatted right on the back of his mother's neck.

"Well, you don't have to worry about that for now." He hesitated. "I'm going to kill Tito Hernandez and his whole crew."

For some reason, she already knew that. She was worried but she was also satisfied he had the manpower to do the job successfully. She knew so much about the men he had accompanying him, she almost felt sorry for the mob.

"Son, I'm not here to try to discourage you because I know that won't do any good. Just be careful and realize you're going against a small army of fools who were born to die. Cocaine is their god and their devil, and human life means nothing to them," she said, wiping a tear from her eye.

"I think I can handle this, Mother, and if for some odd reason something happens to me, at least I will be sending the message that our family ain't to be fucked-with," he said, shedding a tear himself now.

"The only thing I ask is that you go stay at the new house with Camille while I'm gone. Make sure she's okay and not stressed; that wouldn't be good for the baby."

"BABY?! Well, well, I'm finally going to be a G-momma. About time!"

The 747 TWA flight 925 landed right on time at Vegas International, in the city that never sleeps. Las Vegas, Nevada, is the place where it all began for the mafia. The money came when the

number-one gangster of all time built the first hotel in the dessert. So, by rights, the mafia families always felt they had the right to build up or underground in the city. It was theirs; they were Christopher Columbus to Nevada.

Rickey Hammond Jr. entered the black limo waiting on him. He didn't have any intention of staying in Vegas more than eight hours. He already had a return flight booked to get back home. The only luggage Rickey even carried was his pool stick. The driver of the car looked at Rickey and proceeded to the destination.

They drove through downtown and Rickey was amazed at all the sights. He had actually never been to Vegas before, but he knew now wasn't the time to be thinking about pleasure. They passed a place called The Rivera. The lights were lit up, telling people to come see the greatest magic show on earth. He knew it couldn't possibly be the greatest magic show. He knew he and his father had pulled off the greatest magic show on earth. The Horseshoe was advertising its new poker tournament and the MGM had Lionel Richie. There was something going on everywhere in Las Vegas.

Rickey knew he was taking a chance, but if he wanted things to ever go back to being almost-normal, he had to do what he had to do. He'd set up the meeting with the CCC to return the copy of the blueprint he had. He knew his father's friends would figure out he had it and would come, trying to take it back themselves. He knew his brother had called them to town to figure out what happened, and his father had assured him they would figure it out sooner or later. He said a silent prayer for his own safety as they got closer and closer to his final destination. If Tito was a businessman, the meet should go smoothly and he could return home. He could kiss his mother and hug his brother, knowing everyone could sleep peacefully at night.

The limo finally turned away from all the glamorous lights and huge buildings. The driver took a turn on a road that led into the mountains and the air began to get thinner, making it hard to breathe for a person who wasn't use to it. He had looked at the map himself and knew some of their secrets. He knew the entrances and the exits in Arizona and Cali, and he knew what casinos were on board and cleaned money with some of the portions the clientele lost. He knew more than he should, but he wouldn't let that be known.

The car pulled up to a location and two guards ushered them through a fence. When they came to a stop and the driver opened the door, he noticed a rugged-looking man in a white linen suit with two guards on each side of him. He knew he was Tito Hernandez, the man he'd come to see. Tito looked like the man from the beer commercials—one who could smile and shake your hand, and with his free hand, shoot you in the head—but he didn't feel an ounce of fear at all. He knew that was his father's blood running through him. He looked square, and Rickey knew that look had always gotten him through. Many people, such as Jabo, always had him figured wrong. He was one who would forgive a person, but never forget the wrong they had been done to him. When he got all the way out, he had his pool stick under his arm. The guards pointed their heavy artillery at him until Tito motioned for them to back down.

They patted his body down and looked inside the case; as far as they were concerned, he was clean. It appeared Hammond's son had come in peace and wanted to leave in one piece. When Tito took a moment to study the young man in front of him, it was like he was seeing a ghost. Rickey Jr. looked like his father and was built just like him. They shared the same complexion and the height may have been no more than an inch in difference. It was amazing to Tito, made him think about the second time he'd met Rico.

Rico had already delivered the package a month earlier. When Tito first saw him, he took a liking and gave him a nice tip and a couple of kilos of cocaine to take back to Milwaukee with him. He was a master at studying people, and he knew when he met Rico that he had heart and would be what he needed to run the Midwest. Their relationship had lasted many, many years, and they'd both benefitted from it.

Now, even though his seed stood there looking just like his father, Tito knew they had different demeanors. Rickey Jr. didn't come off to him as a man who had a hustler's mentality, but more so as a man who was willing to die to save his family from any further problems that may come about.

"Come in, young man. I believe you have something that belongs to my family," Tito said.

"I believe I do," Rickey replied, following Tito.

ogHe looked around the place as he trailed Tito and saw what real money could do. He had only seen houses this decked-out in magazines or on television. He was surprised to walk past a pool table that sat in a game room. Tito told the guards he would be all right and they were dismissed. Rickey watched them as they hesitated to walk off and leave their boss. He thought that was very noble of them to be so loyal. He wished the people who rented chairs in his salon were that loyal.

"I respect you for coming," Tito said, offering Rickey an expensive cigar.

Rickey didn't smoke and waved his offer off.

"No, thank you, but I will have a shot of that there," he replied, pointing at a clear bottle of what looked to be cognac. He knew it had to be top shelf because the bottle was made of crystal.

"Ahhhhh, you know your liquor, I see. This here we serve at one of my clubs for nine hundred a shot," he said, pouring.

"I see why," Rickey replied after taking a sip of the smoothest liquor that had ever graced his pallet.

"Have a seat, young man. I know you didn't come here to sightsee, but like I said, I respect your courage for coming. How was your flight?"

"The flight was fine," he replied, placing his pool stick case between his legs.

"There has been a lot of death going on in your city. It's a shame we had to lose your father in the midst of it all. Your father was a good soldier and the streets were his battleground, as they are mine as well. There is a code we must live by and respect, and each and every soldier who goes to war in the streets knows that. Your father was smart, but he should have stuck to the code," Tito said, putting out his cigar.

"Mr. Hernandez, what I'm doing here is the last wish of my father. I really didn't come to make friends or small talk. I came so that me and the rest of my family can put this behind us and live our lives in peace. This is what he wanted, so this is what I'm doing," Rickey said, hesitating for a minute.

"Trust and believe I understand your position and your power, sir, but Rico knew the life he was choosing and the codes that accompanied the style. He chose to die for that and may God rest his soul, but after this, if my family has any problems, may God have mercy on the perpetrator's soul," he continued, adjusting his pool case.

"You speak like a true man, young Hammond," Tito replied, watching Rickey Jr. open his pool case.

Rickey reached inside and handed Tito the tube. It was like he was handing a fat kid a piece of double-fudge chocolate cake by the smile that came across Tito's face.

"Would you like one more drink?" Tito asked.

"No, sir; the one was plenty. If you would just tell your driver I'm on my way out, I will just make my way back to the airport."

Forty

The GS 400 Lexus pulled to the back of the house and Don D. got out, ready to go make love to his queen before hitting the road. He had no idea he had an uninvited guest inside, waiting to take his life. Pork Chop and Doll heard the car, and she urged him to get back in the closet, where they had found a second bag full of money and three kilos. He also had the money from the basement and under the sink, and now he was ninety percent satisfied. One more thing and he knew his mission was complete.

Doll's skepticism had begun again after Pork Chop arrived. The evil look in his eyes made her know she wasn't that bad of a person, but she knew it was too late to turn back. She was surely going to abort the baby she was carrying once she got down to Texas with her other cousin. She just glad she hadn't told anyone she was having a baby.

She'd thought about it right before hearing his car—how stupid she was to go along with the plan. She had been with a lot of men, all ballers, and none of them had catered to her like Don D. She knew she was just eye-candy to them or a piece of fly-ass they could point their finger at and say they'd knocked off. But Don was different. He talked to her about the moon and the sun, about business, about the future, and even about small things she'd never had the chance to share with anyone else. She realized, when it was all said and done, she was going to miss him—miss the romantic side of a man who was undeniably all hers.

She had a quick flashback of the first time they had gone to breakfast and the place didn't have any steak sauce for her meat. Don had gotten up, run to the grocery store, and was back before her steak and eggs arrived at the table. No one else would have done that. Now she was forced to stick to her MO and let her cousin take it all away from her. The plan was set. When he came in, she was supposed to have him take her in the bedroom and start making love to him. Pork Chop was going to emerge from the closet and kill him. Plain and simple, one, two, three, and it was going to be over, just like that.

Her mind was going in fifty different directions when she heard his key finally turn the lock. When he came in smiling, he noticed right away the look on her face. She was looking like she had just lost her best friend and he wasn't use to that.

"You okay, honey?" he asked as she started putting her fingers to her lips motioning for him to be quiet.

She'd had an instant change of heart and wasn't going to be part of her baby's father's death.

Pork Chop was in the closet, getting impatient, wondering what was taking her so long. He started thinking about his dead girlfriend and smiled, knowing he was getting revenge for her death.

Doll snatched her jacket and whispered for Don D. to get back in the car and drive. She jumped in the passenger side as he backed out the driveway.

"What-the-fuck is happening, baby?! We left the door open with a half million in the house and some dope."

"Listen, honey, what I'm about to tell you is about to be some fucked-up-shit. So, once I'm finished, I will accept any consequences I have coming; just know that I love you with all my heart," she said.

Sweat started to bead on his forehead and fear floated around in his intestines as he wondered what she was about to say.

"What-the-fuck you talking about, Doll? You're scaring me."

"Just shut up, Don, and listen! Stop talking so much," she insisted.

"Okay; go ahead."

"Well, remember when Cedilla told you I was from B-more? She wasn't lying, as we both know. I lied to you because Brock is my first cousin and he got out of jail a little while ago."

"Brock? Who is Brock?"

"Washington; My last name, Don, is Washington. Brock is Brock Washington. You know him as Pork Chop."

She explained everything they had planned, and when she finished, she told him she'd never had intention of falling in love with him.

"So I was a mark, a trick, all along?"

"Yes, but I fell in love," she replied.

Don wanted to shoot her just like he had the other girl back home.

"I'm having your baby," she blurted out.

He hit the steering wheel, bruising his hand. She began to cry because she had exposed herself when she couldn't go through with what her cousin had wanted to do to him.

"You made me fall in love with you!" she cried, hitting him in the shoulder.

He grabbed her and hugged her tightly.

"Muthafucka . . . This-shit is fucked-up," he said, kissing her forehead.

"He's in our home, waiting on you. He has the money and the dope in a car up the street already; now he wants your life."

As she expressed her concern, he assured her she didn't have to worry about her cousin. He wasn't going to get away with murder and he sure wasn't getting away with his stash. She knew her cousin's plan had backfired and he wasn't going to make it to see another day. It was all part of the dirty game the streets taught people how to play. She fabricated a little about how he'd found her, but that was because she wanted to keep her man when it was all over with. She would even consider marrying Don.

It only took ten minutes for his whole click to show up. They met on the corner, and Don told Doll to take the Lexus and ride, not to return until he called her. He should have killed Brock Washington years ago, but now his death was imminent. Don told J.C. and Shorty Mac, who just happened to be with J.C., the burglar was holed-up in his house, hiding in the bedroom closet.

When they entered the house, Don D. acted like he was talking to Doll, who was nowhere around.

"Come on, baby, you know you want it. Let's go in the bedroom," loud enough to make sure Pork Chop would hear him from the closet.

Pork Chop licked his lips, knowing it was about to go down. He could get it over with and get-the-fuck out of Dodge.

J.C. had his MAC-10 and was ready to bust-a-cap in whoever's-ass for fucking-with his family. Don D. jumped on the bed, acting like he wanted Doll to hurry up.

"Get all them clothes off, baby! Yeah, that's it. Now come to bed with daddy."

Brock Washington took the bait. He burst out the closet, yelling, "WHAT'S UP NOW, MUTHAFUCKA!"

But when he looked into the face of three guns, he knew he was outdone, outnumbered, and outgunned. His only chance was to try to let off a round and take someone with him. Shorty Mac saw the look in his eyes, and before Pork Chop's trigger finger could move, he was full of holes. He fell to the floor looking like a sprinkler, blood gushing from the many different holes in his body.

Don filled his cousin and the plug in on the story, lying to protect his girl. He knew she really loved him; otherwise, she would have let him die and made off with the money and his work. He knew there was a reason he loved her.

~ Forty-One ~

The time had come. Everyone was at the hanger and Peterson had the engines roaring to go.

"Send some killers to kill some killers," Dixon said.

Don D. had almost stayed back because he felt bad leaving Doll behind, but he had put her downtown in the Hyatt until he returned. Oliver had told Dibiase they needed more firepower, and Shorty Mac had come through with about twenty of his men from Peoria. It was all that was needed. They boarded the plane and Dibiase kissed the gold cross he wore around his neck for good luck.

The plane ride was comfortable. Peterson had himself a nice plane, and J.C. and Shorty Mac were kidding about getting themselves one. The back of the plane had a large bathroom and three rooms with double beds in each room. Dibiase was amazed at how small the plane looked from the outside but how much room was actually inside the jet. He now understood why Jay-Z wanted one for himself. They all were seated as the liftoff started. There was no turning back, that was for sure. Oliver wanted to go over some tactical strategies with everyone before they arrived. Of course, it wasn't for Dixon and Peterson's sake, but for the civilian company along with them.

"Look, now, I want to come out of this with no casualties on our end. If you all listen, we can get in there, do this, and get-the-fuck out of there," Oliver said.

"We know some of you guys got some bodies under your belt, but this-shit here ain't like nothing in the street. We are sure some of Hernandez' men have special military training, which will give them a slight edge," Dixon added.

"But they ain't got one of these," J.C. said laughing, holding up his special gun he'd gotten from T-Glaze.

"Now, settle down and listen to what I've got to say," Oliver said, knowing how important it was that they did just that.

Dixon already had a satellite view of the place where Hernandez was. It was like Fort Wayne, but that wasn't a deterrent at all for them. Every one listened and learned something new from hearing him talk. When Oliver finished, they all calmed down and relaxed, most of them wondering if they would see tomorrow.

Shorty Mac sat next to Dibiase and they talked for a while. Shorty told him he understood him getting out the game. When Dibiase asked him why he stayed, Shorty simply replied that he had a lot of people counting on him to eat. That must be what hustlers said because that was exactly how his father use to think. It was more so about the lives he had been responsible for now, making sure everybody else was good.

It took Peterson close to four hours and they were now crossing into Nevada air space. He radioed to the tower, letting them know he was ex-military, training his kids how to fly. They took the bait and gave the plane clearance. He was happy because he already had a designated spot picked out to land.

"This is it, boys. We're about to land," Peterson said through the speakers.

Everyone's adrenaline started to pump faster and they were as ready as they ever were going to be. Dibiase hugged Don D. and J.C. and said to them they were all brothers for life. He thanked everyone else for joining them and putting their lives in harm's way for him as well. Peterson landed the plane and they deplaned. It was about a mile hike to the Hernandez estate and J.C. sparked the first blunt.

"Watch out your-ass doesn't get pricked by a cactus," Dixon said, laughing.

The silver Lotus was flying up the back road, doing over one hundred miles an hour. Draco Hernandez had only been to the United States twice before, but now, because so much was going on, he'd decided to pay his son a visit. It was going to be a surprise, but he wasn't there for pleasure. He had gotten a wire telling him Tito was married to his sister. Draco felt the heat rise to the top of his head knowing his daughter was alive and his own son had married her. There was no forgiving his actions.

Draco saw a plane flying low and overlooked it because it wasn't a federal or military plane. He just needed to get to his son's place and have words with both him and his daughter. He still didn't understand where Julia had been all these years or how Tito had found her—until he realized everything that had happened years ago had been set up by his son. Tito had known he would have to leave Colombia and he wanted to take over things in the United States. Tito had paid the men to come in and kill Draco's wife—his own mother—and kidnap his own sister. His plan had worked out—until now.

The Lotus had made it to the front gate and the guards all drew their weapons down on the car. Draco let the door up and stepped out. They were all astonished, looking at the big man. He was the boss of bosses, the top dog. They rushed over to him, apologizing and kissing his hand.

"Take me to my son!" he demanded.

Oliver, Dixon, and Peterson led the pack as they neared the estate. Oliver screwed on his silencer and Dixon looked through the binoculars to see what awaited them. The place was secured, but not as heavily as they'd anticipated. There was a silver luxury car sitting outside the fence with a few guards around it admiring its beauty. There were four men on the low roof and several more in the yard.

"Cuz, you good, man?" J.C. asked Don D., who was just reading a text from his phone.

"Yeah, I'm good," he lied.

The text he'd read was not to be discussed right now. He knew he would deal with it when he made it home.

"Let's get these muthafuckas!" Shorty Mac said, giving Dibiase some dap.

"Let's do it!" Dibiase replied.

Oliver let off the first two shots that sounded like a whisper, but both bullets struck their targets with precision, catching the car-admiring guards in the neck, ending their lives instantly. Peterson gave a signal and Dixon let off his shots now. He caught two of the guards, but one had gotten down off the roof and alerted everyone they were under attack. Hernandez' people didn't know if it was the police or another family.

The gun battle ensued, and Dibiase and his men were having good luck. They were knocking off Hernandez' men one by one. Dibiase and Shorty Mac followed Dixon around back, while the rest of them stayed and sprayed the front of the estate. It wasn't long afterward that Don D. took one in the chest. He fell to the ground, clutching his chest. Oliver got to his side, instructing him to breathe, but he knew from where the bullet had struck he wasn't going to make it. He knew Dibiase and J.C. were going to be hurt.

The three of them made it in the house with little resistance as they killed each of Hernandez' men who got in the way.

"For these punks to be so tough, they ain't-shit," J.C. said, taking his eyes off the mission.

A bullet struck him in the shoulder, but before the guard could get another round off, Dibiase had dropped him with two in the head.

"You all right, bro?" Dibiase asked.

"Man, I just got popped! What do you think?!" he replied.

Dixon looked at it and saw it was just a flesh wound.

"You'll be fine; hit the blunt again." Dixon laughed.

They split up in the house, seeing the guards on the inside were all done. They were looking for one person now and Dibiase wasn't stopping until he found him. He and J.C. came to a door that looked like an office and entered it. There was a head of hair sitting in a chair facing the back wall, which was a giant shark tank.

"TURN AROUND, TITO! IT'S OVER!" Dibiase yelled.

"HE SAID TURN AROUND, MUTHAFUCKA, OR TAKE IT IN THE BACK."

Just then an older man emerged from a closet holding a nine millimeter. He looked at Dibiase and knew exactly who he was. Draco smiled before putting the gun in his mouth and pulling the trigger. Dibiase and J.C. walked up and spun Tito around. Blood was coming from his nose and mouth. It was obvious he was dead.

"Damn! You think his own father killed him?" J.C. asked.

"Shit, that's the way it seems," Dibiase replied.

He looked at the two empty glasses and the tube on his desk. Dibiase opened the tube and saw the same map as the one on his mother's neck. It was crazy, not adding up. If they had the map, why was there so much going on like they didn't have it?

They turned to leave, and as they were going out, Dibiase turned back to look one more time. What he saw let him know what had happened. A great white shark had come up to the glass with a bloody, solid-gold pool stick in its mouth.

"Yeah, let's get-the-fuck out of here. Our mission is complete!"

~ Epilogue ~

On the ride back, J.C. couldn't help shedding tears. Don D. was gone now. He looked at his phone and read the last text.

Baby, the Feds came and got me from the hotel. Brock killed a woman in my apartment and they have me under investigation.

J.C. lit a blunt and passed it to Dibiase, who took it and hit it hard.

"Man, you sure you're getting out the game?" J.C. asked.

"I'm sure, bro. This ain't the life for me."

*Other Books by
Swift Sloan . . .*

IN HIS WORLD ANYTHING LESS THAN
THE TOP WASN'T AN OPTION
MOTIVATION
MASTERING THE GAME
BOOK BY
SWIFT

MOTIVATION
PT.2 "THE CHASE"

A NOVEL BY SWIFT

RH PUBLISHING PRESENTS

A NOVEL BY
SWIFT

MOTIVATION 3
"THE EXIT"

WWW.SWIFTNOVELS.COM

follow us on social media

twitter   @Swift414   Instagram   @Swift414
facebook   Swift   goodreads   Swift

EMAIL: TALK2US@RHPUBLISHINGS.COM
RH PUBLISHING, LLC P.O. BOX 11642 MILWAUKEE, WI 53211

Book Order Form

	Qty.	Price/each	Total
Motivation 1: Mastering the Game	_____	$9.99	$_____
Motivation 2: The Chase	_____	$10.99	$_____
Motivation 3: The Exit	_____	$12.99	$_____
The Black Dibiase: Return of the Goon Squad	_____	$13.99	$_____
Order Sub-Total:			$_____
Shipping & Handling: 1ˢᵗ Item		$3.99	$3.99
Shipping & Handling: Additional Items	_____	$1.99	$_____
Order Total:			$_____

Mailing information: Please print legibly.

Name: _____

Address: _____

Apt. No.: _____

City, State, Zip: _____

Telephone No.: _____

Email: _____

If you have any questions, please contact us at:
talk2us@rhpublishings.com

*Please send the completed order form
with your check or money order to:*

RH Publishing
PO Box 11642
Milwaukee, WI 53211

Credit/debit cards orders are welcome through our website:
www.swiftnovels.com

Thank you for your order.

Made in the USA
Columbia, SC
16 January 2018